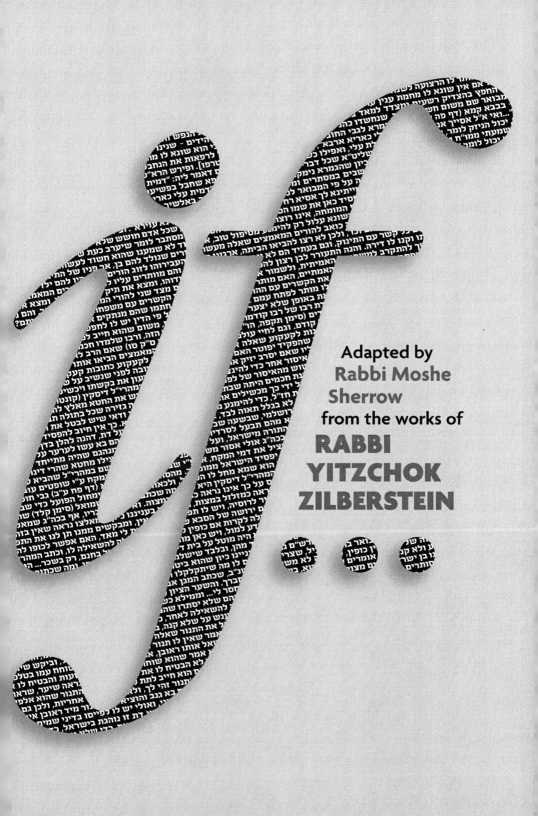

if

Adapted by
Rabbi Moshe Sherrow
from the works of
RABBI YITZCHOK ZILBERSTEIN

FIRST EDITION
First Impression … November 2012

Published and Distributed by
MESORAH PUBLICATIONS, LTD.
4401 Second Avenue / Brooklyn, N.Y 11232

Distributed in Europe by
LEHMANNS
Unit E, Viking Business Park
Rolling Mill Road
Jarow, Tyne & Wear, NE32 3DP
England

Distributed in Australia and New Zealand
by **GOLDS WORLDS OF JUDAICA**
3-13 William Street
Balaclava, Melbourne 3183
Victoria, Australia

Distributed in Israel by
SIFRIATI / A. GITLER — BOOKS
6 Hayarkon Street
Bnei Brak 51127

Distributed in South Africa by
KOLLEL BOOKSHOP
Northfield Centre, 17 Northfield Avenue
Glenhazel 2192, Johannesburg, South Africa

ARTSCROLL SERIES™
WHAT IF
© *Copyright 2012, by* MESORAH PUBLICATIONS, Ltd.
4401 Second Avenue / Brooklyn, N.Y. 11232 / (718) 921-9000 / www.artscroll.com

ISBN 10: 1-4226-1316-X / ISBN 13: 978-1-4226-1316-0

Typography by CompuScribe at ArtScroll Studios, Ltd.
Printed in United States of America
Bound by Sefercraft, Quality Bookbinders, Ltd., Brooklyn N.Y. 11232

Table of Contents

Preface   17
Introduction   21
Acknowledgments   27

Sefer Bereishis

Parashas Bereishis
Pure Profit   31
Family Loyalty   33
Manufacturer's Instructions   35
Professionalism and Emotion   37

Parashas Noach
Vegetables a la Mode   39
Granting Permission Against One's Will   41
Natural Resources   42

Parashas Lech Lecha
Irreplaceable Tefillin   44

Social Security   45

But You Promised!   47

Applying the Lessons We Learn   49

Parashas Vayeira

Speed Versus Beauty   52

Overbooking   53

Medical Ethics   55

Personal Responsibility   57

Parental Rights   58

Chanukah Gelt!   59

Parashas Chayei Sarah

Everyone Has One   61

A Doctor With No Compunctions   62

Be Careful Whom You Ask   65

A Match Made in Heaven   66

Parashas Toldos

No Place Like Home   68

The Money-Making Umbrella   70

Sign on the Microdotted line   71

Car Switch   73

Overlooked, but Not Forgiven   76

Eisav's Kibbud Av   77

Easy as Pi   79

Parashas Vayeitzei

My House for a Slice of Bread   81

Who Owes Whom   84

Would You Mind Moving, Please   87

Fair Exchange Is Not Robbery – Or Is It?   88

Does Family Always Come First?   90

The Walls Have Ears   92

True Honor   94

Parashas Vayishlach

Doing Kindness at the Expense of Others 96
Are There Free Rides? 99
An Underhanded Acquisition 100

Parashas Vayeishev

May We All Hear Good News 102
Are All Men Created Equal? 104
Misdirected Renovation 105
Stop – Thief! 106
You or Me? What's the Difference? 108
The Right Place at the Right Time 109
Advertising 112

Parashas Mikeitz

Picture Perfect I 114
Health Insurance 115
Picture Perfect II 117
Birds of a Feather 119
Finders Keepers 120

Parashas Vayigash

Buy in Bulk 122
Best Buy 124
Practice Makes Perfect 125

Parashas Vayechi

Quiet Contribution 126
Right Address, Wrong House 128
Eviction Without Notice 130
Hashem Runs the World 131

Sefer Shemos

Parashas Shemos

Free Babysitting	137
Misplaced Gratitude	139
100 Percent Leather	140
It's the Ambiance	142
A Matter of Faith	144

Parashas Va'eira

The Right Match	146
Measure for Measure I	147
The Oldest Trick in the Book	150
Conditional Air	153

Parashas Bo

The Absolute Truth	155
True Service	156
Subtle Lighting	158
Into the Fire	159
Whose Matzah Is It?	161
How Much Would You Give to Do a Mitzvah?	163
Leil Shimurim	165
There Is No Place Like Home	167

Parashas Beshalach

Buckle Your Seatbelt!	169
Determining Your Budget	170
Mitzvah Accessories	172
In Honor of Shabbos	173

Parashas Yisro

High-Volume Service	175
A Difficult Mitzvah	177

True Honor 178
The Best Seder 180

Parashas Mishpatim

The Best Things in Life Are Free 182
The Man Who Cried, "Ambulance!" 183
Medical Expenses I 186
Medical Expenses II 187
Dangerous Shame 188
False Security 190
In Absence of X-Ray Vision 192
Check Changing 194
Being Holy at Someone Else's Expense 195
Majority Rules 197
Israeli Healthcare 199
The Whole Truth 200

Parashas Terumah

A Modern-day Holdup 202
Unnecessary Money 204
Undue Dues 206
The Dye Is Cast 207
Priorities 209

Parashas Tetzaveh

Defective Merchandise I 211
Defective Merchandise II 212
Peace Plan 214

Parashas Ki Sisa

Rare Photos 216
Minimizing the Damage 217
It's for the Kids 219
Phone Home 220
It's a Living 221

Parashas Vayakheil

A Diagnosis in Honor of Shabbos — 223
Fare Is Fair — 224
A Living Torah — 226

Parashas Pekudei

It Pays to Be Nice — 227
Whose Mitzvah Is It? — 229
An Expensive House Call — 231
Going the Extra Mile — 234
Shul Business — 235

Sefer Vayikra

Parashas Vayikra

A Father's Blessing — 239
The Privilege of Ownership — 241
The First or the Most — 242

Parashas Tzav

One Dizzy Chicken — 244
No Time to Eat — 246
Can You Take It With You? — 248

Parashas Shemini

You Have the Right to Remain Silent — 249
Please Pass the Ketchup — 251
To Eat or Not to Eat — 252
Mandatory Attendance? I — 254
Bac-Os — 255

Parashas Tazria

The Preferred Sandek — 257

Family First   258
Care for Tefillin   260

Parashas Metzora

Classified Information   262
Service Call   264
Trojan Couch   266
Color Coordination   269
Wet Paint   271

Parashas Acharei Mos

It's Only Water   273
Special Delivery   275
The Yolk Is on Whom?   276
To Call or Not to Call I   277
To Call or Not to Call II   279

Parashas Kedoshim

A Business Expense   280
Driver's Test   282
A Choice of Mitzvos   283
Mandatory Attendance? II   285
Keeping Your Co-workers   286
Uh! Uh! Nu!   288

Parashas Emor

Kiddush Hashem   289
Priorities   291
Which Mitzvah to Choose   292
The Chofetz Chaim's Preference   294
Cramped Quarters   296
The Best Way to Live   298
Oops! Sorry   299

Parashas Behar

Conflicting Interests	301
Too Cheap to Be True	302
A Misinformed Seller	305
Seller Beware	306
Your Life Has Priority	309

Parashas Bechukosai

The Right to Remain Silent	312
Measure for Measure II	314
Absolute Value	316

Sefer Bamidbar

Parashas Bamidbar

Going Down?	321
Hashem Knows	322

Parashas Nasso

An Outstanding Loan Payment	324
Would You Care for Another Cheese Blintz?	326
Shalom Bayis — At What Cost	327

Parashas Beha'aloscha

Age Before Beauty	329
Steak Out	330
Sensitivity	332

Parashas Shelach

The Situation Is Not So Grave	334
Too Easy	336
To Give Him Another Chance	338

Parashas Korach

Know Your Place	340
We Want to Pay!	341
A Picture Is Worth …	342
Taking a Risk to Do Mitzvos	344

Parashas Chukas

Seize the Moment	347
In the Absence of a G.P.S.	349
"Has Anyone Seen My Contacts?"	350
You Get What You Pay For	351
Caution in Repaying a Loan	353
Theft Deterrent	355
Accidental Insurance	356

Parashas Balak

Be Kind to Animals	358
Using the Law for Your Own Purposes	360

Parashas Pinchas

Shul Policy	362
Jackpot!	363
Priority to Be Chazzan	364

Parashas Mattos

False Alarm?	366
Expensive Garbage	369
And You Shall Be Clean	371

Parashas Mas'ei

Metered Parking I	373
Metered Parking II	375
Defensive Driving	376
With a Broken Heart	378

Sefer Devarim

Parashas Devarim

Picking Your Mitzvos	383
One in the Hand …	385
First Come …	387
Preferential Treatment	389
Talent Versus Experience	391
Sounds the Same	392

Parashas Va'eschanan

Wedding Album	394
A Mitzvah or an Aveirah	395
One Reader or Two	398
It's Not Easy Being Green	399
Guard Your Tongue	401
True Chinuch	402
Save Some for Me	404
It Is Not Yours to Trade	406

Parashas Eikev

Maximize Your Potential	408
Bar Mitzvah Pose	409
Precious Time	411

Parashas Re'ei

Two Mitzvos at Once	413
Keeping the Peace	415
Questionable Public Relations	417
A Matter of Accounting	419
A Free Mitzvah?	420
My Day Off	422
Dressing Up	423

Parashas Shoftim

A Profitable Investment	424
Medical Secrets	426
A Help or a Harm I	428

Parashas Ki Seitzei

Finders Are Not Always Keepers	432
Where Is Your Gratitude?	433
As Long as It Stands	435
A Help or a Harm II	436
Structural Defect	439
Cardboard by the Pound?	440

Parashas Ki Savo

An Incomplete Present	442
Honoring One's Parent: At What Price?	445
Just Desserts	448

Parashas Nitzavim

Good Things Come Anyway	451
In the Footsteps of Our Sages	453
Practice Makes Perfect	455
Mitzvos Take Time and Money	457

Parashas Vayeilech

Maximizing Your Potential	460
A Sure Sign	462
Under Surveillance	465

Parashas Ha'azinu

A Captive Audience	467
Do I Have To?	469

Parashas V'zos HaBerachah

Mass Labor	471

Giving Tzedakah at the Proper Time   473
The Most for Your Money   474

Glossary   477
Index   483

Preface

A Song of Praise to the Master Composer

By Rabbi Yitzchok Zilberstein[1]
Rav of Ramat Elchanan

The story is told of an older man who began to study Torah. Although he applied himself diligently, he struggled to understand the Gemara. He saw young boys who knew far more than he, and whose grasp of the material far exceeded his own.

Despite the challenges, the fellow always remained upbeat.

But now the man had been diagnosed with cancer, and as he felt his end was drawing near, he grew frustrated at the limited knowledge that resulted from his significant investment of time and effort.

He discussed the situation with the rabbi who was guiding him.

"*Rebbi*, I have had it! Gemara is just not for me. I see younger students who are able to learn an entire page in an hour, and in

---

1. Translated from the Preface Rabbi Zilberstein wrote for this book.

the same amount of time I barely learn a few lines, and I barely understand even that little bit! Why should I continue to waste my time? The people around me study so much; do my few lines make a difference to anyone?"

The rabbi sat his student down and shared a story:

"Yesterday I heard of a world-famous conductor who was once sitting with his biographer, and together they listened to the recording of a complex classical composition.

"When the rendition ended, the conductor turned to his companion and asked, 'Did you notice anything unusual about the overture we just heard?'

" 'It was quite amazing, but I heard nothing unusual,' replied the man.

" 'Well,' said the conductor, 'this piece was arranged to be played by an orchestra that includes 14 violins. But I am certain that only 13 violins were playing. One violin was missing.'

"The skeptical biographer concluded his session and left the maestro's home. Was the assertion true? Was it possible that through the rich sounds of the full orchestra a person could detect that one violin was missing?

"The next day, the biographer began his research. Sure enough, the day that the recording was made, one violinist had called in sick and no replacement was found.

"What was imperceptible to almost anyone else was easily discerned by the master conductor. One part was not played. One crucial set of notes was missing. The performance was incomplete.

"The same is true in life.

"We are each in this world to play our unique part in the Symphony of Life. You may view your role as small and insignificant, but to the Master, the Conductor on High, that symphony — with all its accomplished Torah scholars and all the righteous people — is incomplete, as long as one musician is missing.

"Your absence will certainly be noticed by Hashem. You are a unique part of the orchestra, with your unique capabilities. You should not be discouraged by your difficulty or lack of understanding, because Hashem asks only that you learn His Torah to the best of your ability.

"By playing your part, you are completing the Symphony for the Master of the Universe."

<hr />

When the Jewish family gathers around the Shabbos table and discusses *divrei Torah* they are similar to a great musical choir that has assembled to sing songs to Hashem. There is nothing more pleasurable to Hashem than this.

The *pasuk*[2] tells us, "And Moshe gathered," from which *Chazal* derive that there is a special mitzvah to gather together on Shabbos to learn Torah. Therefore, we deeply thank Rabbi Moshe Sherrow, who chose to excerpt and adapt the *Chashukei Chemed* series for the purpose of uniting Jewish families in discussing practical halachic questions, giving young and old the opportunity to join together in discussing matters and principles that reflect "the Word of Hashem" — halachah.

I hereby bless the exceptional Torah scholar Rabbi Moshe Sherrow, *shlita*, that he should succeed in glorifying the Torah and bringing those who *"desire His ornaments"*[3] closer to Hashem, the Master Composer, Who has chosen us from all of the nations and given us His Torah.

May he grow and succeed in exalting the Torah and strengthening it.

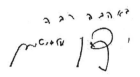

<hr />

2. *Shemos* 35:1.
3. The meaning of *Chashukei Chemed*.

Introduction

הַמִּזְבֵּחַ עֵץ שָׁלוֹשׁ אַמּוֹת גָּבֹהַּ ... וַיְדַבֵּר אֵלַי זֶה הַשֻּׁלְחָן אֲשֶׁר לִפְנֵי ה׳
The Altar was of wood, three cubits tall ... He said to me,
"This is Table that is before Hashem"
(Yechezkel 41:22)

he Gemara in *Chagigah*[1] asks why the *pasuk* changes its subject from an Altar to a Table. It answers that both R' Yochanan and Reish Lakish taught that when the *Beis HaMikdash* was still standing, it was the function of the Altar (*Mizbe'ach*) to atone for a person's sins. Now that the *Beis HaMikdash* is no longer extant, atonement is achieved by means of a person's table.

Rashi explains that a person's table atones for him, as it is the means whereby one can invite guests and thereby accrue merits for oneself. In addition, the Gemara in *Shabbos*[2] quotes Rav Yehudah in the name of Rav as saying that hosting guests is an even greater merit than greeting the *Shechinah!* Whereas the *Beis HaMikdash* was a place where the Presence of Hashem was apparent, a person's dining-room table has the potential to fulfill an even greater purpose: hosting guests.

1. 27a.
2. 127a.

Avos D'Rabbi Nassan[3] relates the following story: Once, R' Yochanan ben Zakkai was leaving Yerushalayim. R' Yehoshua, who was following him, surveyed the site of the destroyed *Beis HaMikdash*. R' Yehoshua lamented, "Woe is to us over that which is in ruins — the place where the Jews received atonement for sins." R' Yochanan answered him, "My son, do not be distressed, as we have an atonement of equal measure, and that is doing kindness, as the *pasuk* says, 'I desire kindness, and not an offering.'"[4]

Tosafos in *Chagigah* quotes a different source regarding the ability of one's table to effect atonement. The Gemara in *Sanhedrin*[5] quotes R' Yochanan in the name of R' Yose ben Kisma: גְּדוֹלָה לְגִימָה שֶׁהִרְחִיקָה שְׁתֵּי מִשְׁפָּחוֹת מִיִּשְׂרָאֵל — "Eating is of such importance that it caused two nations to be distanced from the Jewish nation." This refers to Ammon and Moav, whose members are restricted from marrying most Jews as a consequence of their actions when they did not provide bread and water to the Jewish people when they left Egypt.

Rashi in *Sanhedrin* explains that "eating" refers to that which is fed to guests. I would like to humbly suggest that the emphasis on "eating" is because one must eat in order to live. When one feeds a guest, he is providing him with sustenance, i.e. the energy to live. Sustaining the life of those created in the image of Hashem also preserves their souls within their bodies, and thereby sustains the presence of Hashem in this world. This may be why hosting guests is even more important than *Kabbalas P'nei HaShechinah*, because feeding guests is not merely greeting the Presence of Hashem, but sustaining people whose souls are an extension of that Presence.

However, in order for this to be true, there would seem to be a precondition. The Mishnah in *Pirkei Avos*[6] teaches in the name of R' Shimon that three people who ate together at one table and did not speak words of Torah, it is as if they have eaten from sacrifices

---

3. 4:5.
4. *Hoshea* 6:6.
5. 103b.
6. 3:4.

to the dead (idol worship) … whereas three people who ate at one table and did converse in words of Torah, it is as if they have eaten from Hashem's Table, as it says, "He said to me, 'This is the Table that is before Hashem.'"[7]

In order for the table to be considered as having sustained the living, one must include words of Torah at the meal. To sustain the body without sustaining the soul, to feed the flesh and ignore the spirit, is to deprive the person of the nutrition that is essential to be truly alive. Only when one attends to the needs of his eternal soul can he be considered as having eaten from Hashem's Table. This is the very same *pasuk* that is quoted in reference to the table's ability to function as a means of atonement for a person, as effective as the Altar itself. A table without words of Torah is likened to a sacrifice to a foreign god, whereas words of Torah transform a table into a place of holiness, where one sits in the presence of Hashem.

The *pasuk*[8] records that Aharon and all the elders of Israel came to eat bread with Yisro, the father-in-law of Moshe, before Hashem. *Rashi* explains that we are to learn from this *pasuk* that when one enjoys a meal where *talmidei chachamim* are present, it is as if he is benefiting from the radiance of the *Shechinah*. Again we find that a meal that is infused with spirituality, in the presence of Torah scholars, is not merely a mundane experience, but an exalting opportunity to rise to levels of holiness. It is an opportunity to have contact with Hashem Himself.

Everything we have presented until now is pertinent to a standard meal. How much more so when one partakes of a *seudas mitzvah*, where the meal itself is the object of service to Hashem, does one have the opportunity to come closer to Hashem.[9]

Even greater is *seudas* Shabbos, the Shabbos meal. Shabbos is a taste of the World to Come, when one has the opportunity to bask in the Presence of Hashem. The Shabbos meal is a fulfillment

---

7. *Yechezkel* 41:22.
8. *Shemos* 18:12.
9. See *Machzik Berachah, Orach Chaim* 250.

of the injunction to honor the Shabbos and enjoy the Shabbos.[10] On Shabbos, the pleasures of this world are infused with spirituality when they are enjoyed in honor of the Shabbos. In return for according this honor to Shabbos, the *Navi* promises us, אָז תִּתְעַנַּג עַל ה' — "Then you will delight in Hashem."[11]

If a failure to bring food could distance nations from the Jewish people, how much greater is the power of a Shabbos meal to bring families closer together and closer to Hashem. Especially when meals are infused with spirituality, they have infinite power to bring everyone there together, since spiritually all Jews are one.

Imagine a Shabbos meal that is attended by *talmidei chachamim*, and is graced with words of Torah. מַה נּוֹרָא הַמָּקוֹם הַזֶּה — *"How awesome is this place!"*

———————◆◆◆———————

The inspiration for this *sefer* came to me years before I was introduced to the *sefarim* of Rabbi Yitzchok Zilberstein. The Chofetz Chaim Heritage Foundation produced a tape titled, "Mining the Treasures of the Shabbos Table." On the tape, Rabbi Paysach Krohn suggested that a great springboard for Shabbos-table discussions is to prepare engaging questions in halachah that lend themselves to everyone present participating and offering an opinion. I tried this with the steady guests at my Shabbos table (my children), and had amazing success. In addition to making them think and learn to offer an opinion, it is enriching educationally, and establishes a framework for endeavoring to understand the opinions of the Torah giants whose rulings guide us.

When Rabbi Zilberstein began publishing the *Chashukei Chemed* series containing actual halachic questions arranged according to the topics of the *Daf HaYomi*, I realized that it was a gold mine for Shabbos-table discussions. I wrote to him requesting permission to

———————

10. *Yeshayah* 58:13.
11. Ibid. v. 14.

cull and adapt questions from the 12 volumes already printed, and received the reply, "Permission is granted with love!"

The answers to the questions are a rich harvest of Gemara and *Shulchan Aruch*, Responsa *sefarim*, as well as the *poskim* of our generation. This enabled me to invite these *talmidei chachamim* to our table, and experience enjoyment as one who would be sitting at the Table of Hashem.

May it be the Will of Hashem that this *sefer* find favor in His eyes and in the eyes of His children, to draw us closer to Him, and to reap the benefits of the Shabbos table. And may we merit the rewards of the proper observance of Shabbos, with the coming of the Mashiach, quickly in our days.

Moshe Sherrow

Yerushalayim

Cheshvan 5773

Rabbi Zilberstein writes in each volume that the purpose of the *sefer* is to inspire people to learn Torah. ***It is not to be used to issue halachic rulings.*** Each person should present any inquiries to his own *Rav* and comply with his decision.

If such a statement can be made for the original work, how much more so does it apply to this *sefer*, whose author is so much farther from the original sources. Still, it is our hope that many will be enriched and inspired by this presentation.

Some questions conclude with וצ"ע, which means that more research is required to reach a final conclusion.

Unless otherwise indicated, or in the mention of a *gadol* or *posek,* the name of the protagonists in each question are fictitious.

Please avail yourself of the extensive Glossary at the end of this book.

Acknowledgments

First and foremost, I thank the *Ribono Shel Olam* for placing me מִיּוֹשְׁבֵי בֵּית הַמִּדְרָשׁ וְלֹא מִיּוֹשְׁבֵי קְרָנוֹת.

I am indebted to HaRav HaGaon Rav Yitzchok Zilberstein, *shlita,* for having taught me so much through his *shiurim* and *sefarim,* and for so graciously granting his permission to share his Torah with Klal Yisrael.

To my parents, who should live long and healthy lives, for their constant love and encouragement, and for having provided me with the skills and tools necessary to make me who I am today.

A special thank you to my other set of parents for having raised my wife, before I even knew them, and for all of their love and support ever since. May they continue to see *nachas* from all of their offspring, for many years in good health.

Everlasting הַכָּרַת הַטּוֹב to all of my *rebbeim* who have molded me and instilled in me the love of Torah and appreciation of the paramount importance of Torah learning. I am forever grateful to the Rosh Yeshivah, Rav Doniel Lehrfeld, *shlita,* for setting me on the path to become a *ben Torah* and for opening the yeshivah's door for me בְּשָׁעַת הַדְּחָק, and לְהַבְחִ"ל to the Rosh Yeshivah, Rav Nosson Tzvi Finkel, *zt"l,* for hosting me in the Mir Yeshivah, prodding me to rise ever higher, and being an example of what it means to be an עָמֵל בַּתּוֹרָה.

I thank Rabbi Paysach Krohn, *shlita,* for his enriching inspiration and for being the catalyst for this book.

My deep appreciation to Rabbi Hillel Geller, *shlita,* for his extensive efforts in thoroughly reviewing and editing my version of Rav Zilberstein's Torah and offering crucial suggestions that had had a profound impact on this *sefer.*

It has been an honor and a pleasure to work with the team at ArtScroll/Mesorah. Mrs. Judi Dick's insightful comments added immeasurably to this work, Eli Kroen's eye-catching cover design is delightful, Mendy Herzberg coordinated this project through its many stages, Avrohom Biderman worked closely with me to ensure that every detail was addressed, Miss Rivky Plittman developed the creative page design and typeset the book, and Mrs. Faigie Weinbaum and Mrs. Mindy Stern proofread. I am grateful to each of them for their efforts to make this book accurate and beautiful.

Continued gratitude to my loving children for their participation in our Shabbos-table discussions.

To thank my wife ... I will suffice with the fact that she knows. May we all be זוֹכֶה to be מְקַבֵּל פְּנֵי מָשִׁיחַ צִדְקֵנוּ בִּמְהֵרָה בְיָמֵינוּ אָמֵן.

Moshe Sherrow

Cheshvan 5773

ספר בראשית

Sefer Bereishis

פרשת בראשית
Parashas Bereishis

Pure Profit

וַיִּקַּח אַחַת מִצַּלְעֹתָיו

And He took one of his sides

(2:21)

 Harav Shimon Goldneck is an outstanding *talmid chacham* in serious financial straits. His hat is old and in poor condition. A wealthy man who davens in the shul would like Rav Shimon to have a new hat. May the wealthy man purchase a hat, then switch the old hat for a new one without Rav Shimon's consent, or would this be considered stealing?

 It seems that this is permissible. The Gemara in *Sanhedrin*[1] relates that an apostate challenged Rabban Gamliel, "Your G-d is a thief! Does it not say in the Torah that Hashem made Adam sleep and while he was sleeping Hashem took part of Adam and fashioned it into a mate?"

---

1. 39a.

The disbeliever's daughter asked permission from Rabban Gamliel to respond to her father, which he granted.

The girl asked her father,[2] "Please call a policeman!"

"What happened?" the apostate asked.

"Burglars came to our house last night and stole a silver pitcher, and they replaced it with a gold one!"

The man responded, "They should come to us every night!"

The conclusion to be drawn from the Gemara is that an act that benefits the victim is not considered stealing at all.

However, this would seem to be contradicted by the Gemara in *Bava Metzia*[3] that teaches that one may not steal, even if his intention is to repay double. *Rashi* explains that the Gemara is discussing an instance in which the "robber" wanted to give a gift to his "victim" and he knew that the victim would not accept it. This is prohibited even though he is taking with the sole intention of giving!

The *sefer Divrei Shaul*[4] answers that the prohibition is against causing the victim pain while waiting for the theft to be repaid. If, however, the beneficiary is not aware of his "loss" until he has already received his present, there is no pain, and therefore it is permitted.

The *Ahavas Eisan* answers[5] according to the *Rosh*[6] that if one has the means to pay more than he is taking, and the payment is available, he may take something from its owner, since doing so is a benefit for the one from whom he is taking.

According to both answers, it would seem to be permissible to switch Harav Goldneck's hat for a better one, since the replacement will be immediate, and therefore there is no pain of loss, and the *Rav* is receiving a clear benefit.

However, it is not so simple. Perhaps the *Rav* is one who despises gifts,[7] and he would not want his hat to be switched. Nevertheless

---

2. Translation based on *Rashi* 91a and *Maharsha*.
3. 61b.
4. Cited in *Margalis HaYam*.
5. Brought in *Ein Yaakov*.
6. In *Perek HaKoness*.
7. In accord with the verse (*Mishlei* 15:27), "one who hates gifts will live."

it would seem that there are two reasons why this is not a concern.

1) The *Bach*[8] writes that unless someone expresses that he does not want to accept gifts, the general consensus is that gifts are desirable. The *S'ma*[9] quotes the *Mahari Vi'el* that one cannot assume that his friend is agreeable to accept a gift, and therefore one can only acquire a gift for his friend when he has his friend's consent. Nevertheless, the *Ketzos HaChoshen* and *Nesivos HaMishpat* maintain that the Gemara and *poskim* are replete with the concept that a gift is desirable and does not require the express consent of the recipient.

2) The *S'dei Chemed*[10] quotes the *Minchos Zikaron*, that with regard to gifts to a *talmid chacham,* there is no issue of *"sonei matanos yichyeh,*[11] one who hates gifts will live," since one who supports *talmidei chachamim* receives great benefits in return.

In summary, it would seem that it is permissible to switch the hat unless there is reason to believe that the *talmid chacham* objects to receiving gifts (e.g., he has, in the past, refused to accepts gifts).

Family Loyalty

עַל כֵּן יַעֲזָב אִישׁ אֶת אָבִיו וְאֶת אִמּוֹ

Therefore a man shall leave his father and his mother
(2:24)

 There was once a couple who were blessed with a baby boy. The parents took a strong dislike to the baby's face, simply put, as his nose was crooked, and the shape of his chin did not appeal to them. They even refused to

---

8. *Hagahos HaBach, Bava Metzia* 12b.
9. *Choshen Mishpat* 195 § 11.
10. *Ma'areches Shin, Klal* 13.
11. *Mishlei* 15:27.

take the baby home from the hospital! A *chesed* organization arranged for the baby's adoption by a couple who had no children of their own, and who knew how to appreciate this gift from Hashem. The biological parents signed a document that they would have no relationship now or in the future with the child.

The adopting parents cared for all the child's needs, and raised him as their own. When he came of age they married him off and bought him a house.

Suddenly the child, now an adult, had a desire to acquaint himself with his biological parents. He located his adoption file and discovered his biological parents' identity. Despite his urge to meet his natural parents and form a relationship with them, he knows that this will cause pain to his adoptive parents. They feel that after all of the dedication expended in raising him, they are his true and only parents. How could he develop a relationship with the people who refused to have him as their child? Should he pursue his plan to meet his natural parents?

 Rav Chaim Kanievsky answered that there is no halachic reason to prevent him from meeting his natural parents. Although they severed their ties with him forever, he is not obligated by their commitment.

There is a constructive purpose in his meeting them; it will give him the opportunity to fully identify his family members, in order to prevent his children from inadvertently marrying a relative, which would constitute a forbidden relationship. However, he should initiate contact with them in a way that will not cause pain to his adoptive parents. He is obligated to honor the parents who raised him, perhaps even more than his natural parents. The Gemara in *Bava Metzia*[12] states that one must return the lost object

12. 33a.

of one's *rebbi* before that of his father. Although his father brought him into this world, his *rebbi*, who taught him Torah, is responsible for bringing him into the World to Come. His adoptive parents, as well, are credited for his share in the World to Come since they are responsible for his religious upbringing. Indeed, *Sefer Chassidim* writes,[13] "If the rabbi refused to teach unless he was paid, and the salary was paid by a benefactor, the lost object of the benefactor has priority (even over that of the *rebbi*)!"

Moreover, the adoptive parents have more of a share in his continued existence and survival in this world than his natural parents, and he would probably have to save the lives of his adoptive parents before he would save that of his birth parents!

That being the case, his desire to meet his birth parents and any halachic obligations he might have to them must take into consideration his primary responsibility to his adoptive parents.

<hr />

Manufacturer's Instructions

וַיֹּאמֶר הַנָּחָשׁ אֶל הָאִשָּׁה

The serpent said to the woman

(3:4)

 Aharon bought an expensive *esrog* from a dealer. The *esrog* was very beautiful, but had a tinge of green. Aharon asked the dealer how one could hasten the ripening process to make the *esrog* yellow. The merchant

13. *Siman* 585, cited by *Shach, Yoreh De'ah* 242 § 66.

responded, "Put it in the microwave for five minutes until it's done." The words were meant as a joke, but since Aharon was unfamiliar with microwaves, he asked his neighbor, who owned one, to carry out the *esrog* dealer's instructions. When his neighbor returned with a dried, black and burnt *esrog*, Aharon was horrified. He returned to the dealer and demanded that his money be refunded, since Aharon had only followed instructions. Does Aharon's claim have a basis in halachah?

 The dealer did not damage the *esrog* directly; he merely offered an opinion. At most, it is a *"gerama"* (an indirect cause) for which one cannot collect in a *beis din* and carries only an obligation *b'dinei Shamayim*. In our case there should be no obligation at all even *b'dinei Shamayim*, since the dealer never intended to cause the damage.[14]

However, the Gemara in *Bava Kamma*,[15] as brought in *Shulchan Aruch*,[16] obligates anyone who is paid to offer an opinion to pay for damage that results from his advice. It would seem that one who pays for an *esrog* has paid for guidance pertaining to the care of the *esrog* as well.

Specifically in our case, since the vast majority of people are familiar with microwaves, and would understand that the dealer was only joking, it would seem that the dealer is not liable because he did not have to suspect that his words might be heeded.

If an article of clothing is cleaned according to the label's care instructions and is ruined because the wrong label was inadvertently attached to the garment, then the manufacturer must refund the cost of the clothing since the customer paid for the cleaning instructions as well.

In our case, it would seem that the neighbor should be the one

14. See *Meiri* in beginning of *Perek HaKoness*, that any *gerama* done unintentionally does not create an obligation to pay, even *b'dinei Shamayim*.
15. 100a.
16. *Choshen Mishpat* 306:6.

to reimburse his friend, since he knew that the microwave would ruin the *esrog*.

—◆—

Professionalism and Emotion

 By the time the soldier felt the snake tightening its grip around his legs, it was too late for him to do anything but scream. The other soldiers in his unit ran to see what had happened, but when they realized it was a snake, they froze. They were afraid that angering the snake would cause him to bite their friend. Suddenly their commanding officer appeared with the unit's sniper. He ordered the sniper to shoot the snake in the head. The soldier whose leg was being squeezed by the snake objected hysterically that the sniper should not be given the job. The sniper and the soldier in danger had been at vicious odds for a long time, and now the sniper would have a perfect excuse not to be careful, and to shoot his helpless rival in the leg. Alternatively a sniper could be brought from a nearby unit, but the second marksman's aim was not as good as the first's, and calling the second one might actually result in the soldier being shot in the leg. Should the commanding officer acquiesce to the soldier who objects to the first sniper, because of his suspicion that the latter may allow his emotions to interfere with his assignment, or is there greater danger in calling the less expert marksman?

A There is certainly basis for the soldier's concern. The Gemara in *Kesubos*[17] states that a person cannot serve as a judge in a case involving someone he dislikes, because in that capacity, he will not be capable of seeing any merit in that person's case. Similarly, the Gemara in *Bava Kamma*[18] states that one who wounds someone else and is obligated to pay the medical expenses cannot offer his own services to heal the wound; rather, he must pay a doctor. The reason for this is because the victim can say that he considers his attacker like a lion waiting to pounce.

However, the Gemara also states that if the one who made the wound offers to bring a doctor from somewhere else, his victim can counter, "A distant doctor blinds an eye!" *Rashi* explains that a local doctor is more careful than a visiting one, since a local doctor is more concerned about his reputation. Therefore, it would seem that the superior marksman should be chosen. He will be careful not to damage his reputation as an expert, and thus will not want to mix personal issues into his professionalism, especially in sight of the many soldiers who had gathered.

---

17. 105b.
18. 85a.

פרשת נח
Parashas Noach

Vegetables a la Mode

וְאַתָּה קַח לְךָ מִכָּל מַאֲכָל (עי׳ כלי יקר)
And as for you, take yourself of every food
(6:21)

1) On Friday afternoon Aharon saw the owner of a vegetable store throwing out his old produce. Aharon asked him, "Why throw out all of it? Some of it is good."

"Because I feel like it," came the reply.

Aharon asked, "Can I at least take the good stuff?"

"You could," he answered. "But pay me a dollar a pound!"

Since the storekeeper is throwing away the vegetables anyway, can Aharon take them without paying?

Similarly, when farmers destroy their surplus crops in order to regulate prices, could a truck driver carrying the surplus distribute the vegetables to poor people instead?

2) Meir was in the supermarket on Friday afternoon. The owner told him that his ice-cream freezer broke, and there is no time to call a technician before Shabbos. Since the ice cream will melt and spoil by the time Shabbos is over, is it considered *hefker*?

 As long as the owner so desires, he may retain ownership of his merchandise. Although this should be obvious, a reference to this idea can be inferred from the fact that Noach was commanded to take food for all the animals in the *teivah*, without taking from others. The *Kli Yakar* explains that even though the flood would destroy any food Noach did not take, it was nonetheless forbidden for Noach to take it because it still belonged to its current, albeit temporary, owners.[19]

Certainly the farmers, who have good reason to destroy their vegetables, have the right to do so, and may enforce their rights. So too the storekeeper, whose ice cream was still good, may still charge the regular price.

The *sefer Orchos Mishpatim* discusses a case of one who broke a bottle of whiskey in an inn during Prohibition. Immediately afterward the king's officer came to search the inn for forbidden liquor. Had the whiskey been found, it would have been confiscated, and its owner fined. Even so, he obligates the man who broke it to pay damages, since the bottle belonged to its owner at the time it was broken. In the case of the vegetables as well, they are not yet ownerless, even though they stand to be, and Aharon must pay for whatever he takes.

***

19. Editor's Note: Perhaps in Noach's case, the people could have repented and avoided the flood. That is why their money remained theirs, as opposed to our cases where the spoilage is unavoidable. Perhaps that is why the *Kli Yakar* is not a definitive proof.

Granting Permission Against One's Will

אַךְ בָּשָׂר בְּנַפְשׁוֹ דָמוֹ לֹא תֹאכֵלוּ

But flesh; with its soul its blood you shall not eat

(9:4)

 1) A man petitioned the city clerk in Tel Aviv for a license to open a tattoo parlor. The clerk refused the petition for religious reasons, as tattooing is a violation of halachah. The man threatened the clerk that he will take the matter to a higher city official, and the clerk will lose his job. May the clerk issue the license in order to save his job?

2) Reuven asks Shimon to feed him a limb of a living animal, and threatens him that if Shimon will not fulfill his request, he will destroy Shimon's property. May Shimon accede to the request, or does Shimon have to suffer the loss of his property, just as one is obligated to lose all of his money in order not to violate any other Torah prohibition?[20]

 The *Maharil Diskin*[21] proves that in a case where one is forced to comply with a request to provide means with which to violate a prohibition, there is no violation of *lifnei iver*[22] by fulfilling the request. Perhaps the *Maharil Diskin* is in agreement with the *Mishpetei Shmuel*,[23] who explains that when

---

20. As is explained in *Shulchan Aruch, Yoreh De'ah* 157:1.
21. *Kuntrus Acharon, Siman* 145.
22. *Lifnei iver* (lit. before a blind person [you shall not place a stumbling block]) refers to the prohibition against enabling others to transgress a prohibition.
23. *Siman* 134.

one provides his friend with the means to violate a prohibition, it is as if he himself is rebelling against the mitzvah. That, however, can be considered rebellious only when one does so willingly. When one is coerced, he does not appear as one who is rebelling against the mitzvah. Therefore, if one would comply in order to protect himself from even a monetary loss, there would be no prohibition of *lifnei iver*, since he is not doing so of his own volition, and therefore does not appear as one who is disregarding the will of the Torah. According to this, the clerk may indeed grant the license. The same applies to Shimon acceding to Reuven's request.

Natural Resources

וְאַךְ אֶת דִּמְכֶם לְנַפְשֹׁתֵיכֶם אֶדְרֹשׁ

However, your blood which belongs
to your souls I will demand

(9:5)

1) **Yossi's dentist recommended** an extremely expensive treatment for his infected tooth. Is it permissible to extract the tooth, simply because extraction is less costly than treating the tooth?

2) Chanoch's finger was wounded in an accident, and he had to make a decision. He could have the finger treated in an attempt to heal it, or he could have the finger amputated. Chanoch chose to amputate, yet the doctor believes that the only reason he did so is to be able to collect disability insurance. Should the doctor honor his patient's decision?

The Torah forbids[24] cutting down fruit trees even in war-time, as it is a destructive act. Similarly, one may not destroy useful property without valid reason. This is the prohibition of *"bal tashchis."*

The Gemara[25] states that there is a prohibition of *"bal tashchis"* on one's body as well as one's property. Therefore, since a limb or tooth is worth much more than the potential profit, it would seem that one may not remove it unless absolutely necessary, due to the prohibition of *bal tashchis*.

The *Shulchan Aruch* rules[26] that if one asks his friend to cut off the first person's hand, and promises that the friend need not fear that he will be asked to pay for damages, the friend must pay the damages regardless of the promise. According to this, the doctor might even be liable to pay, if he honors the wishes of his patient. וצ"ע.[27]

24. *Devarim* 20:19.
25. *Bava Kamma* 91b.
26. *Choshen Mishpat* 421.
27. See above, end of Introduction.

פרשת לך לך
Parashas Lech Lecha

Irreplaceable Tefillin

וְאֶת הַנֶּפֶשׁ אֲשֶׁר עָשׂוּ בְחָרָן

And the souls they made in Charan

(12:5)

The tourist visiting Russia had brought a pair of *tefillin* with him. The Jews there implored him to leave his *tefillin* with them so that they could have one kosher pair of *tefillin* to share with their fellow inhabitants. The tourist, although he would not have to miss even one day of the mitzvah, refused because the *tefillin* in question belonged to his grandfather and were very precious to him. Does he have to leave them his irreplaceable *tefillin*, or not?

The *Maharasham*[28] writes that we cannot force one who has a *Megillah* to lend it to one who does not have one. He proves this from the *Rashba* brought by the *Rema*[29] who rules that if a father does not know how to circumcise his

---

28. Vol. II, 96.
29. *Yoreh De'ah* 261:1.

son and there is someone present who could but he demands payment, it is as if the baby does not have a father, in which case the obligation falls upon *beis din* to circumcise the baby and *beis din* should force the man to circumcise the baby.

One may infer that had the obligation not been upon *beis din*, the man could not be forced to perform the circumcision.

Even though the *Shulchan Aruch*[30] rules that in a place where *sefarim* are rare, *beis din* can force someone to lend his *sefarim* to others (with the provision that they will pay solely for wear and tear), which would imply that we can force someone to allow others to use his object for a mitzvah, that case is different since it involves mass *bitul Torah*.

According to the *Maharsham*, since our case involves the mass negation of the mitzvah of *tefillin*, we should force him to leave his *tefillin* as long as he is compensated for their fair value.

Social Security

וְאַנְשֵׁי סְדֹם רָעִים וְחַטָּאִים לַה' מְאֹד
*Now the people of Sodom were wicked and
sinful toward Hashem, exceedingly*
(13:13)

 An argument arose among the tenants of an apartment building. One tenant claimed that since there had been several burglaries in the neighborhood an intercom should be installed so no one could enter the building without being "buzzed" in. The neighbors claimed that

---

30. *Choshen Mishpat* 292:20.

the likelihood of a break-in in their neighborhood was still slight, and installing the intercom would prevent poor people from entering the building to request *tzedakah*. What should be done?

 The Gemara in *Bava Basra*[31] relates a dispute whether neighbors can compel one another to install a gate and a door at the entrance to their courtyard to prevent passersby from looking into their yard. The Gemara asks if it is a good thing to have a gate that closes, as there was a *chassid* who was frequented by Eliyahu HaNavi, and when the *chassid* erected such a gate, Eliyahu stopped appearing to him. *Rashi* explains that this occurred because such a gate prevents poor people from being able to enter.

The *Chazon Ish* asks:[32] Why did the Gemara find it necessary to bring this story? Even without the story we could understand that one should not erect a barrier that would prevent poor people from collecting *tzedakah*.

The *Chazon Ish* offers two answers: 1) The Gemara is teaching us that sometimes it is possible for even a devout person to inadvertently harm others without being aware of the implication of his actions, and even that act, albeit unintentional, would still result that Eliyahu HaNavi would stop coming to him.

2) Without the story, it would seem that one does not have to be available to benefit poor people to the point of allowing people to look into his yard. This, in fact, was the opinion of the *chassid*. Eliyahu maintained that this was not fitting for the *chassid*, and therefore one could not force his neighbor to act likewise.

According to the *Chazon Ish*'s first answer, even when there is a possibility of a burglary, one should not erect such a gate. But according to the second answer, one does not have to suffer a loss for the sake of poor people unless he wants to emulate the behavior

---

31. 7b.
32. *Bava Basra* 4 § 7.

of a *chassid*. Certainly if burglary or loiterers are an actual concern there would be no reason not to install such a door.

Yet it could be that in this case, according to *all* opinions one could install such a door. The Gemara only says that for the sake of poor people one must put up with having others look into his property. This, in itself, does not entail a financial loss, and one could take caution not to do activities in his yard that require privacy. In our case, however, one would be left unprotected, so his own loss would take precedence and would outweigh his responsibility to benefit the poor.

On the other hand, if the neighbor really wants to install the door to stop people from collecting money from him, and he is merely using the possibility of burglary as an excuse,[33] according to the *Mishpatim Yesharim* he would have no right to make such a claim.

━━━━◆◆◆━━━━

But You Promised!

וַיַּחְשְׁבֶהָ לּוֹ צְדָקָה

And He reckoned it to him as righteousness

(15:6)

 Pinchas bought his wife a new oven to replace their old one. He placed an advertisement in the newspaper, offering their used oven for sale. The ad read: "USED OVEN, in excellent condition, asking 2,000 shekels," and included Pinchas' phone number.

That day he received a phone call from someone who was interested in the oven. He claimed that he did

---

33. See "Using the Law for Your Own Purposes," *Parashas Balak* (p. 362).

not have an oven nor did he have 2,000 shekels to pay for one. He asked if Pinchas would consider giving the oven away for free.

Pinchas thought about it, and decided to give away his oven to someone less fortunate than himself. He replied in the affirmative. An hour later there was a knock at the door, accompanied by a request for the oven. Pinchas asked if he was the man with whom he had spoken on the phone. The man replied that he was. Pinchas gave him the oven and closed the door.

Five minutes later, there was another knock on the door. The newcomer identified himself as the man who had called, and reminded Pinchas that he had agreed to give him the oven for free.

He apologetically informed the man that he had just given away the oven to someone who pretended to be him.

Pinchas was sure that the first man had been an imposter who assumed that Pinchas would give him the oven if he asked, but had never actually spoken to Pinchas on the phone. Now Pinchas wonders if he has to give 2,000 shekels to the second man who arrived at his door, since he promised to give him the oven as a gift.

 It makes sense that Pinchas is exempt, since he never promised to give the poor man *an* oven, but rather a specific oven. He never accepted responsibility to ensure delivery of the oven. Even if a person is obligated by a verbal pledge to give *tzedakah*, in our case, there would be no obligation, as Pinchas never accepted responsibility to deliver it. Therefore, since the oven was stolen, it is the poor man's loss.

Regarding if Pinchas was remiss in not verifying the identity of the first man who came to his door, it could be that perhaps he was slightly negligent with regard to the case of the poor man's property, and some form of appeasement would be appropriate.

It is to the benefit of all poor people that one who agrees to give away his oven should not be liable if the oven is lost, so that people will not be afraid to give away their property for fear of such eventualities.

Applying the Lessons We Learn

כִּי גֵר יִהְיֶה זַרְעֲךָ

That your offspring shall be aliens

(15:13)

There was once an elderly widower who had a son and a daughter. When his health had deteriorated to the point where he was no longer able to care for his basic needs, the son suggested that his father be placed in a nursing home. The daughter refused to consider this, and she took her father into her home, to care for all of his needs.

One day the father attended a *shiur* on the *Pesach Haggadah,* and the words he heard struck a chord within him.

In the *Haggadah* it says "And I gave Eisav the mountain of Seir as an inheritance, and Yaakov and his sons went down to Mitzrayim." The *Beis HaLevi* questions the relevance of Eisav's inheritance to the *Haggadah.* He explains that the Mishnah states that one who swears not to benefit from the sons of Avraham is allowed to benefit from all gentiles. Although some gentiles are descendants of Eisav and Yishmael, they are not considered descendants of Avraham. The *Rambam*[34] explains that since Hashem promised Avraham that his descendants would be strangers in a strange land, and only Yaakov and his children fulfilled this prophecy, only they are considered true descendants of Avraham. Based on this, the *Beis HaLevi* explains that we mention Eisav's inheritance to prove that Eisav has no claim to Eretz Yisrael, as he received his portion right away without having to suffer the exile in a strange land. Yaakov and his children, who suffered as the children of Avraham, deserve to possess the Land that was promised to Avraham's children.

The widower heard this beautiful explanation, and decided that perhaps these words were applicable to his situation as well. His daughter did everything for him, tolerated him, and worked very hard to tend to his needs. She deserves to inherit him. His son, who did nothing for him, and never suffered the burden of his father's maintenance, did not deserve more than a small fraction of his father's estate. Before he makes an appointment with his lawyer to change his will, he would like to know if it is appropriate to do so.

The Gemara in *Bava Basra*[35] states that if a man gifts his assets to others and does not leave an inheritance for his children, although he is able to do so, the *Chachamim* disapprove of his behavior. The *Levush*[36] explains that since the Torah set a specific order of inheritance, *Chazal* saw that it was improper to bypass the Torah's "will" (no pun intended) by giving away one's estate to others. The *Chasam Sofer*[37] writes that

---

34. *Perush HaMishnah, Nedarim* 31a.
35. 133b.
36. *Choshen Mishpat* 282.
37. *Responsa, Choshen Mishpat* 151.

perhaps one could give gifts while he is still living, as a person may spend his money as he wishes, but he mentions that from the Gemara in *Kesubos*[38] it seems that one cannot give a gift during his lifetime in order to distribute his estate as he wishes. The *Rashbam*[39] says that even giving one child more than another child is forbidden.

In our case, even though the son's behavior toward his father was improper, the *Rambam*[40] writes that even under such circumstances, the *Chachamim* disapproved of changing the order of inheritance.[41]

If, however, the father feels that if not for his daughter's care, his money would have gone to pay a nursing home, and he is changing his will to his daughter's advantage because of his gratitude toward her, and not to punish his son, perhaps it would be permissible. The *sefer Imrei Yaakov*[42] concurs with this ruling. Especially if he leaves his son the value of four *zuzim* (between 5 and 10 dollars) in order to provide a fulfillment of the Torah's order of inheritance, according to the *Tashbetz* and the *Baal HaItur*,[43] it would be acceptable to do so.

---

38. 53.
39. *Bava Basra* 133b.
40. *Hilchos Nachalos* 6:11.
41. See *S'ma* 282 § 1.
42. As cited in the *Ketzos HaChoshen* pg. 16.
43. *Choshen Mishpat* 282 § 2.

פרשת וירא
Parashas Vayeira

Speed Versus Beauty

וַיְמַהֵר אַבְרָהָם הָאֹהֱלָה

So Avraham hastened to the tent

(18:6)

 Yaakov had a kosher *esrog* in his possession on the first day of Succos, but it was not particularly "beautiful." However, if he would wait for an hour or two, he would be able to get one that was more beautiful. What is more important, to do the mitzvah without delay, or to do the mitzvah more beautifully?

 The *Shvus Yaakov*[44] discusses this very issue, and although he originally proves that *zerizus* (alacrity) is preferred, he concludes that if the reason for the delay is to do the mitzvah in an enhanced manner, it is likewise considered expedient to wait in order to subsequently perform the mitzvah more beautifully.

---

44. Vol. I, *Siman* 334.

This issue is relevant every month in deciding if *Kiddush Levanah* should be recited even during the week, on the first possible night, or after Shabbos, which is considered a preferred time since people are still dressed in their finery and the spirit of Shabbos is still upon them.[45] The *Mishnah Berurah* brings a difference of opinion between the *poskim*, to wait or not.

In the case of the *esrog*, the *Tosefes Bikkurim*[46] says that one could still beautify the mitzvah later in the day even after he has fulfilled his obligation earlier, since *Tosafos* says that the entire day is included in the glorification of the mitzvah.[47] Therefore he should use his own *esrog* first, and take his *lulav* again with the other *esrog* later without a *berachah*. (This seems to disagree with the position attributed to Rav Chaim Brisker, that one cannot beautify this mitzvah if one has already fulfilled his obligation.)

Overbooking

וַיִּקַּח חֶמְאָה וְחָלָב
He took cream and milk
(18:8)

 Yosef and Binyamin were best friends. Binyamin married before Yosef and moved to Eretz Yisrael. Soon afterward Yosef was engaged, and called his friend Binyamin with the news. Yosef so much wished that his best friend would personally participate in his *simchah*, that he offered to send him two tickets for himself and

---

45. See *Mishnah Berurah* 426 § 20 and *Sha'ar HaTziyun* 21.
46. *Siman* 651.
47. *Tosafos, Succah* 39a.

his wife to fly in for the wedding. Binyamin was over-joyed and looked forward to his friend's *simchah*.

Binyamin arrived at the airport in plenty of time for the flight. When he arrived at the counter, they informed him that they had given his seats to other customers who had priority. However, they would give Binyamin a large monetary compensation for his inconvenience. As a result, Binyamin never boarded the plane, as he would have missed the wedding. When Yosef arrived in Eretz Yisrael two weeks later, he went with Binyamin to a *rav* to ask to whom the compensation belongs: to the one who paid for the tickets, or to the inconvenienced traveler?

 It seems clear that the company's intent is to compen-sate the traveler for his inconvenience. He is the pas-senger on record, and he could possibly sue the airline for causing him a loss.

In addition, one cannot claim that it was Yosef's money that earned a profit, since the sale of the tickets was void, and Yosef's money was returned. Yosef's money merely caused Binyamin to profit, but that does not entitle Yosef to any more than the price he paid for the tickets.

Moreover, had Binyamin wanted, he could have told the airline that he forgives them, and does not want the compensation. Then there would be no profit. Therefore Binyamin is entitled to keep the money, as is the halachah[48] of an agent who received an over-payment. The agent is allowed to keep the extra money.

One might contend, however, that that case is completely dif-ferent, since in the case of an overpayment, there was no intent to give a gift to anyone. In the case of the airline, they gave the gift willingly. If we will decide that Yosef is entitled to the gift, Binyamin would not be allowed to refuse to part with it! וצ"ע.

---

48. *Choshen Mishpat* 183:6.

Medical Ethics

Now Sarah was listening at the entrance of the tent

(18:10)

 Dr. Shulman pioneered a new surgical procedure that will revolutionize the way surgeons approach certain cases. He delivered a lecture on the subject in an auditorium and charged an admission fee. Several doctors refused to pay, but listened to the lecture from the lobby, to learn the technique without paying. Is that permissible, and must they pay for the benefit of learning the new technique?

 The *Rambam*[49] writes that one who blew a stolen *shofar* on Rosh Hashanah has nevertheless fulfilled the mitzvah, because the mitzvah is to hear the sound, and sound is not something that can be stolen. *Rabbeinu Mano'ach* explains that sound and voice are not tangible items. Similarly, the *Shulchan Aruch*[50] rules that if one read from a stolen *Megillah* on Purim, he has fulfilled his obligation. The *Mishnah Berurah* says the reason is because voice cannot be stolen.

Our case is different than that, because one who hears the *shofar* or the *Megillah* has not taken anything from the owner of the *shofar* or the owner of the *Megillah*. In our case, the doctors have

---

49. *Hilchos Shofar* 1:3.
50. 691:11.

taken Dr. Shulman's wisdom. The *Shulchan Aruch*[51] rules that one who agreed to pay a doctor an inflated fee must honor his agreement, as he has acquired the doctor's wisdom, and wisdom has no price. We see that wisdom has great value, even though it is transferred through voice.

Responsa *Amudei Aish*[52] dealt with someone who owned a book that taught the craft of dyeing, and someone else copied the book and learned the craft. Does the copier have to pay for his use? The *Amudei Aish* answered: If the copier had intention to steal the book, he does not have to pay for its use, just like any other thief who returns a stolen item. [The Sages decreed an exemption in order to promote the return of stolen objects, in order to encourage the thieves to repent.[53]] If, however, he had no intention to steal, only to use, perhaps he should pay because of his benefit at his friend's expense. Now that he knows the craft, he might take away customers from the owner of the book.

The *Amudei Aish* points out that this is not the typical case of one who benefits from someone else's loss who is required to pay. In those cases the benefit itself creates a loss to the owner. For example, one who lives in his friend's apartment without permission makes the walls slightly dirty from his use of the property. Nevertheless, he concludes that even a loss that is not directly connected to the benefit would still require payment.

Responsa *Divrei Malkiel*[54] draws the same conclusion. Someone developed a nostrum and received approval from the health ministry. Someone else produced the same product and duplicated the first one's labels. The *Divrei Malkiel* ruled that the second one must pay half the cost of the license. Even if the duplication of the labels by the second one caused only an indirect loss to the first one, e.g., taking away customers, and would therefore not obligate him to pay for damages, nevertheless, the benefit of having his

51. *Yoreh De'ah* 336:3.
52. 12.
53. See *Shulchan Aruch, Choshen Mishpat* 363 with the *Sm'a's* commentary.
54. Vol. III, 157.

product licensed obligates payment since it involves even an indirect loss.

In contrast, the *Maharsham*[55] was asked about a case of someone who opened a business and bequeathed the rights to his daughter. Subsequently, someone else opened the same business and caused heavy losses to the first one. The *Maharsham* ruled that although the second person was not allowed to open his business because he was infringing on the first one's rights (*issur hasagas g'vul*), still the first one does not own the idea and cannot give it to his children. He concludes that they should come to a compromise.

In summary, according to all opinions, one may not listen to the lecture from the lobby without paying, since he is infringing on the rights of the lecturer. However, if he has already done so, he would not have to pay, because he may rely on the opinion of the *Maharsham*.

Personal Responsibility

כִּי יְדַעְתִּיו לְמַעַן אֲשֶׁר יְצַוֶּה אֶת בָּנָיו

For I have loved him, because he commands his children

(18:19)

 A person had two *esrogim*. He chose one for himself, and the other could be given either to his friend who does not have one, or to his own minor child. To his friend he has an obligation of *"arvus"* as all Jews are responsible for each other. To his son, he has an obligation of *chinuch*. Which has precedence?

---

55. Vol. 2, 202.

Rav Elyashiv ruled that he should give it to his son. Even though the obligation of *chinuch* is only *mi'd'Rabbanan* (of Rabbinic origin) and *arvus* is *mi'd'Oraisa* (of Biblical origin) the obligation of *chinuch* is a father's personal mitzvah, while his friend's mitzvah is primarily his friend's responsibility. One's own mitzvah takes precedence over an obligation which is his friend's.

This can be compared to a person who borrowed money but is also a guarantor on his friend's loan. If he currently has money available to repay only one of them, it is obvious that he should pay back his own loan first. So, too, in our case, his own responsibility comes first.

———◆———

Parental Rights

וַיִּשְׁמַע אֱלֹקִים אֶת קוֹל הַנַּעַר

G-d heard the cry of the youth

(21:17)

 A child contracted a serious disease, and his mother requested that it remain a secret because she does not want to be looked upon with pity as an unfortunate person. Is it proper for the mother to take that approach, or is it improper since if people would know about the child's illness, they could *daven* for him?

 The Gemara[56] explains the *pasuk* in *Mishlei*,[57] "One who has a worry should discuss it with others." *Rashi* says the reason for this is in order to seek advice. The *Aruch*[58]

---

56. *Yoma* 75a.
57. *Mishlei* 12:25.
58. *Erech "Sach."*

explains that this is so people will *daven* for him. According to both reasons it would seem that the mother's request is inappropriate since she is contradicting the words of the wisest of all men, who instructs us to let our problems be known.

The Gemara in *Berachos*[59] also teaches us that one who becomes ill should not let it be known on the first day lest his fortune become ruined, but afterward he should let it be known. Therefore, the child's possible benefit should outweigh the mother's personal discomfort.

<hr />

Chanukah Gelt!

אִם תִּשְׁקֹר לִי וּלְנִינִי וּלְנֶכְדִּי

That you will not deal falsely with me, nor with my son,
nor with my grandson

(21:23)

 A grandfather sent a large sum of money to Israel to be distributed among his grandchildren for Chanukah *gelt*. A doubt arose as to whether his great-grandchildren also deserved a portion, or only grandchildren. Who is entitled to Chanukah *gelt*?

 The Responsa *Mishkenos Yaakov*[60] brings a similar case, of a man who lay on his deathbed and gave instructions to give a certain amount of money to each of his grandchildren. One of his grandchildren had children, and there was uncertainty if the great-grandchildren were also entitled to the gift.

59. 55b.
60. Cited in *Pischei Teshuvah, Choshen Mishpat* 247 § 2.

The response was that a grandchild refers only to a child's child. This is explicit in Avimelech's vow,[61] ". . . that you will not deal falsely with me nor with my son, nor with my grandson," where *Onkelos* translates "grandchild" as "my son's son." *Rashi* comments that a father's love extends only as far as his son's son.

Although someone might contend that when people speak, great-grandchildren are sometimes referred to as "grandchildren," wherever there is no reason to assume that they had a different intention than the Torah's definition of grandchildren, we follow the interpretation of the Torah. The *Mishkenos Yaakov* concludes that even if someone will argue that there is still room for doubt, it must be noted that the gift of a man on his deathbed is only binding as a Rabbinic enactment, whereas inheritance is Torah law. Therefore the great-grandchildren cannot reduce the inheritance of the heirs unless we have a solid basis to believe that his intention was to give to the great-grandchildren as well.

However, the assumptions that we would apply to Chanukah *gelt* may be different than those of a bequest, as the motivation for giving Chanukah *gelt* is to bring about a love for Torah. Since the Torah instructs us to teach our children and our children's children, and the *Ramban*[62] explains that the mitzvah is to convey throughout the generations the monumental events that transpired at *Har Sinai*, to all of our offspring, perhaps the Chanukah *gelt* was intended for the great-grandchildren as well.[63]

---

61. *Bereishis* 21:23.
62. *Devarim* 4:9.
63. Editor's Note: There is a difference of opinion between the *Aruch HaShulchan* (245:9) and the *Shulchan Aruch Harav (Hilchos Talmud Torah* (1, 8) whether the mitzvah to teach Torah to one's offspring includes a person's great-grandchild.

פרשת חיי שרה
Parashas Chayei Sarah

Everyone Has One

תְּנוּ לִי אֲחֻזַּת קֶבֶר עִמָּכֶם

Grant me an estate for a burial site with you

(23:4)

A man purchased a plot in a cemetery many years before he planned on putting it to use. The cemetery workers did some digging in order to pour cement in preparation for using the area. To their surprise they found a buried treasure that had been hidden by thieves many years earlier. Are the owners of the cemetery entitled to keep their find, or does the treasure belong to the man who bought the plot, since eventually the treasure would be found in his land on the day of his burial?

Rabbi Nissim Karelitz ruled that the intention of the managers of the cemetery was to sell the land for use only after the buyer had died, and not while he is still alive. As long as the buyer is alive, ownership of the land is retained by the cemetery.

Tosafos[64] in *Bava Basra* notes that halachic power of attorney is transferred together with four *amos* of land (the approximate area of a person's grave). This structure is used even if the person conveying authority does not now own any land. *Tosafos* explains that everyone ultimately will own the land in which he will be buried. According to the aforementioned ruling, however, the land only belongs to him after he dies.

Indeed, the *Kovetz Shiurim*[65] asks: If a man did not yet own a plot, how can he use it to transfer power of attorney? He answers that since we are sure that he will eventually acquire the land, it is considered as if he already owns it.

It would seem that although this knowledge is sufficient to transfer power of attorney, it is not a sufficient level of "ownership" to acquire items left on the property; therefore, the treasure belongs to the cemetery owners.

A Doctor With No Compunctions

אַרְבַּע מֵאֹת שֶׁקֶל כֶּסֶף בֵּינִי וּבֵינְךָ מַה הוּא

Four hundred silver shekels; between me and you –

what is it?

(23:15)

 An elderly man suffered from a plethora of infections and illnesses. The bacteria in his body developed a resistance to antibiotics, and the doctors had given up

---

64. 44b. A full discussion of this halachic mechanism is beyond the scope of this work.
65. *Siman* 192.

hope. His children heard of an expert doctor who specialized in this problem. When the expert heard details of the man's condition, he decided to take advantage of the tragedy and demand an exorbitant fee. The children were amenable to paying the expert's fee, but were hesitant to endanger other sick people by setting a precedent of paying an unfair price for his services. Doing so could endanger lives if people are unable to procure such exaggerated sums of money. What is the right thing to do, to hire the doctor, or watch their father deteriorate?

 One may not buy an overpriced item. The *Tur*[66] tells the story of an officer who sent his servant to the marketplace to buy a fish. The servant found only one fish and the seller demanded a price of one golden coin. A Jewish tailor outbid the servant, and eventually bought the fish for five golden coins. The officer sent for the tailor and asked him why he had overpaid for the fish, and had not let his servant buy it. The *Beis Yosef*[67] explains, that the Jew was accused of two wrongdoings. Firstly, that he had paid a higher price than the fish was worth. (Such an action impacts negatively on the economy.) Secondly, he had shown a lack of respect to the officer. Thus it is clear from the first accusation that one may not overpay for a product, as doing so accustoms merchants to raise their prices.

In life-and-death matters, the *Mishnah* in *Gittin*[68] teaches that one may not redeem captives for more than their value, due to the harm this can cause to the rest of the world. The Gemara debates whether the reason is in order not to tax the funds of the community, or in order not to encourage kidnaping. The difference between the two reasons would be if the captive had a wealthy

---

66. *Orach Chaim* 604.
67. Ad loc.
68. 45a.

father. There would be no expense to the community, although one might be encouraging kidnaping.

Perhaps according to this second concern, one should not pay an exorbitant fee for a doctor either, so as not to encourage doctors to charge unfairly. This, however, would be relevant only if it were the children's money. If the money comes from the father's assets, a man may redeem himself at any price.[69]

In truth, there are three reasons not to compare these cases.

1) In our case, the danger comes from the sickness, not from the fee. Whereas paying an outlandish ransom may bring about kidnaping, paying a doctor may bring about a cure, not the sickness.

2) A doctor is hired for his wisdom,[70] and therefore any price may be considered fair.

3) There is an opinion that in a case of life and death one may pay even an exorbitant ransom.[71]

Therefore, the children should engage the doctor's services, regardless of who will pay the unfair fee.

---

69. See *Shulchan Aruch, Yoreh De'ah* 252:4.
70. As explained in the *Ramban* and *Rashba* in *Yevamos* 106a.
71. See *Pischei Teshuvah, Yoreh De'ah* 252 § 4.

Be Careful Whom You Ask

לֹא תִקַּח אִשָּׁה לִבְנִי מִבְּנוֹת הַכְּנַעֲנִי

That you not take a wife for my son from the daughters of the Canaanites

(24:3)

 Raphael received a phone call from someone inquiring about his friend Shmuel for the purpose of a *shidduch*. Raphael and Shmuel happened to be walking together at the time, and when Shmuel became aware that he was the subject of the inquiry, he decided to take the phone call. Shmuel excitedly described himself in glowing terms, in a way that no one else could have, or would have. Raphael wants to know: does he have an obligation to call the inquirer and inform him the information he received was exaggerated, or can he just remain silent?

 This would be a case of *"geneivas da'as"* since Shmuel stands to gain undeservedly by presenting himself as just a friend, and not the subject of the conversation. A friend would not have given such an exaggerated report. Therefore, perhaps Raphael should call back, and say he was not the one who gave the previous information. It was actually a very close friend of Shmuel's, who gave a slightly exaggerated picture of Shmuel.

However, the matter is unclear, as people who call for information are aware that friends sometimes are very enthusiastic when providing *shidduch* information, and will sometimes exaggerate.

This being the case, no damage will result from what Shmuel had said about himself, and Raphael need not call back.

A Match Made in Heaven

אָנֹכִי בַּדֶּרֶךְ נָחַנִי ה'

As for me, Hashem has guided me on the way
(24:27)

 Noach was under the impression that Menashe had wronged him, and Noach wanted to settle the score. Noach was also upset with a certain *yeshivah bachur*, and he decided to settle both matters at the same time. He called the boy and proposed a match, Menashe's daughter. The boy inquired about the girl, and accepted the proposal. Noach arranged a time for the boy to come to the girl's house to meet her. The boy arrived promptly and knocked on the door. Menashe opened the door, and asked the boy what he wanted. The boy replied that he was there to meet his daughter. Menashe found himself in a very awkward and embarrassing situation since he had never been told about the match! Menashe inquired as to the identity of the *shadchan*. When the boy replied that it was Noach, everything became clear.

Menashe felt sorry for the boy, and invited him into the house. He gave him some refreshments, and the two shared *divrei Torah*. Menashe was actually impressed with the boy, and it struck him that maybe this was an act of Divine Providence. They decided to arrange a real meeting and a short time later the boy and girl were engaged.

Noach heard of the turn of events and demanded a matchmaker's fee. After all it was his effort that brought about the meeting. Do they have to pay him?

A Responsa *Avnei Nezer*[72] records a case of a matchmaker who proposed a match between Reuven and Shmuel's younger daughter. In the end Reuven got engaged to Shmuel's older daughter without the involvement of the matchmaker. The *Avnei Nezer* rules that no payment is due, since the matchmaker never intended to make this match. Since he only proposed a match for the younger daughter, he has no right to be paid for the older one's match.

Certainly here, since Noach had no intention of matching anyone, he does not deserve any payment.

In addition, Noach might have to pay the boy for causing him embarrassment. Even though in the end the boy benefited, at the time it was only an act of damage, and the sweet ending only came about afterward.

---

72. *Choshen Mishpat* 36.

פרשת תולדות
Parashas Toldos

No Place Like Home

כִּי עָיֵף אָנֹכִי

For I am exhausted

(25:30)

Rivkah arrived home with her newborn infant. She was anticipating some much-needed rest, when the drilling began. It seems that her neighbor decided to renovate his apartment, and today was their first day of construction. Rivkah begged the neighbor to send the workers away, if only for a few hours, so she could rest, but the neighbor claimed that stopping the project would cause a significant loss, as well as delaying the completion of his renovations, which he desperately needed. Could Rivkah prevent the neighbor from building?

According to halachah, a protester cannot stop his neighbor from building since the project is short-term and is considered a normal use of one's apartment. The

Chazon Ish[73] writes that even though the *Rivash*[74] maintains that a sick person could protest against a neighbor's banging or milling wheat, and claim the noise is detrimental to the sick person's health, that right to protest is limited to those activities that do not constitute essential living. Normal use of one's apartment cannot be curtailed. Therefore, one is allowed to do renovations for a short period of time.

However, since we are dealing with a potentially life-threatening situation since Rivkah has nowhere else to rest, and if the noise continues, her health will suffer, the neighbor must stop construction. Rivkah, however, must compensate her neighbor for any expenses he incurs on her behalf, since he has a legal right to build. It is only her condition that prevents him from doing so, and therefore she must pay him as in any case of *pikuach nefesh*, where the rescuer must be paid for his expenses.

If Rivkah has another apartment where she could go to rest, she must go there. In such a case there is no *pikuach nefesh*, and her neighbor is entitled to complete the renovations.[75]

---

73. *Bava Basra, Siman* 13 § 11.
74. See *Rema, Choshen Mishpat* 156:2.
75. Rav Zilberstein explained that a hotel room would not be a satisfactory option, as she needs an apartment. That would be a major expense, and she is not obligated to such an extent to satisfy her neighbor's needs.

The Money-Making Umbrella

וַיִּמְצָא בַּשָּׁנָה הַהִוא מֵאָה שְׁעָרִים

And in that year he reaped a hundredfold

(26:12)

 Dan bought a new umbrella for $10. Instead of putting his name and phone number on the handle, he affixed the following note: This umbrella cost me $10. If I lose it, don't bother returning it; just send $1 to the following address …

Dan promptly lost his umbrella and over the next two years received not less than $50 in the mail, dollar by dollar. It seems that the umbrella kept getting lost and Dan hit the jackpot. Is Dan entitled to keep all the money? Additionally if someone finds such an umbrella, does he have to send a dollar to Dan's address? Perhaps the umbrella was lost by a subsequent owner, and Dan is no longer entitled to the money.

 It would seem that Dan could keep the money, even though he intended to sell the umbrella to the first person who sent him a dollar. As the finder did not remove Dan's address, it is probable that he did not intend to acquire the umbrella. Anyone buying a second-hand umbrella would remove the original owner's name and address.

Even though the Gemara in *Bava Metzia*[76] rules that one who finds currency with someone's name on it need not return it to

76. 25b.

that person, since money transfers from hand to hand and we may assume that the money was not lost by the original owner, our case is different. Whereas we do not expect the person who found currency to remove the name of the previous owner because money is soon spent, an umbrella, in contrast, is something that one buys to keep, and if one intended to acquire it, he should have removed the previous owner's name. Therefore, if the finder wishes to keep the umbrella in question, he should send one dollar to the address and remove the note, since Dan is still the one and only owner. Until his name is removed from the umbrella, Dan may keep all of the money he receives.

<hr />

Sign on the Microdotted line

אָנֹכִי עֵשָׂו בְּכֹרֶךָ

It is I, Eisav your firstborn

(27:19)

 When Avraham made a wedding for his daughter, he received a substantial check from his friend Yaakov as a gift for the new couple in honor of the occasion. Avraham noticed that the signature on the check was missing, and he assumed that his friend had accidentally forgotten to sign the check. Avraham did not feel comfortable asking his friend to sign the check, so he just set it aside and forgot about it.

Now Avraham was making a wedding for his son.

Again he received a generous check from his friend Yaakov, and again the check was not signed. It was not likely that Yaakov would make the same mistake twice. It seemed that this was his custom, to send unsigned checks. Avraham forged Yaakov's signature and cashed the check.

Later, Avraham regretted his hasty action. He obviously should not have forged his friend's name. He would like to know if he has to return the money to Yaakov, or perhaps since Yaakov sent the check, he did intend to give the gift, and the lack of signature may have been just an oversight.

Had Avraham also sent Yaakov similar gifts for his family's *simchahs*, it would have seemed that Yaakov intended to reciprocate in kind, as the *Shulchan Aruch*[77] writes that when one marries a woman, it is the practice that his friends give him money to help pay wedding expenses. This is not actually a gift because the understanding is that when the giver will marry he will receive in return. Since that was not the situation, Avraham should take note of how Yaakov greeted him after the check was cashed, or how he treated Avraham's son. If Yaakov seemed unhappy, he probably did not intend for the check to be used. He was just giving the appearance that he wanted to send them a gift, but in reality was hoping that Avraham would not want to approach him to validate the check.

The Gemara in *Bava Metzia*[78] asks: If someone had gone to his friend's field and separated *terumah* without his permission, how do we determine if the separation is valid?[79] If the owner of the field will come to him and complain, "Why did you not take from

---

77. *Even HaEzer* 60:1.
78. 22a.
79. In order to effect a change in the status of someone else's fruit, i.e. to declare a certain portion of the fruit to be *terumah*, one would have to have the permission or acquiescence of the owner.

the better quality fruits?," then we will know that the owner did not mind that his field was tithed without his permission. It is clear that the owner's reaction is a reliable barometer of whether he was agreeable to someone else tithing his field.

Rava qualifies this rule as holding true only for someone who took *terumah,* because it is a mitzvah. In a case of someone who gave a gift, we cannot rely on the fact that the owner seems to agree. Perhaps he is only acting as if he agrees because he is embarrassed to say that he wishes that the gift had not been given. In our case, however, where Yaakov sent a check, and people do not normally give unsigned checks, one could use such an indication to decide if the check was meant to be cashed.

Of course, this will be effective only if Yaakov realized that the check was cashed. Again, it must be stressed that Avraham should not have forged Yaakov's name and presented a falsified document.

Car Switch

וְלֹא הִכִּירוֹ כִּי הָיוּ יָדָיו כִּידֵי עֵשָׂו אָחִיו שְׂעִרֹת

But he did not recognize him because his hands were hairy like the hands of Eisav his brother

(27:23)

 Zalman rented a car from his friend Yonasan. They settled on a price for four days. Zalman picked up the key and went to where Yonasan's car was parked. When Zalman returned the key four days later, Yonasan came out to check that the car had not been damaged. When Yonasan saw the car that was returned, he asked Zalman, "This is the car you drove?"

"Yes," the reply came.

"But this is not my car!" exclaimed Yonasan. "This is my neighbor's car. He's been sick in bed this week, so he did not even realize his car was missing."

The cars were identical, and for some reason Yonasan's key worked in his neighbor's car. Now the three, Yonasan, his neighbor, and Zalman, came to a *din Torah*, to decide who should get paid for the rental: The one who provided the rental car, the owner of the car, or no one, since by taking the wrong car, Zalman never actually rented a car from anyone.

 The *Shulchan Aruch* rules:[80] One who took his friend's boat and used it, when it was not being offered for rent, needs to pay for any depreciation the boat suffered.[81] If the boat was available for rent and the one who took it had intended to rent the boat, then since he took it without permission, the owner of the boat could charge the rental fee or the depreciation. If the one who took it intended to steal the boat, he pays only the depreciation.

In our case, had the neighbor's car been available to rent, we would have to decide if Zalman took the car with the intention of renting it, since he thought that it was Yonasan's car, in which case he would have to pay either the rental fee, or the depreciation of the car (the neighbor's choice). Or, perhaps since he had already rented Yonasan's car, he had no intention to rent the neighbor's car as well. If that is so, then he inadvertently "stole" the neighbor's

---

80. *Choshen Mishpat* 363:5.

81. The reasoning behind this halachah is because one who steals has to pay for the item's value at the time it was taken. Therefore, any depreciation is the responsibility of the one who took the boat. If the boat was offered for rent, and it was taken with the intention to rent, the reason he has to pay is that the one who took the boat had the benefit of having the boat. This entitles the boat's owner to collect the rental.

Alternatively, the boat's owner could collect the depreciation. Since the rental occurred without the consent of its owner, the owner is entitled to be compensated for any losses he incurred. If there was no benefit at all, then the owner could only collect his losses, and not the rental, since there was no rental benefit.

car, in which case he would pay only for any depreciation in the value of the car. It would seem that he took the car with the intention to rent, since he had no intention to steal the car.

The question remains if Zalman actually benefited from having the neighbor's car, since he had in any case rented Yonasan's car. The case of the *Shulchan Aruch* is when one actually benefited from taking the boat. Since Zalman already had a rented car, he might not have to pay for the rental, since he never received the benefit of having a rented car.

It also needs to be clarified if Yonasan deserves to be paid for the rental since it was not his fault that Zalman did not take his car. The car was rented to Zalman, whether he used it or not. The *Shulchan Aruch* rules[82] that when Zalman paid Yonasan, the rental took effect, and therefore Yonasan may keep the money. It would seem that Zalman does not need to pay the neighbor since he already rented Yonasan's car, and Zalman should just reimburse the neighbor for the gas that he used and any loss to the value of the car.

---

82. *Choshen Mishpat* 198:6.

Overlooked, but Not Forgiven

וְהָיָה כַּאֲשֶׁר תָּרִיד

Yet it shall be that when you are aggrieved

(27:40)

רש"י: וְיִהְיֶ לְךָ פִּתְחוֹן פֶּה

And you will have a claim

 Boruch owns a dog. The dog darted into a neighbor's house and fled with a steak between its teeth. The neighbor did not mention the incident until two years later, when a disagreement arose concerning a different matter. The neighbor added the cost of the steak to his list of claims. Boruch was shocked. "That was two years ago, and you never said a word. Surely you forgave me for that old story. You have no right to bring it up now after you have already forgiven me." Is Boruch right?

 The *Maharshal*[83] contends that one who forgave his friend, even if he did not verbalize the forgiveness, indeed has no right to ask for what he has already forgiven. He brings a proof from the halachah in *Kesubos*[84] that a woman who does not request to be paid her *kesubah* for twenty-five years can no longer ask for it, even though she never actively relinquished her claim.

The *Ketzos HaChoshen*[85] argues that we never find that one's thoughts can change the status of their property even to make something *hefker* or *hekdesh*.

---

83. On the *Sma"g, Mitzvas Asei,* 48.
84. 104a.
85. 12:1.

Therefore, if in truth the neighbor had forgiven Boruch in his heart, his right to claim the loss would be dependent on the difference of opinions mentioned above. According to the *Maharshal* the claim has already been forgiven, whereas according to the *Ketzos* it has not. However the neighbor's silence itself does not actually prove that Boruch was forgiven. It is quite likely that the neighbor never forgave Boruch, but decided to wait for an opportunity to mention it, when making an issue over the damage would not disturb the harmony between the neighbors. Therefore, the neighbor could certainly demand to be paid for the steak if he maintains that he never forgave Boruch.

Eisav's Kibbud Av

יִקְרְבוּ יְמֵי אֵבֶל אָבִי

May the days of mourning for my father draw near

(27:41)

 A Jewish couple married and had a son shortly before the outbreak of World War II. The wife was killed in the Holocaust, and the husband was taken in by a German woman who registered him on her passport as her husband. Unfortunately, he eventually did marry her and they had a son. The Jewish son had lost contact with his father as he had been smuggled to a distant country before the war began.

One day the Jewish son received a call from a lawyer's office in Europe informing him that his father had died, leaving an inheritance of $50 million, of which each son was entitled to half. He immediately traveled to that city, and arrived before his father had been buried. An argument erupted between the Jewish son and his gentile brother. The gentile son wanted to bury the body next to that of his mother, in the gentile cemetery. The Jewish son wanted to bury his father in the Jewish cemetery next to the wall, as the halachah prescribes for one who has married a non-Jew. The matter was brought to court, and the judge decided that the body should be cremated and each son should receive half the ashes to do with as he wishes.

The Jewish son was horrified by the ruling. He was advised by his lawyer to offer the gentile brother a generous sum of $50,000 for the right to bury his father as he wished. The Jewish son thought it was a great idea and made the offer.

Once he realized that the father's honor was so important to his Jewish brother, the gentile son decided to make the most of the offer. He insisted on keeping the entire inheritance of $50 million, in order to give up his right to half of his father's body!

The Jewish son understood that there was no other way for him to bury his father, and courageously forfeited his entire inheritance for the mitzvah of burying his father.

Was the son actually obligated to forgo such an enormous sum of money in order to properly bury his father? Even though one is obligated to honor one's parents, the *Shulchan Aruch* rules[86] that any expense involved in honoring one's parent is the responsibility of the parent.

The *Shulchan Aruch* rules[87] that if one distributed many gifts and left only a small inheritance for his heirs, the heirs are obligated to bury him. The reason the obligation is upon the heirs, instead of those who received the gifts, as

86. *Yoreh De'ah* 240:5.
87. *Choshen Mishpat* 253:31.

explained by the *S"ma*, is because the heirs take the place of the one they inherited, and that which they received as an inheritance belongs to the one they inherited. As such, when they pay for the burial, they are paying with the money of the deceased. In the *Perishah*, he adds that accepting the inheritance carries with it the obligation to bury the one who left it, and the *beis din* will take the money by force, if necessary, to provide for the burial.

According to this, the Jewish son was obligated to forgo his rightful share of the inheritance in order to provide for his father's burial. Although it did not go directly to pay for the burial, but was needed to buy off the extortionist, it is still the father's money with regard to insuring a proper burial, and the son is not entitled to anything before the proper burial is facilitated.

Easy as Pi

אֵם יַעֲקֹב וְעֵשָׂו
Mother of Yaakov and Eisav
(28:5)

רש"י: אֵינִי יוֹדֵעַ מַה מְלַמְדֵנוּ
I do not know what it teaches us

 Reb Chaim Alpert was an excellent Gemara *rebbi* who loved his students. One day he challenged his students to find how many times in the entire *Shas*, *Rashi* uses the phrase "I do not know." Reb Chaim offered $100 as a prize for the student who would toil to get the right answer. One of the pupils found the answer all too easily, with the assistance of his home computer. Does the *rebbi* have to honor his offer and award the boy for a job well done?

A In *Sefer Shoftim*, Shimshon posed a riddle to the *Plishtim* and offered a prize of 30 suits and 30 cloaks to the one who would solve it. The *Plishtim* pressured Shimshon's wife to reveal the answer. The *pasuk* says that Shimshon indeed gave them 30 suits, but no mention is made of the cloaks. The *Radak* points out that either Shimshon gave them cloaks as well, even though it is not specified in the *pasuk*, or since Shimshon had a claim against the *Plishtim* for having obtained the answer unfairly, he gave them only suits. The *Malbim* also explains that Shimshon gave only half the prize since it was in doubt whether they deserved the prize at all.

Certainly in our case the point of the contest was to get the boys to search, to strive, and to exert themselves to examine the *Shas*, not to show proficiency with a computer. Certainly the *rebbi* intended the boys to put forth their own effort. Therefore, perhaps the *rebbi* should give half the money, just like Shimshon gave half the prize, since the answer was reached through an undesired means.

Moreover, even though the *rebbi* promised the boys the prize, he could not be accused of dishonesty if a prize was not forthcoming. The *rebbi* could explain to the boys, who were aware of the *rebbi's* true intentions, that under these circumstances no reward is deserved.

פרשת ויצא
Parashas Vayeitzei

My House for
a Slice of Bread

וְנָתַן לִי לֶחֶם לֶאֱכֹל

And will give me bread to eat

(28:20)

A man, who had been wealthy before he was rounded up by the Nazis, lay in his barracks in a concentration camp on the brink of starvation. He felt that if he did not eat something very soon, he would not last until morning.

He announced that he was willing to sell his mansion to anyone who would give him a slice of bread. A Jew who was lying next to him agreed to the offer. They finalized the deal with a legal "*kinyan*," and the seller was able to survive.

The very next day the Allies liberated all the Jews from the camp, and shortly afterward the buyer came to collect the house from the seller. The seller claimed that the sale was invalid, as he had sold it under duress. Since he was about to die at the time, he felt he should not be bound to his word. To whom does the house belong?

The Gemara in *Bava Kamma*[88] relates the story of a man who escaped from prison and must cross the river immediately so the prison guards will not catch him. There was a ferry standing at the riverbank, and the escapee offered the captain several times his usual fee in order to secure passage across the river. The Gemara states that the ferryman deserves only his regular wage, as the fugitive may claim that he never intended to pay such a high price, and promised to do so only because he was desperate to escape. The *Shulchan Aruch*[89] quotes this ruling as the halachah.

The *Ramban*[90] applies this halachah to a case of a man who is ill and requires medicines. Even if he promises his friend an exaggerated sum in order to secure the medicine, he has to pay only the fair value. If, however, he needed to pay a doctor's fee, he is paying for the physician's wisdom, which is very valuable, and therefore has to pay whatever the doctor charges.

Similarly, we find that Eisav asked Yaakov for lentil stew, and Yaakov gave Eisav bread and lentil stew. Some explain that Yaakov was concerned that Eisav was in danger of dying from extreme hunger. Since Yaakov wanted to acquire the birthright in return for the stew, he was afraid that Eisav would claim afterward that the sale is not valid, because Eisav had agreed to the sale only under duress. Therefore, first Yaakov gave Eisav bread. After he had already eaten, Yaakov gave him the stew, so that the sale was with Eisav's complete agreement.

In our case, perhaps the wealthy man could claim that he

88. 116a.
89. *Choshen Mishpat* 264:7.
90. *Yevamos* 106a.

offered the house only because he was desperate, like a sick man who needs his medicine. However, there is a difference. The man with the bread was not obligated to forgo his own portion. All of the prisoners were starving, and a man's own life has precedence. Every piece of food was essential for survival. The wealthy man cannot claim that he was only fooling his neighbor into doing something he would in any case be obligated to do, because there was no obligation for the man to give up his own ration. The *Mordechai*[91] explains that in the case of the ferry, the ferryman had an obligation to save the prisoner, as did the man who owned the medicine. That is why the one being saved can claim that he was exaggerating when he promised to pay more than the fair value, since the provider was obligated anyway to save his petitioner. This is not so for someone who had a piece of bread in the concentration camp, when he so desperately needed it himself.

Moreover, under such desperate conditions the bread is actually equal in value to the house. The Gemara in *Gittin*[92] tells of Marta bas Beisus who was fabulously wealthy. She lived at the time of the siege on Yerushalayim. One day, she sent her servant to the marketplace to buy some food, but there was no food to be bought, as the storehouses of grain had been burnt. When she discovered that there was nothing to eat, she threw her gold and silver into the marketplace, and said, "What do I need these for!" Maybe this is meant to teach us that at such desperate times, food is more valuable than gold and silver. This being the case, the price the man offered was not inflated.

There may, however, be a different reason why the sale may not be binding. Since the Nazis confiscated all Jewish property and the seller could not take possession of his property even via legal process, it is not considered to be in his possession to sell! The *Nesivos*[93] explains that if one could lose possession of his real estate, e.g., he had no witnesses that it was his, he could not

---

91. *Bava Kamma* 174.
92. 56a.
93. 363 § 1.

donate it to the *Beis HaMikdash*, because it is not considered in his possession. If so, in our case as well, it would seem that the sale may not be valid since the owner had lost control of his property. וצ״ע.

<hr />

Who Owes Whom

עֲשֵׂר אֲעַשְּׂרֶנּוּ לָךְ
I shall repeatedly tithe to You
(28:22)

 A fund-raiser arrived at the home of a wealthy man to solicit a donation. The donor responded that his financial situation was not what it had been in the past, and he could not afford to give as he previously had. However, he had once loaned 50,000 shekels to a certain man, and was unable to collect the loan because of the borrower's reluctance to repay. The loan would probably never be repaid, but the fund-raiser was welcome to try to collect the entire loan, and any money he could recover from it would go to benefit the institution for which he was collecting. The collector accepted the offer, and was given the loan contract.

As the collector was leaving, he bumped into someone. It was none other than the one who had borrowed the 50,000 shekels. The collector asked him why he had come, and he answered that he had come to pay back an outstanding debt. The collector was amazed! He happily pulled out the loan contract and relevant documents, proving that the loan had been transferred to his institution. The borrower suggested that they go into the house together.

An argument erupted. The collector claimed that the loan belonged to his institution, as it had been donated just minutes beforehand. The wealthy man claimed that the donation had been a mistake. He had only given over the loan because he thought that it was hopeless. Had he known that the borrower was right outside his house, he never would have given away his rights. The borrower claimed that since the loan had been given to *tzedakah*, he did not have to repay the loan! Who is right?

One cannot verbally give a loan away to *tzedakah*.[94] The *Shach* explains that this is because the loan is not in the donor's possession to give. In this case, however, a document, i.e., the loan contract, changed hands, and that is a valid transaction. While the *Nesivos*[95] maintains that the transfer of the contract must be accompanied by a written consent, the *Mishpat Shalom*[96] in the name of the *Maharashdam* argues that whatever the custom is, it is sufficient to transfer ownership. Nowadays, since people sell checks by merely handing them over, that is considered a legal sale.

As far as the donation being a mistake, Rav Chaim Kanievsky ruled that the money belongs to the institution. Although the borrower had been right outside at the time, until the money is returned to the hand of the lender, it is considered lost. Since the loan had been taken so long ago and the borrower had escaped paying until now, therefore, nothing was certain until it was actually repaid.

Rav Elyashiv saw the case from a different angle. If we knew that the wealthy man had not given a tenth of his earnings to

94. *Shulchan Aruch, Yoreh De'ah* 258:8.
95. 201 § 1.
96. Ad loc.

tzedakah (or a fifth, according to his wealth), which he probably had not, perhaps he intended that if the institution would be successful in recovering the entire loan, it would be applied to his personal debt to *tzedakah*. It is logical that he would be happy that the *tzedakah* had succeeded in collecting his lost money, even though initially he would have liked to have the money himself.

In *Maseches Kallah*[97] the following story is told: R' Tarfon was very wealthy but did not give the proper amount to *tzedakah*.[98] When R' Akiva offered to invest R' Tarfon's money for him, R' Tarfon gave R' Akiva 4,000 gold pieces. R' Akiva took the money and distributed it to poor people. In the end, R' Tarfon kissed R' Akiva on the head and called him, "My teacher and my master" — my teacher in wisdom and my master in conduct.

The commentary *Kisei Rachamim* explains that even though R' Tarfon did not give the proper amount to *tzedakah*, R' Akiva did not confront him, but rather used a ploy to accomplish his goal without embarrassing R' Tarfon. Even the holy *Tanna* R' Tarfon had been obligated to give more than he had given, and in the end, had been happy that he merited to give more.

---

97. 1, 21.
98. Certainly the great R' Tarfon gave a tremendous amount to *tzedakah*, but according to his Torah greatness and wealth, R' Akiva understood that he should have given even more. Indeed, it is prohibited for an individual to take the license to do a similar act.

Would You Mind Moving, Please

לֹא עֵת הֵאָסֵף הַמִּקְנֶה

It is not yet time to bring the livestock in

(29:7)

 Dovid came out of shul and found his car surrounded by parked taxis from a nearby taxi stand. He did not have to look far to find several cab drivers sitting on a bench, leisurely eating their breakfast. When Dovid explained that they were blocking his car, they casually replied that they were eating now, and did not wish to be disturbed. They would move their cars soon, they promised, and Dovid did not respond. He simply walked away and dialed the cab company. "I need a cab on 351 Grove St." and hung up. He ordered a few more cabs to various destinations and the cab drivers' meal came to an abrupt end, as they went to answer the calls of their dispatcher. Did Dovid do the wrong thing by sending them on a "wild-goose chase"?

 One who orders a cab, and does not ultimately travel with him, must pay the driver any expense he had on behalf of the caller. By ordering the cab to his house, the caller had already hired him for a job and must compensate him.

In our case, however, the drivers were not willing to move their vehicles. Dovid may take matters into his own hand, as is stated in *Shulchan Aruch*:[99] If one filled the avenue with jars, preventing pas-

---

99. *Choshen Mishpat* 412:2.

sage, if a passerby smashed them maliciously [in order to pass], he does not need to pay.

In our case, as well, Dovid may cause them the expense in order to secure his ability to move.

However, Dovid should not send them to a distant destination in order not to cause them more of an expense than is necessary. Also, he should be careful in his wording so as not to imply that he is waiting in the place to which he sent them, as that would not be true, and is also unnecessary.

━━━◆◆◆━━━

Fair Exchange Is Not Robbery — Or Is It?

כִּי אֲחִי אָבִיהָ הוּא

That he was her father's relative

(29:12)

רש"י: אֲנִי אָחִיו בְּרַמָּאוּת

I, too, am his brother in deceit

 As Mr. Cohen studied the screen of the store's surveillance system, he was shocked to witness his worker appropriating merchandise. It was one of his better-working employees, and he did not want to fire him. In addition, Mr. Cohen did not even want to confront his employee about the offense, and he knew that if he would deduct the value of the merchandise from his employee's paycheck, his employee would not notice.

Mr. Cohen knows clearly that his worker indeed stole the merchandise and there is no way to judge him favorably. May Mr. Cohen deduct money from his employee's paycheck without confronting him?

 The Gemara in *Berachos*[100] tells us that Rav Huna had a sharecropper who helped himself to much more than his fair share of the crop. Rav Huna in turn withheld the branches from the harvest, which by common custom should have been given to the sharecropper. When Rav Huna's colleagues criticized him for his behavior, he responded that he was only doing so in order to minimize his loss. His colleagues retorted, "This is what people say, that one who steals from a thief enjoys the taste of stealing."

Rav Elyashiv, in his *sefer He'aros*, asks, Why is Rav Huna criticized? Could we not say that Rav Huna simply exchanged the branches for his fair share of the harvest? Rav Elyashiv answers that Rav Huna did not have a right to exchange branches for the stolen fruit. The fruit and the branches are two separate accounts.

According to this, one would not be allowed to deduct from the salary in exchange for the merchandise, because although merchandise has value, it is not *money*. However, if the worker had taken money from the business, one would be able to take it from his pay, since there is no exchange of goods and Mr. Cohen is only taking money to replace the money that he is owed.[101]

---

100. 5b.
101. See *Mordechai, Bava Kamma, Perek HaMeini'ach* § 30.

Does Family Always Come First?

אַךְ עַצְמִי וּבְשָׂרִי אָתָּה

Nevertheless, you are my flesh and blood!

(29:14)

Rochel and Leah were shopping for groceries. Leah asked the storekeeper for a bottle of olive oil. The storekeeper replied that the oil was out of stock but would be available the following day. Leah was perturbed as she was in the middle of a recipe and needed the oil that night. Rochel offered that she had a little olive oil at home that she did not need. Leah could borrow it from her so she could proceed as planned. Leah was relieved and arranged to pick up the oil later that afternoon.

An hour later, Rochel received a call from her mother, with a request for a little olive oil. Her mother had also checked at the store and they were out of stock.

Both Rochel's mother and Leah need all of the oil. According to halachah, one who reneges on an offer is lacking trustworthiness. The question remains, however: Is Rochel obligated by *kibbud eim* (honoring one's mother) to give her mother the oil even though it was already promised to Leah, or perhaps it is more important that she keep her word and give it to Leah as planned?

The *Shulchan Aruch*[102] writes: One who commits himself with an oral agreement should keep his word, even though no payment has been made. One who does not

---

102. *Choshen Mishpat* 204:7-8.

keep his word has exhibited a lack of faithfulness and is disdained by the *chachamim*. So too, one who said he would give his friend an inexpensive gift, and did not do so, has exhibited a lack of faithfulness.

If Leah would be a poor person as well, by offering the oil to her, it would be considered a vow to give *tzedakah*. Certainly the mitzvah of honoring one's mother would not absolve her from her vow, and Rochel would have to give the oil to Leah.

If Leah is not poor, perhaps her mother's need would come first. Rav Zilberstein brings a difference of opinion, regarding an inexpensive gift, if the words themselves transfer ownership or not. Even though the oral agreement is certainly not binding to the extent that one could renege *although he is certainly obligated not to do so*, the question remains if the words actually create a transfer of ownership. A ramification of this would present itself in a case of someone who told his friend that he would give him a gift and subsequently died. Would his heirs be bound by his words? If it is only an obligation on the person who promises, to keep his word, the heirs would not be bound by his statement (Rabbi Akiva Eiger on *Shulchan Aruch*[103]). Conversely, if the words themselves actually transfer ownership, even the heirs would have to honor the wishes of their inheritor (*Mishnas Ya'avetz*[104]).

In our case, it would seem that according to both opinions, *kibbud eim* would not take precedence either to take away from Leah that which Rochel had already granted, or to stop Rochel from keeping her word, as the Torah did not obligate one to fulfill the mitzvah to honor one's parents when improper behavior is involved.

On the other hand, the *Rema*[105] brings an opinion that if the price of the item in question rose, one could retract his words and it is not considered a lack of faithfulness. Thus, one could

---

103. *Choshen Mishpat* 204.
104. Ibid. 33.
105. Ibid. 204:11.

argue that since the oil has the potential to be a vehicle to perform the mitzvah of *kibbud eim*, it could be considered that the value of the oil has changed and Rochel could retract her previous offer.

The Walls Have Ears

וַיִּקְרָא לְרָחֵל וּלְלֵאָה הַשָּׂדֶה

And summoned Rachel and Leah to the field
(31:4)

 Azriel had valid reason to believe that his competitor Zev was plotting against him. Zev had attempted several times to sabotage Azriel's business and, until now, had been unsuccessful. Azriel would like to try to protect himself for the future, but he needed to know what Zev was planning next.

If he could, would it be permissible for Azriel to eavesdrop on Zev's conversations? May Azriel plant a listening device in Zev's home in order to protect himself?

 When people are unable to use their own property without having their neighbors watch them, the limitation of using their property for private activities is called *hezek re'eyah*.

The Responsa *R'em*[106] notes that we do not find that *hezek shemiah*, limitation of use of one's property out of fear of being overheard, is considered improper.

---

106. *Siman* 8.

The *Meiri*[107] contends that there is no necessity to protect from *hezek shemiah*, because people are careful to conceal their conversations. One may infer from the *Meiri* that eavesdropping on someone else's conversation would be improper.

The Responsa *Halachah Ketanos*[108] rules that one may not try to discover his friend's secrets, because there is no difference between one who gossips to his friend and one who gossips to himself!

In addition, one who eavesdrops is guilty of stealing (as *Rabbeinu Yonah* considers all damages that one does to his friend to be included in the prohibition against stealing) of *geneivas da'as*, and of transgressing *ve'ahavta l'rei'acha kamocha*.

It is apparent that the *R'em* does not argue in principle, and contends only that the bearer of the secret will naturally protect himself, as it is known that the walls have ears. But certainly if one was careless, it does not give his friend permission to listen.

If, however, one suspects that his neighbor intends to harm him, one may protect himself by monitoring his neighbor's conversations.

Another example where eavesdropping may be permitted would be in the case of a teacher or a parent who is responsible for his student's or child's development. Listening to the youth's conversations may be permitted in order to guide and educate the child in the proper path.

————◆————

107. *Bava Basra* 2a.
108. Vol. I, 276.

True Honor

וַתִּגְנֹב רָחֵל אֶת הַתְּרָפִים

And Rachel stole the teraphim

(31:19)

 Jay sent his children to Jewish schools and ate only kosher food. He kept Shabbos in his home, but there was one area where he felt he could not do what was right. His store was open on Shabbos.

Of course, all the store's workers were non-Jews, as were the customers, but the store was known to be owned by a Jew, and he received all the profits from the sales that took place on Shabbos. In his lack of faith, he claimed that a majority of his livelihood came from business transacted on Shabbos, since that was when most of his customers received their weekly pay and were able to shop in his store.

His son begged him to close his store on Shabbos, but the son's cries fell on deaf ears.

The son came to ask if he is permitted to run away from home until his father pledges to close the store on Shabbos. On the one hand, such an act would cause his parents pain and embarrassment. On the other hand, the likelihood was that his father would acquiesce. What should the son do?

 It would seem that such a tactic it prohibited. One may not cause a father pain, even if the father is a sinner. Even though he does not have to honor a sinful father,[109] he may not hit him, or curse him.[110] The *Zohar*[111] explains that

---

109. See *Rema, Yoreh De'ah* 240:18.
110. See *Shulchan Aruch* 241:4.
111. Vol. I, pg. 164.

the reason Rachel Imeinu did not merit to raise her son Binyamin is because she caused pain to her father Lavan, even though her intent was to stop him from idol worship.

The *Ya'avetz*[112] asks: Why was Rachel punished? We find that King Chizkiyah is praised for dragging his wicked father's corpse because he had been an evildoer.[113] Rav Chaim Kanievsky answered that perhaps the *Zohar* is relevant specifically in the time before the Torah was given. At that time, honoring parents was more stringent than other mitzvos. Chizkiyah lived after the giving of the Torah, and then perhaps one could cause their parents pain in order to prevent them from sinning.

The *Shiyurei Berachah*[114] quotes the *Zohar* as the final halachah and therefore even in our times it would seem to be prohibited. It is possible that even according to the *Zohar* one could cause pain to parents to prevent sin, if one is sure to appease them afterward.

Perhaps a different possible answer to the *Ya'avetz's* question can be suggested based on *Rashi*.[115] It might be that *Chizkiyah* dragged his father's corpse to atone for his father's misdeeds, by sanctifying Hashem's Name and showing that evildoers will be punished. Accordingly, one may not cause pain to a parent to prevent them from sin unless it will cause a sanctification of Hashem's Name.

In our case, however, aside from the desecration of Shabbos that was caused by keeping the store open, doing so is a blatant desecration of Hashem's Name. If the son will run away, it will become public knowledge and sanctify Hashem's Name when people hear that he ran away for the sake of Shabbos.

[This incident actually took place, and when the boy ran away, the parents indeed conceded and closed their store on Shabbos. Not only did the parents eventually forgive him, but they thanked him and were very proud of him for what he had done.]

---

112. Quoted by the *Nitzotzei Zohar*.
113. *Pesachim* 56a.
114. See footnote 2.
115. Ad loc.

פרשת וישלח
Parashas Vayishlach

Doing Kindness at the Expense of Others

וַיִּקַּח מִן הַבָּא בְיָדוֹ מִנְחָה
Then he took, from that which had come in his hand
(32:14)

 At Mutty's wedding they placed exquisite *siddurim* in a beautiful array on all of the tables as gifts for the guests to take home. There were not enough *siddurim* for all of the guests, so Yehudah wanted to set one aside for his friend Zevi, who would be coming to the wedding later. May Yehudah do so, or is the rule "first come, first served"?

 The Gemara states in *Kesubos*[116] in the name of R' Yochanan, "One who collects a debt for his friend to the detriment of other debtors (because the borrower

---

116. 84b.

does not have enough money to pay everyone) is not considered to have collected the debt, and must return the money to the lender."

In contrast, the Gemara in *Bava Metzia*[117] states, also in the name of R' Yochanan, "One who picks up a lost object (which one is allowed to keep) for his friend's sake, has acquired the object for his friend."

The commentaries on the Gemara note that there is an apparent contradiction in the two statements. How can one acquire an item for his friend if, by doing so, he is depriving others of the opportunity to take it for themselves? It is for this very reason that we do not allow collecting the debt of one's friend where others will be negatively affected. What is the difference?

Tosafos answers that in the case of a lost object, since he could have taken it for himself, he may take it for his friend as well. In the case of the debt, he has no ability to collect money from the debtor for himself, as the lender does not owe him anything, so he may not collect for his friend, when it is at the expense of others.

The *Ramban* notes that according to this, if the collector had his own debt to collect, then he may collect for his friend. The *Ramban* disagrees with *Tosafos*, and contends that one can be considered to be harming others only when he takes an object to which the other people had rights. A lost item does not belong to anyone. When one acquires it, he is not taking it away from anyone, and therefore he can take it for whomever he wants. Only in a case of a debt, where a person's assets are bound to the debt, is a person considered to be harming others when he collects for one of the creditors.

Our case would seem to be dependent on these two opinions. According to *Tosafos*, Yehudah may not take a *siddur* for Zevi, since Yehudah already took one for himself and has no right to take another one. Since he has no right to take (another one) for himself, he may not take one for his friend, either. According to the *Ramban*, since the *siddurim* do not belong to any one of the guests,

---

117. 10a.

they are similar to a lost object, and by taking one for Zevi, he is not interfering with rights that anyone already has on the *siddur*, he is merely preventing them from acquiring something new. If this is so, Yehudah could take a *siddur* for Zevi.

In our case, it is arguable that even *Tosafos* would agree that Yehudah may take a *siddur* for his friend. Since the hosts who gave out the *siddurim* indiscriminately want their guests to have one, and it does not matter to them which guests will get one, the hosts' desire to give the *siddur* to their guests may give Yehudah a right to take for his friend, who is also a guest at the wedding.

However, even if he has a **right** to do so, it is inconsiderate to a guest who would like to take a *siddur* now, and out of sensitivity and propriety one should leave the *siddur* for others to take.

It is apparent that one traveling on a bus may not save a seat for someone who will board the bus at a later stop, since he is preventing others from taking a seat on the bus (if similar seats are not readily available). Certainly, since the others paid for a seat on the bus, one is interfering with their rights to take that which is rightfully theirs. An exception to this would be if it is generally accepted to do so; for example, a wife saving a seat for her husband, or a father for his children.

Even if Zevi had asked Yehudah to be his agent to take a *siddur* for him, although *Rashi* in *Bava Metzia* writes that he may do so, *Tosafos* argues, and the *Shulchan Aruch* rules like the opinion of *Tosafos*.[118]

———◆———

---

118. *Choshen Mishpat* 105:1.

Are There Free Rides?

וַיֹּאמֶר נִסְעָה וְנֵלֵכָה

And he said, "Travel on and let us go"

(33:12)

 Three boys ordered a taxi to take them on an inter-city trip. En route they passed someone waiting to hitch a ride, and they invited the boy to join them on the ride for free. When they reached their destination the three boys jumped out, promising to return momentarily with the cab fare. After 15 minutes, the driver and the remaining boy realized that the boys had exited the building from the rear and run away. It became apparent that the boys had never intended to pay, and therefore their invitation for a free ride was meaningless, since they were not going to pay the driver's fee. Now, the driver demanded that the remaining boy pay. The boy countered that the driver saw he had been waiting for a free ride. Why should he pay? Who is right?

 The *Rema* rules:[119] "One who invites his friend to eat, [where it is not apparent that it was a gift], and subsequently asks for payment, must be paid and we do not assume that it was a gift." The *Shach* qualifies, that if the invited person had elsewhere to eat without having to pay, he does not have to pay. Here as well, it would seem that the boy should not have to pay since he could have "hitched" for free.

However, this is only on the condition that he could have waited until he would get a ride for free. If he was in a rush, he has to pay the value of his benefit since he was driven by cab to his

---

119. *Choshen Mishpat* 246:17.

destination. Even though he did not intend to hire the driver, it is similar to a case in the Gemara[120] that discussed children whose father borrowed a cow, and died without telling them that he did not own the cow. The children, thinking the cow was their father's, slaughtered the cow and ate it. They are required to pay for the benefit they had, even though they never intended to pay for the meat. A *beis din* should determine the value of traveling in a taxi based on the location and the time of day, and notify the hitch-hiker how much he owes the driver.

An Underhanded Acquisition

וַיַּעֲנוּ בְנֵי יַעֲקֹב ... בְּמִרְמָה
Yaakov's sons answered ... cleverly
(34:13)

 Reuven placed a case of olive oil in his shul with a sign: "18 shekels a bottle." Shmueli passed by and wanted to buy a bottle, but he did not have any money. He decided to earn a bottle for himself by changing Reuven's sign from "18 shekels" to "20 shekels." After nine people paid for oil, Shmueli took a bottle for himself. After all, he was responsible for the extra 18 shekels that were in the box. When he arrived home, his conscience began to bother him. Does he need to return the money, and to whom?

---

120. *Bava Kamma* 112a.

A If Shmueli would have been acting on behalf of Reuven, the extra 2 shekels per bottle would belong to Reuven. In our case, Shmueli acted on his own behalf, and he had no right to use someone else's merchandise to generate a profit for himself. The *Shulchan Aruch*[121] rules that if someone rented out an apartment that did not belong to him, and the owner of the apartment did not intend to rent it out, the renter does not need to pay rent to the owner. Even though the renter was willing to pay when he came to live there, he still has no obligation to follow through since no actual rental transpired, as the apartment did not belong to the one who rented it out.

Consequently, the would-be profiteer does not need to pay the owner either, because no rental ever took place. Even if the renter did pay rent, the money would have to be returned to him, since it was paid in error.

In our case as well, even though the buyers were willing to pay 20 shekel per bottle, the money was paid by mistake, since neither the seller nor an agent of his ever requested such a price, and therefore the extra 2 shekels per bottle must be returned. Even though Reuven did not do anything wrong, he is still left holding money that does not belong to him, and he must return it. However, if Reuven could not be found after collecting his money, Shmueli would have to pay back all the people to whom he caused an additional expense, since they spent extra money because of him.[122]

It would seem that once Shmueli returned the money to all the buyers, he could keep the bottle of oil he had taken, since Reuven already received all the money he was entitled to, based on the original price of the oil. ‏וצ"ע‎.

---

121. *Choshen Mishpat* 363:9-10.
122. See *Rema, Choshen Mishpat* 14:5.

פרשת וישב
Parashas Vayeishev

May We All Hear Good News

וַיָּבֵא יוֹסֵף אֶת דִּבָּתָם

And Yosef would bring evil reports

(37:2)

 Zaydie Goldberg had been in the hospital for a long time. The family tried to ensure that someone was at his bedside around the clock. When none of the family members were available, they would hire an aide to tend to Zaydie. One day, during the attendant's shift, Zaydie passed away. Should the attendant call the family with the bad tidings, or should he wait for the hospital to inform them?

 The Gemara in *Megillah*[123] explains that when Esther refused Mordechai's request to go to Achashveirosh, Hasach, who had been the messenger between them

---

123. 15a.

until now, allowed others to carry the response to Mordechai. The Gemara derives from this that one should not be the bearer of bad news. The Gemara in *Pesachim*,[124] as well, records that R' Yehoshua bar Idi did not want to report the death of Rav Kahana to the Rabbis. Instead, he ripped his garment and wore it backward, and entered the room crying. The Rabbis said, "He is dead!"

R' Yehoshua responded, "I did not say so. One who spreads bad tidings lacks intelligence!"[125]

That said, it would seem that the attendant should not call.

Nevertheless, the *Sefer Chassidim*[126] writes that the behavior of not spreading bad tidings is specifically when there is no constructive purpose. If there is something positive that can be done as a result of the information, it is a bigger sin not to tell. For example, it would be proper to tell someone that his relative is ill in order that he may tend to the illness or visit him before his death. Another example would be to allow him to pray for him, or to be able to identify the body to allow his widow to remarry. Hasach did not want to report Esther's refusal to Mordechai because Hasach did not agree with Esther's approach to the matter, and felt that Mordechai was correct.

In this case, if there is a benefit to inform the family earlier, e.g., to allow them to make funeral arrangements, one should indeed inform them immediately. In the Gemara in *Pesachim*, there was no need for the Rabbis to know immediately.

---

124. 3b.
125. *Mishlei* 10.
126. Chapter 802.

Are All Men Created Equal?

וְעָשָׂה לוֹ כְּתֹנֶת פַּסִּים

And he made him a fine woolen tunic

(37:3)

 Is one allowed to treat each of his children differently if one child needs more loving attention and care to boost his self-esteem? Do the parents have to be wary of causing jealousy when one child receives more than another, when the children's needs are not the same?

 The Gemara[127] states: "A person should not single out one child **from among his children,** as we see that a little silk caused Yosef's brothers to be jealous and caused the Jewish people to be exiled to Egypt."

The *Chasam Sofer*[128] infers that this is specifically when the child is **among the other children,** i.e. all the children are of similar stature. However, when one child stands out from the rest, they all need to show him respect, and there will be no jealousy. This is why Yaakov Avinu felt he was not being unfair when he presented Yosef with a special striped robe. He felt that Yosef stood out from all the brothers by virtue of his wisdom. Unbeknown to Yaakov, his other sons did not notice anything special about their brother Yosef, and thought him to be immature.

We find[129] that after revealing himself to his brothers, Yosef gave Binyamin five portions at the meal, and he was apparently

---

127. *Shabbos* 10b.
128. On *Maseches Shabbos* ad loc.
129. *Bereishis* 45:22.

not concerned of causing jealousy. The *Eitz Yosef*[130] explains that it was understood that Yosef would want to appease Binyamin for making him undertake the journey down to Mitzrayim.

Based on this, the other children in the family should be made to understand that this child is different, requiring the parents to make greater efforts to meet his needs, and that his siblings should offer him help and encouragement as well. The other children need to be told that their parents will be there for their special needs as well.

Misdirected Renovation

וַיִּשְׁאָלֵהוּ הָאִישׁ לֵאמֹר מַה תְּבַקֵּשׁ

The man asked him, saying, "What do you seek?"

(37:15)

 Michoel, Gavriel, and Raphael lived on the same floor of an apartment building. Michoel hired a contractor to redo the bathroom in his apartment.

The workers came up the steps of the building, and met Gavriel. They asked him, "Which is Michoel's apartment?" Gavriel, who was in the middle of a dispute with Raphael, pointed to Raphael's apartment. The workers found the door unlocked, and proceeded to take apart Raphael's bathroom and install a new one.

When Raphael came home, he asked the workers what they were doing, and they told him how they had come to his house. Raphael informed the workers that they could ask Gavriel for their payment, since Raphael had installed a new bathroom just a few months earlier,

---

130. In his commentary on *Ein Yaakov* ad loc.

and had no need for a new one. Is Gavriel required to pay?

A The *Shulchan Aruch* rules:[131] One who hires a worker to work for him, but then showed the worker his friend's property, needs to pay the worker's full wage, and can collect from his friend whatever benefit his friend received. According to this ruling Gavriel should have to pay the worker, except for one detail; Gavriel never hired the workers, he merely pointed to Raphael's apartment.

Even so, it seems that Gavriel has to pay. This is similar to one who shows thieves his friend's merchandise. For merely pointing out his friend's property, he needs to pay for his friend's loss.[132] There is no difference between causing his friend to lose his money at the hands of robbers, or causing the workers to lose their money by installing the bathroom in the wrong house.

———◆———

Stop — Thief!

וְהִיא שָׁלְחָה אֶל חָמִיהָ
She sent word to her father-in-law
(38:25)

רש"י: לֹא רָצְתָה לְהַלְבִּין פָּנָיו
She did not wish to make his face pale

 Q Chaim regretted taking his new briefcase to yeshivah that day, as an hour after he arrived, it disappeared. Several days later, he saw a boy in the hallway carrying

131. *Choshen Mishpat* 336:1.
132. *Bava Kamma* 116b.

the missing briefcase. Chaim wanted to scream to get back his briefcase.

Is he allowed to publicly embarrass a thief to compel him to return it, or must he take him to *beis din*?

 The Gemara in *Berachos*[133] states, "It is preferable for a person to throw himself into a fiery furnace rather than embarrass his friend publicly." We learn this from Tamar who gave Yehudah the choice to admit his guilt, even as she was being taken out to be put to death by burning for a crime that she did not commit.[134]

Rav Elyashiv, in his *sefer He'aros,*[135] mentions that the Gemara in *Berachos*[136] teaches us that one who sees his friend wearing *shaatnez* (an article of clothing that contains a mixture of wool and linen) should rip it off of him, even in public. Obviously, one is allowed to shame his friend in order to save him from a (Biblical) prohibition. If so, how could Tamar refrain from shaming Yehudah and thus not preventing him from facilitating her death and the death of her unborn fetuses?

Perhaps we could differentiate between physical shame and emotional shame. To expose the covered parts of someone's body is a great embarrassment. Yet one who suffers such embarrassment, in order to keep the laws of the Torah, is to be honored for such commitment. However, one who is embarrassed for a crime that he committed is embarrassed to a much greater degree. To expose Yehudah, in such a way, would perhaps not be permitted. And if so, even to compel a thief to return stolen items by shaming him might be prohibited.

This applies only when there is another way to retrieve the object (e.g., going to *beis din*). If the only way to have the object returned is through public humiliation, it would be permitted.

---

133. 43b.
134. *Bereishis* 38:25.
135. *Bava Metzia* 59.
136. 19b.

You or Me? What's the Difference?

וְהִנֵּה תְאוֹמִים בְּבִטְנָהּ

There were twins in her womb

(38:27)

Two friends went to the computer store and each bought the same model of an expensive printer. The printer came with a certificate of warranty for two years. One month later, one of their printers stopped working. The person looked for his warranty and receipt, but could not find them. May he take his friend's certificate of warranty to the store to get the service, or is that dishonest?

He is not stealing from the store, since his printer is also under warranty; he simply cannot find his certificate. This is implied by *Tosafos* in *Gittin*.[137] However, if his friend's name appears on the warranty, and he would have to pretend that he was the one for whom the warranty was written, perhaps that would be considered a lie, and would be prohibited, even though he is entitled to the same service.

---

137. 27a.

The Right Place at the Right Time

וַיְהִי ה' אֶת יוֹסֵף

Hashem was with Yosef

(39:2)

Mr. Gold was a successful businessman who had left yeshivah long ago. However, he maintained set times for learning at the beginning and end of his day. One day he received a visit from a fund-raiser. Mr. Gold decided to take advantage of the visit to help him understand a certain topic he had been studying. He asked the fund-raiser if he could explain a certain passage in the Gemara. The collector, although scholarly, was not able to decipher the passage, as he had not learned it recently. He apologized and was awarded a generous donation in appreciation for his efforts.

As the collector was leaving the Gold's home, he met a fellow collector and decided to give him a tip. "Reb Shimon," he said, "I was just with Mr. Gold and I know that he is having difficulty with a certain Gemara. It would be worth your while to review the Gemara well before you go to see him." Reb Shimon decided to take advantage of the opportunity and quickly went to a nearby shul to plumb the depths of the Gemara. When he felt he was proficient in the passage in question, he returned to Mr. Gold's house.

As if on cue, Mr. Gold, who was even more perplexed by the first man's failure to shed light on his difficulty, proceeded to ask Reb Shimon if he could enlighten him in understanding this particular Gemara. Reb Shimon easily answered all of Mr. Gold's questions, leaving the latter openmouthed at the genius of someone who had such clarity in a difficult passage without even preparing! Mr. Gold gave double his usual donation to this yeshivah out of respect for the erudite collector.

Reb Shimon accepted the check, but later his conscience started bothering him. Had he tricked Mr. Gold into giving a donation that he did not deserve?

 The *Shulchan Aruch*[138] rules that it is forbidden to fool one's friend. For example, if one intended to open a new barrel of wine and his friend just arrived at his home, he may not open the barrel in front of him, giving him the impression that the barrel is being opened in his honor. But if one was following his regular routine and his friend misinterpreted his actions as being done in his honor, he need not correct the error. For example, Binyamin was traveling and met his friend Reuven at the airport. If Reuven is honored because he thinks that Binyamin came to greet him, Binyamin does not have to clarify Reuven's misunderstanding, since nothing was done to mislead Reuven, and Reuven misjudged the situation on his own.

In our case, Reb Shimon did something that led Mr. Gold to the wrong conclusion. It would seem that Mr. Gold was tricked and the magnanimity was undeserved.

However, Rav Chaim Kanievsky ruled that there was no dishonesty involved here, only *Hashgachah Pratis* (Divine Assistance). He supports his ruling with a story that happened to Rav Yitzchok Elchonon Spektor who was traveling to accept a Rabbinical position. The wagon driver stopped at an inn to rest, and although the rabbi was very tired from the trip, he asked the innkeeper if perhaps he could have a *sefer* from which to learn. The innkeeper replied that he did not have any holy books except for a *siddur*

---

138. *Choshen Mishpat* 228:6.

with the commentary of *Derech HaChaim*. The Rabbi accepted the *siddur* and opened it to the page that contained the laws of *Krias HaTorah* (Reading the Torah).

The next day when Rabbi Yitzchok Elchonon arrived at his destination, a question arose in shul concerning the Torah reading — the exact question that the Rabbi had perused several hours before. Rabbi Yitzchok Elchonon ruled as he had seen in the *Derech HaChaim*. The scholars of the city began to debate the ruling, bringing proof from earlier and later sources. Finally, one member offered, "Let's bring the *siddur* 'Derech HaChaim,' and see what he rules." That ended the debate, and all were impressed with Rabbi Yitzchok Elchonon's ability to issue such a complex ruling.

Subsequently, when Rav Yitzchok Elchonon traveled to a different pulpit, he chanced upon a particular *Tosafos*. The following day when he arrived, he found the scholars of the city debating the subject discussed by that very same *Tosafos!* Rav Spektor resolved their dispute based on the aforementioned *Tosafos*, due to Divine Assistance. This is not trickery, and there is no obligation to reveal that the information was just learned recently. Only if one receives honor for something that he does not know, while others assume that he does know it, must he reveal that the honor is undeserved.[139]

In our case, Reb Shimon was a proficient scholar, albeit he would not have been able to answer Mr. Gold's question had he not recently seen the Gemara. Heaven saw to it that he should hear about the Gemara before visiting Mr. Gold.

A similar vignette involves a rabbinical student who went to be tested for *semichah* (rabbinical ordination) by Rav Betzalel Zolty. While he was waiting for the *Rav*, he went to a local *beis medrash* and opened a *sefer*. When the test began, Rav Zolty questioned him on the exact same material that the student had just seen in the *sefer*, so he was able to answer immediately. Rav Zolty was so impressed by the comprehensive answer, that he saw no further

---

139. See *Yerushalmi Shevi'is* 10:3.

need to test him and informed him that he had passed. That is Divine Assistance, and not trickery.

Advertising

וְאֵת שַׂר הָאֹפִים תָּלָה

But he hanged the Chamberlain of the Bakers

(40:22)

A *tzedakah* **organization sought funds** to help a *Yid* who was in prison and faced a possible sentence of death by hanging. They decided to advertise, hoping that the momentum of advertisements would produce a greater response from the public. The first in the series of posters read, "Get ready for a great mitzvah." "Stop the hanging!" "Details to follow."

They invested thousands of *shekalim* in the campaign, hoping that the interest of the public would build. Then they would publicize the second poster telling of the plight of a *Yid* facing a terrible sentence.

The day before the second sign was scheduled to be posted, a company that manufactured clothes dryers advertised in the same format as the fund-raisers: "It is a great mitzvah to buy a dryer, stop the punishment of hanging wet laundry." The campaign was so successful that everyone was convinced that the original poster was also due to the initiative of the dryer company. The *tzedakah* organization saw no reason to hang their second poster, and printed smaller ones instead. The response of the public was smaller as well.

Can the *tzedakah* organization demand payment from the dryer company for using their advertisement campaign without permission?

 Certainly the dryer company acted wrongly, and are considered sinners for their actions. *Tosafos* explains the Gemara:[140] If one fisherman puts down bait in an area of the ocean and attracts other fish, then any other fisherman who fishes in the immediate vicinity is considered a sinner. Here too, the organization put down "bait" and the dryer company took the benefit for itself.

As far as there being a financial obligation, the *Divrei Malkiel*[141] ruled in a similar case. Berel produced a nostrum, and received a license from the Health Administration after to much effort and expense. His friend Shimon from a nearby city produced a similar drink and printed labels identical to Berel's. He went on to sell his product under the same name as Berel's. Berel, the original producer, claimed that Shimon had no right to benefit from his investment. The *Divrei Malkiel* ruled that through his actions, Shimon had expressed that Berel had actually acted on behalf of both of them, and therefore Shimon needs to share in Berel's expenses. Shimon in effect has become a partner with Berel in the investment, even though that was not Berel's original intention. He adds that Shimon is actually taking away business from Berel and has no right to do so. Under such circumstances, certainly Shimon needs to compensate Berel for his efforts, which led to Shimon's business success.

In our case, it seems that since the dryer company revealed their amenability to the expense of the advertisement campaign for their own benefit, they have become partners in the endeavor. And since they caused the *tzedakah* organization to lose their entire investment, the dryer company should pay the entire cost of the original poster.

140. *Bava Basra* 21b.
141. Vol. III, 157.

פרשת מקץ
Parashas Mikeitz

Picture Perfect I

וַיַּכֵּר ... וְהֵם לֹא הִכִּרֻהוּ

(He) recognized ... but they did not recognize him

(42:8)

Simcha Cohen hired a photographer to take pictures at his wedding. He was very anxious to see how the pictures would come out, as he had many *Gedolim* at his wedding. The photographer was highly professional, and in all of his years in the business he had never had such a mishap. One of the films from the wedding was exposed to light, and all the pictures on that roll were ruined! The photographer was horrified, and did not know how he would face his client, until he came up with an idea.

He took pictures from a different client's *simchah*, and was able to make a collage combining pictures of *Gedolim* and pictures of Simcha's wedding. The job was so well done that Simcha did not even notice that the pictures were not taken at his wedding.

Afterward, the photographer felt that maybe he had acted improperly. Perhaps he had no right to take money under false pretenses. After all, he had been hired to take real pictures, not to make a photo collage. Does he have to reveal the truth to his client?

A This question was posed to Rav Elyashiv. The *Rav* answered that maybe initially the photographer should not have misrepresented the pictures, but now that he has already sold them, he does not have to return the money. Since the customer was more than satisfied with the finished product, and all he wanted was a picture to remind him of the *Gedolim* who attended his wedding, he received the product for which he had hired the photographer. Even if the photo is a counterfeit, the client is satisfied that his money was well spent.

Health Insurance

אָנֹכִי אֶעֶרְבֶנּוּ

I will personally guarantee him

(43:9)

 An elderly woman donated her entire house to a yeshivah in return for a commitment from the yeshivah's administration to cover her medical expenses. It seemed a very lucrative agreement for the yeshivah, except for the fact that she subsequently contracted a rare disease that brought in its wake medical expenses that exceeded the value of the house that they received. The yeshivah claims that they never accepted responsibility to such a degree. Can the yeshivah be absolved of its obligation?

The *Shulchan Aruch*[142] rules: "One who obligates himself to support his stepdaughter is required to do so whether prices of food are low or high." The *Ta"z* comments: It would seem that this is true as long as inflation is common. If in fact inflation is uncommon, then he is not considered as having obligated himself under such a rare circumstance. The *Beis Shmuel* concurs with this ruling.

The *Maharshag*[143] explains the *Ta"z*, stating that it depends on whether the change in circumstances is something that affected everyone, or something that happened to the individual. If food prices became inflated for everyone, we cannot say that this individual's doomed-for-failure business agreement caused the price rise for everyone. Conversely, if something happened that affected that person's status individually, for example he became poor, we would say that it was his personal misfortune, and he would still be bound by his obligation.

Along these lines, since only this woman became ill with a rare disease, we attribute the additional costs to the misfortune of the yeshivah's administrators, and they need to pay for her recovery even though the expense will exceed the woman's donation. Especially since in effect the woman purchased from the yeshivah the equivalent of an insurance policy, and the yeshivah was willing to take a chance to possibly gain from the agreement, they must honor their commitment.

———◆———

142. *Even HaEzer* 114:1.
143. Vol. II, 226.

Picture Perfect II

וְאֶת גְּבִיעִי גְּבִיעַ הַכֶּסֶף

And my goblet – the silver goblet

(44:2)

Don and Naftali divided their father's estate. Don wanted to assume ownership of his father's store, since it was close to his own business. Naftali would receive his father's apartment in return. Naftali agreed to the division only on condition that he receive his father's *Kiddush* cup, as it held great sentimental value to him. Don agreed to the condition, but felt uncomfortable parting with the *Kiddush* cup, as it was very special to him, as well. Don felt that they should draw lots for the *Kiddush* cup, but Naftali was adamant. Don commissioned a silversmith to fashion a replica of his father's cup, and presented the replica to Naftali. The *Kiddush* cup was an exact replica, and cost the same as its original. No one could tell them apart. Now Don wants to know if he is guilty of stealing, and if the division of their father's property is void.

The Gemara in *Gittin*[144] quotes Rabban Shimon ben Gamliel, who told the story of a man from Tzidon who presented his wife with a *get* on condition that she return his *tallis*. The Rabbis ruled that she may fulfill the condition by giving him the value of the *tallis* in the form of money.

In our case as well, it would seem sufficient that Don presented Naftali with something of equal value.

---

144. 74a.

However, the Gemara concludes[145] that Rabban Shimon ben Gamliel related the incident only in the context of a case where the item in question is not available. If, however, the item is being withheld, money would not be a satisfactory substitute.

The *Shulchan Aruch* rules:[146] "One who makes a condition with his friend to deliver an item may give its monetary equivalent, except in the case of a *get*."

The *Ketzos HaChoshen* explains that this ruling is relevant to a case where the item is not available.

The rationale is that the person who made the condition is not really interested in the money, otherwise he would have asked for the value. By the fact that he specifically requested the item, it is apparent that the item has a special value to him. Only when the item is lost is it understood that money is an acceptable replacement.

In our case, it is clear that Naftali is interested only in the original cup, and perhaps the condition would be binding even if the original cup had been lost!

There is no comparison between this case, and the previous case of the photographer,[147] as a picture is only a memento and has no intrinsic value. A *Kiddush* cup that is suffused with the holiness of the mitzvos for which it was used cannot be duplicated. Don will have to honor his agreement honestly.

-------◆-------

145. 75a.
146. *Choshen Mishpat* 241:7.
147. See *Picture Perfect I* in *Parashas Mikeitz* (p. 116).

Birds of a Feather

אֲשֶׁר יִמָּצֵא אִתּוֹ

With whom it is found

(44:9)

Nachman hired a construction crew to add a bedroom to his house. One day, after the crew had left, Nachman noticed that an expensive pen had been removed from his desk. He ran after the crew, and found his pen in one of the worker's tool belts. Nachman demanded to search the rest of the crew's belongings as well. The workers refused. They claimed that Nachman had no reason to suspect them, as his missing pen had been found, and there was no further evidence that anything else had been taken. Does Nachman indeed have the right to search them?

Yosef's brothers declared:[148] *If you will find the goblet by one of us, he shall die, and we will become your servants.* *Rashi* comments, "Ten people who are together, and one of them is found to have stolen, all ten are accountable."[149] The *Rashbam* has a similar comment. "Your sentence is correct, for you are all partners and such is the custom of merchants, to be punished for each other's misdeeds."

The *Maharil Diskin* on that verse explains the rationale behind such an arrangement, that it is probable that they all stole together and hid the items by one of them for safekeeping. It is only logical that if they could be punished for each other's actions, they could certainly be searched to determine if they had stolen as well.

---

148. *Bereishis* 44:9.
149. *Rashi's* source is the *Midrash, Bereishis* 92:8.

If, however, Nachman does not discover anything in his search Nachman should appease them and bless them.[150]

Finders Keepers

וַיְחַפֵּשׂ ... וַיִּמָּצֵא

He searched ... and ... was found

(44:12)

 Zevulun bought a used car from Yisrael. When the evening of *bedikas chametz* arrived, Zevulun went to his car equipped with his flashlight and vacuum cleaner to rid the car of any *chametz*. When he removed the seats to vacuum, he discovered an expensive diamond ring in one of the crevices between the seats. Perhaps the ring belonged to Yisrael's wife, who may have stuck her hand under the car's seat and lost her ring in the process! Or, over the years, perhaps a different woman had been the unfortunate one to leave her ring behind. As Zevulun pondered the matter further, he decided that the first possibility is the more likely one. Should Zevulun interrupt his *bedikas chametz* to call Yisrael and try to verify the owner of the lost ring?

 According to halachah, one would have to finish his *bedikah* first as one who is involved in one mitzvah is exempt from engaging in other mitzvos. Even if Zevulun had found the ring before he began checking for *chametz*, the mitzvah of *bedikas chametz* would take precedence over the mitzvah of

---

150. See *Berachos* 31b.

returning a lost item, as the mitzvah of *bedikas chametz* has a set time to be done; i.e., the beginning of the night of the fourteenth of Nissan.[151] Certainly, now that Zevulun is in the middle of the *bedikah*, he should not interrupt the mitzvah to busy himself in a different mitzvah.

In our case, however, when the item in question is an expensive piece of jewelry, the *yetzer hara* has many convincing reasons why Zevulun should be allowed to keep the ring for himself. Who says the ring belonged to Yisrael's wife, and even if it did, she probably gave up hope of recovering it, etc. If Zevulun waits to return the ring, by the time he finishes his *bedikah*, he may be convinced that it does not need to be returned! Therefore he should probably place a phone call to Yisrael right away to find out whether the ring could be his. וצ"ע.

---

151. See *Beur Halachah* 336:2.

פרשת ויגש
Parashas Vayigash

Buy in Bulk

לְכֻלָּם נָתַן לָאִישׁ חֲלִפוֹת שְׂמָלֹת

To each of them he gave changes of clothing
(45:22)

Five boys from Shlomo's yeshivah heard about a sale in Manny's Shirt Warehouse. Shirts that usually sold for 150 shekels were on sale for 95 shekels. Since the boys lived far from the store, they asked Shlomo, who lived nearby, to make the purchase for them. When Shlomo arrived at the store he saw that the store had an additional offer. A 500-shekel purchase entitled the buyer to a 150-shekel discount on his next purchase. Since the boys were spending only 475 shekels on the shirts, Shlomo bought a tie for 30 shekels. Now the question arose: Who deserves the 150-shekel gift certificate? Should Shlomo keep it, or should he share it with his friends?

A The Gemara[152] differentiates between a discount that is universal and a discount that was given on a specific purchase, with regard to whether the profit belongs solely to the buyer or if the profit should be divided between the buyer and his agent.

There is an additional fact to consider, as the entire profit was generated because the agent added his own purchase to the total bill.

The *Ri Migash*[153] rules that one who was overcharged for an item to the extent that the transaction is void, and in the interim, before the object could be returned, the purchaser sold the item for a profit, in spite of the fact that the original sale was void, the profit does not need to be given to the original owner, since the profit was earned solely through the initiative of the purchaser.

In our case as well, the gift certificate was given only because of Shlomo's initiative.

The *Maharashdam*[154] asks with regard to the *Ri Migash*: How could someone do business with someone else's merchandise? The *Mishmeres Shalom*[155] says that the *Ri Migash* ruled that the profit belongs to the one who earned it, only if the sale required special effort or talent that not everyone could have produced.

According to this stipulation, Shlomo cannot do business with his friends' money and therefore the gift certificate should be divided among the boys based on the amount of each one's investment. Shlomo will surely be rewarded from Heaven for his initiative to benefit the group, and for going beyond the call of duty. וצ"ע.

---

152. *Kesubos* 98b.
153. Quoted in *Shitah Mekubetzes, Bava Metzia* 65a.
154. *Choshen Mishpat* 147.
155. 332, 4.

Best Buy

לְכֻלָּם נָתַן לָאִישׁ חֲלִפוֹת שְׂמָלֹת

To each of them he gave changes of clothing
(45:22)

Aharon went to buy a suit. The salesman, a hired employee, knows that in a few days there will be a sale with a significant reduction on the suit that Aharon wants to buy. May the salesman inform Aharon of the forthcoming sale?

The salesman may not cause a loss to his employer. If the customer is ready to buy the suit today, why should the salesman disclose information to the customer at the employer's expense?

If the customer is a *talmid chacham*, it seems that the salesman could tell him, because everyone is obligated to honor and support a *talmid chacham*, including the salesman's employer.[156] Similarly, if the customer is a relative of the salesman, he can be informed about the sale, as the salesman has a special mitzvah of ומבשרך אל תתעלם (not to forsake his relatives).

If, however, the customer is entitled to a discount (for example, the store has a coupon), and is just unaware of his eligibility, then he may certainly be informed, as the discount is already deserved. That would not be comparable to the case of a sale that will not occur until a later date [and will be offered by the store owner only at that time].

---

156. See *Bava Basra* 22a.

Practice Makes Perfect

וְאִם יָדַעְתָּ וְיֶשׁ בָּם אַנְשֵׁי חַיִל

And if you know that there are capable men among them

(47:6)

 A *talmid chacham* had a heart condition and needed to undergo complex surgery. The doctors in Eretz Yisrael conceded that they do not do this type of operation on a daily basis, but they maintain that they are proficient in the surgery and their rate of success is 95 percent. In contrast, there is a specialist in the United States who does the same operation every day, and he also says that his rate of success is 95 percent.

The *talmid chacham* wants to know if it is preferable to fly to America to have the specialist operate on him if the success rate is the same in both places. (The doctors are sure that there is no danger for him to travel.)

 Rav Elyashiv answered that certainly one should prefer the doctor in America, since he has more experience operating.

The Mishnah in the beginning of the second *Perek* of *Ta'anis*[157] states that an elderly and experienced *chazzan* is chosen to lead the *davening*. *Rashi* explains that since he is accustomed to leading the *davening*, the words flow easily from his lips and he will not make a mistake. The more practice one has, the less margin there is for error.

Therefore it is preferable to choose the doctor who has daily experience with the operation, although in either case one certainly must *daven* to the Healer of all Flesh that the operation should be successful.

---

157. 15a.

פרשת ויחי
Parashas Vayechi

Quiet Contribution

וַיְחִי יַעֲקֹב בְּאֶרֶץ מִצְרָיִם
Yaakov lived in the land of Egypt
(47:28)

A wealthy *Yid*, known for his warm heart and open hand, donated 30 beds to a local hospital, a very generous and much needed donation. Years later the donor himself contracted an illness that required hospitalization. Simultaneously, a revered *talmid chacham* also became a patient in the hospital, and due to his eminence it was only befitting that he receive a private room in the hospital. The hospital had only one private room available. Should the administrators give the room to the generous donor or the great scholar?

The Gemara in *Shabbos*[158] states: "These are things that a man does, and reaps their fruits in this world, while the principal remains intact for the World to Come ...

---

158. 137a.

bestowing kindness ... and the study of Torah is equal to all of them combined."

Even though the philanthropist owns the mitzvah, the *talmid chacham* still takes precedence. While the donor enabled 30 people to be healed while staying in the hospital, the righteous scholar's merit can keep people out of the hospital! His merit also helps the sick to recover.

Yosef HaTzaddik fed the people in Mitzrayim through two years of famine, but when his father Yaakov came to Mitzrayim, he brought an end to the famine altogether. We see that the merit of a *tzaddik* is greater than the merit of one who distributes money.

However, the *Rema*[159] rules that if there is a custom when one donates a *Sefer Torah* or the like to a shul that the donor may reacquire his donation if he needs to, we follow this custom because the donation was given with that intention (as long as it is the accepted custom). Maybe in our case as well, the implicit intent of the donor was that if he should ever need to stay in the hospital, he should have precedence over anyone else. If so, maybe he should have preference even over the *talmid chacham*. וצ"ע.

---

159. *Yoreh De'ah* 259:2.

Right Address, Wrong House

וְהוּא יִתֵּן מַעֲדַנֵּי מֶלֶךְ

And he will provide kingly delicacies

(49:20)

 One of Avraham's relatives had been hospitalized, and Avraham took responsibility for overseeing his medical care as well as for the welfare of his family. Yitzchak was a messenger from Heaven to help ease Avraham's burden in this difficult time. Avraham felt tremendous gratitude for all of Yitzchak's kindness. When Purim approached, Avraham prepared a large *mishloach manos* basket filled with an entire Purim *seudah* and sent it with a messenger to Yitzchak Stein's house. Yaakov lived in the same building as Yitzchak and had the same last name. It was only natural that the messenger deliver the *mishloach manos* to the first apartment he saw that had the name "Stein" on the door. Yaakov Stein was also a friend of Avraham's, so he did not realize that a mistake was being made. He opened the package and ate every last morsel of the impressive feast.

Meanwhile, Avraham was waiting for a phone call from Yitzchak to acknowledge receipt of the *mishloach manos*. When the phone call was not forthcoming, Avraham called the messenger to verify the delivery. That is when Avraham discovered the mistake.

The following questions then arose:

1) Does Yaakov have to pay Avraham for the *mishloach manos*, or does the messenger have to pay, since it was his mistake?

2) Has Avraham fulfilled his mitzvah of *mishloach manos*, since he never intended to send it to Yaakov?

3) Has Yaakov fulfilled his obligation of eating the *Purim seudah*, since he ate food that did not belong to him?

 It seems that Yaakov, who enjoyed the *mishloach manos* in its entirety, must pay for it, albeit at a discounted price. It is similar to the case of children whose father died and left a cow in his yard. If the children slaughtered the cow and ate its meat, and discovered afterward that the cow did not belong to their father, they have to pay the owner two-thirds of the price of the meat, and the price of the hide.[160] Similarly Yaakov should pay two-thirds of the cost of the *mishloach manos*, and the messenger should pay the remaining third.

Concerning Yaakov's *Purim seudah*, a similar question is debated by the *Machaneh Chaim*.[161] On the one hand, since the food did not belong to him, it would seem to be a *mitzvah habaah be'aveirah* to use it for his Purim *seudah* and therefore, he has not discharged his obligation. This fact not withstanding, once the food was chewed, Yaakov could have acquired it by changing its form (*shinui*).[162] But this still would not help in this case, because Yaakov never intended to acquire the food through making a *shinui*. The *Machaneh Chaim* concludes that since a person wants to do a mitzvah with his own property, he has a subconscious will to pay for whatever benefit he receives from his friend in order to acquire the food, and thereby have fulfilled his mitzvah.

As far as Avraham's fulfillment of the mitzvah of *mishloach manos*, if he insists that Yaakov and the messenger pay him for the food, it is as if he never gave *mishloach manos*, and he has not fulfilled the mitzvah. If he acquiesces to Yaakov's receipt of the food, he will have fulfilled his obligation.

---

160. See *Shulchan Aruch, Choshen Mishpat* 341:4.
161. *Orach Chaim* Vol. III, 53.
162. See *Shulchan Aruch, Choshen Mishpat* 353:1.

Eviction Without Notice

אֲשֶׁר קָנָה אַבְרָהָם אֶת הַשָּׂדֶה

the field that Avraham had bought

(50:13)

Eliezer inherited a house from his father. The house stood empty for a few months, until one day Eliezer received a phone call informing him that someone had broken in and begun living there with his family! Eliezer decided to pay them a visit, and asked the intruder what was going on. The man brazenly declared that he had bought the house, something Eliezer knew to be untrue. Besides, the man could not produce any document to support his claim.

Eliezer had no choice but to engage the services of two muscular men to remove the unwanted intruder.

Afterward, Eliezer's conscience began to bother him. The incident had taken place on a Friday afternoon, and the would-be homeowner and his family, who were *Shomer* Shabbos, had to spend a miserable Shabbos without a roof over their heads. Did Eliezer do the right thing?

Eliezer did nothing wrong. On the contrary, he did the intruder a favor by removing him from the house. Every second that he continued to occupy someone else's house without permission, he was guilty of stealing as well as causing pain to its owner.

This would not be so if someone had rented a house and because of poverty had fallen behind on payments. In such a case — depending on the exact circumstances — since he entered the house with permission and has nowhere else to live, it may be a mitzvah of *tzedakah* to allow him to continue living there if possible. But in our case, where he entered the house without permission, each second he remains is an additional transgression.

Hashem Runs the World

אֱלֹקִים חֲשָׁבָהּ לְטֹבָה

G-d intended it for good

(50:20)

Tzvi was working his way through the *shidduchim* process, and had already met with Rivkah several times. Somehow, Naftali, Tzvi's adversary, discovered Tzvi's situation and decided to use the information to settle an old score between them. Naftali phoned the local newspaper and ordered an advertisement in the next day's paper announcing Tzvi's and Rivkah's engagement. That would certainly cause Tzvi significant embarrassment and teach him not to tangle with Naftali.

Hashem had mercy on Tzvi, and that night, when Tzvi and Rivkah met, Rivkah agreed to finalize their engagement. Tzvi suggested that since it was already late at night, it might be better to wait until the following day, but Rivkah insisted. They called their families despite the lateness of the hour and announced their decision to build a home together.

The next morning they were pleasantly surprised when they saw the newspaper announcing their engagement, and they wondered how someone had managed to include the ad despite the late hour of their engagement. In any event, the ad certainly enhanced their happiness, even though they were clueless as to its source.

A week later, Tzvi received a letter from Naftali. Naftali confessed that he had placed the ad, and explained as well what his motivation had been in doing so. Now he realized that Hashem had protected Tzvi, and Naftali was humbled. He asked Tzvi to forgive him for his evil intentions, and to send a check to cover the cost of the advertisement, since in the end Tzvi had benefited from and enjoyed its placement in the newspaper! Does Tzvi have to pay?

 The Gemara in *Sanhedrin*[163] relates a debate between Geviha ben Pesisa and an apostate. The apostate, frustrated by Geviha's clever answers, threatened to give Geviha such a hard kick that it would straighten Geviha's hunchback. Geviha retorted, "If you were capable of such a feat, you would become famous as a wonderful doctor, and collect an exorbitant fee!"

The *Chida*[164] explains that although a physician does not normally charge for experimental treatments, as the publicity received is already sufficient payment for the doctor's efforts, in this case Geviha voluntarily offered to pay the apostate as well.

In an alternate explanation, the *Chida* suggests that although the *Rema*[165] rules that one who provides a service for his friend is allowed to charge for the service (even if it was unsolicited), that

---

163. 91a.
164. *Pesach Einayim*.
165. *Choshen Mishpat* 264:4.

is only if the intention of the provider was to benefit his friend. If the provider had malicious intent, even if his plan backfired and he benefited his intended victim, no payment is due, as there was no intention to be paid at the time that the act was committed. Geviha's retort was that even though the apostate intended to cause pain, nevertheless Geviha would graciously consider such an act as a kindness worthy of being rewarded!

The conclusion to be drawn from the *Chida* is that when one commits an act with malicious intent, then even if the outcome proved to be beneficial, no payment may be requested.

ספר שמות

Sefer Shemos

פרשת שמות
Parashas Shemos

Free Babysitting

שֵׁם הָאַחַת שִׁפְרָה

The name of the first was Shifrah

(1:15)

A woman wanted to attend shul on Shabbos because one of her friends was making an *aufruf*, but she could not find a babysitter for her 2-year-old son. She decided to make use of the neighborhood's "*gemach*" for lost children, where anyone who found a lost child would bring the child to a designated home, and the child would be cared for until his parents came looking for him. Parents knew to look for their child at that house. The woman took her child to the building of the lost children's station, and asked a child standing outside to bring her 2-year-old to the family in charge. She continued on her way to shul, knowing that her child would be well cared for. Afterward, she picked up her child and did not give the matter a second thought, until the eve of Yom Kippur. Her conscience began to bother her.

She came to ask if she must pay the woman who cared for her child.

Although the woman who left her child clearly acted improperly, there are two reasons why it would seem that she does not have to pay.

1) The services were rendered completely[1] on Shabbos, and one may not ask to be paid for services rendered on Shabbos.[2] 2) Since the woman who watched the child intended to do so as a mitzvah, no payment is necessary. The woman who watched the child never intended to be paid for her efforts. Had she known the truth, she might have agreed to watch the child anyway. Even if she would not have agreed to do so for free, she would also not have undertaken to do so for payment as she is not interested in providing a regular service, and only does so for the mitzvah. Now that she was deceived, she cannot ask for payment just because she was deceived.

However, if the woman had to expend money to watch the child, even if only a small amount, such as giving the child a treat, she could demand to be paid for everything.[3] This would not be considered Shabbos wages since her payment is categorized together with the payment of her expenses.

---

1. Had the services been rendered partially on a weekday, one could charge for Shabbos and the weekday together.
2. See *Mishnah Berurah* 334 § 24.
3. See *Shulchan Aruch, Choshen Mishpat* 363:7; if one benefited and his benefactor had even a small loss, payment is due for the entire benefit.

Misplaced Gratitude

וַאֲנִי אֶתֵּן אֶת שְׂכָרֵךְ
And I will give your pay
(2:9)

 Daniel and Aharon were young married men, learning and living in Lakewood. Daniel had just undergone a very stressful experience, and his friend Aharon decided that the best thing for Daniel would be to get away for a while. Aharon called a mutual friend of theirs who lived in Yerushalayim, and made the following request. "I know you will be traveling to Tzefas for *bein hazemanim*. Why don't you call Daniel and invite him to stay in your apartment, rent free? I will pay the rent and any expenses. Daniel does not need to know."

His friend agreed to Aharon's terms, and called Daniel, who gladly accepted the offer. Daniel spent three weeks in the friend's apartment, in the most beautiful city in the world.

When the friend returned to his apartment he found a letter from Daniel thanking him for his most generous hospitality. The letter was accompanied by an expensive pair of candlesticks, as a gift. Is he entitled to keep the gift when he knows that he was paid in full for the hospitality that he extended?

 He may not keep the candlesticks, since they were given on the basis of a misunderstanding. Even if he gives the rent back to Aharon, it is unclear if that would be a solution, since the present was given in error. There was no kindness on the part of the apartment owner, who extended his hospitality in exchange for payment. He should find a way to return the candlesticks, or their equivalent value, to Daniel without him knowing.

Even though we find that Yocheved, the mother of Moshe Rabbeinu, was paid by Pharaoh's daughter to nurse her own child, the *Netziv*[4] explains that it was permitted for Yocheved to keep the money only because it is the custom of royalty to pay generously for professional services provided to them.

———— ◆ ————

100 Percent Leather

שַׁל נְעָלֶיךָ

Remove your shoes
(3:5)

 Yitzchak walked into a shoestore and requested a pair of leather shoes. The salesman gave him a pair of shoes and told Yitzchak that they were made of leather. Yitzchak bought the shoes and brought them home. His family members insisted that the shoes were synthetic! Yitzchak went back to the store and reported this to the salesman.

The salesman maintained that Yitzchak's family was mistaken, and suggested they go to the shoemaker next door and ask him for his opinion. They immediately headed to the shoemaker.

The shoemaker confidently stated that the shoes were not made of leather. The salesman was furious, and he let the shoemaker know exactly what he thought about his judgment in no uncertain terms. Then he turned to Yitzchak and shouted at him that he

---

4. *Ha'amek Davar, Shemos* 2:9.

refuses to return his money, as the shoes were undeniably leather.

Yitzchak left the store in a huff, after warning the salesman that he would not forgive him.

A few nights later, Yitzchak was walking with some friends, and they noticed the salesman walking with his *kallah*. The friends approached the salesman and reproached him for the way he treated Yitzchak. The *kallah* was shocked.

The next day Yitzchak received a delivery. It was a pair of genuine leather shoes with a note from the salesman saying that since Yitzchak's friends scared and embarrassed him the previous night, Yitzchak could keep both pairs of shoes. May Yitzchak indeed keep both pairs of shoes? Is it possible that Yitzchak's friends did the right thing, embarrassing the salesman in front of his *kallah*?

 It would seem that they acted properly. The Gemara in *Pesachim*[5] relates that the Kohen who was in charge of the shift would make those Kohanim who were impure, and therefore unfit to fulfill their duties in the *Beis HaMikdash*, stand in the eastern gate in order to embarrass them. *Rashi* explains that this was a punishment for those who had not taken the proper precautions not to become impure. They knew that they were meant to serve in the *Beis HaMikdash* the following day, and they should have been more careful. If, for not being careful, one deserves to be embarrassed, certainly a storeowner who tries to cheat his customer, and refuses to accept the Torah's laws, deserves to be embarrassed.

If Yitzchak had no other way to help him recover his money, he was within his halachic boundary to use such pressure to try to force the salesman to come to an agreement with him.

---

5. 82a.

It's the Ambiance

וַיְהִי בַדֶּרֶךְ בַּמָּלוֹן

It was on the way, in the lodging
(4:24)

A man lodged in an expensive hotel. In the middle of the night, he became thirsty, and he decided to help himself to a bottle of water from the well-stocked refrigerator. Since the hotel checks the refrigerator so they can charge the guest for any drinks that were enjoyed, the man woke up early in the morning and bought an identical bottle of water from the grocery store across the street. He then replaced the bottle in the refrigerator, because he knew that the hotel charges three times the price of the grocery store. Does the man need to pay the hotel the difference in price?

If he took the bottle with the intention of buying it from the hotel, he did so under the conditions set by the hotel. The hotel's owners are not interested in having the bottle replaced. They wish to receive the payment that is due to them. Accordingly, he must pay the difference in price.

Even if he took the bottle with the intention that he would not pay, but with the intention to replace the bottle, he is a *gazlan* as the hotel does not permit such a practice. Although a *gazlan* may return the stolen object to the owner, that is only if it is the original object. For example, a *gazlan* may return stolen *chametz* to its owner after Pesach, even though *chametz* owned by a Jew that was not sold is prohibited for any benefit. Nevertheless, since he is returning the same *chametz* that he stole, it is considered payment. He may not return different *chametz* that was in Jewish possession on Pesach as payment. In our case he is not returning the original bottle, and therefore the new bottle is not a viable form of payment.

One could still argue that *chametz* after Pesach has no value, whereas the bottle of water can be sold to the next hotel guest. Nevertheless, it is not a viable payment option, and he cannot claim that he is giving the hotel the water at the same price that they charge their guests. The reason the hotel charges three times the price of the bottle is because they are providing a service for their guests, i.e., that there should be cold water available at their bedside. The guest who returns the bottle to the hotel is not providing the same service for the hotel, and his bottle is worth only its market value.

In addition, the guest cannot claim that the hotel will recover its money when they sell the water to the next guest, because the hotel can claim that they have enough water to sell to the next guest and have no benefit from the replacement bottle.

This is in accordance with what the *Rema*[6] writes in the name of the *Rosh:* "One who does damage to his friend's barrel on market day cannot return a barrel on a different market day, because his friend may claim that he already has a different barrel to sell on that day, and has no need for the barrel to be replaced."

———◆◆◆———

6. *Choshen Mishpat* 304:5.

A Matter of Faith

וַיַּאֲמֵן הָעָם

And the people believed

(4:31)

 A man entered Shimon's bookstore looking for a particular *sefer*. Shimon informed him that unfortunately the book he wanted was not in stock. However, Shimon remembered that a new store that had opened down the block surely carried the *sefer*. Shimon was hesitant to send a customer to his competitor. The truth was that the competitor had lower prices on many items, and Shimon was afraid that the customer would become accustomed to shopping there, and would never enter his store again. Does Shimon have to tell his customer that he could find what he is looking for in the competitor's store?

 The Gemara[7] speaks very harshly against one who prevents others from learning Torah. The salesman should certainly not prevent his customers from learning, due to his personal interests. Even if the book was not for Torah study, so there would be no obligation to refer the customer to a competing business, we know that a person's income is determined on Rosh Hashanah.[8] One who is afraid to do kindness with his customer and his competitor is lacking faith in Hashem.

Sometimes it was decreed upon a person on Rosh Hashanah to have a setback in business. The person may have been designated to lose income, and instead of getting sick ח"ו, and having

---

7. See *Temurah* 16a for the Gemara's explanation of the *pasuk* (*Mishlei* 29:13).
8. *Bava Basra* 10a.

to pay doctor bills, Hashem sent him a competitor to take away customers so that the sickness is not necessary. Shimon should be grateful to his competitor for keeping him healthy! In addition, when the customer sees Shimon's sincere concern for his welfare, — that he would even send him to the competitor — Shimon will earn the customer's esteem as an honest businessman.

פרשת וארא
Parashas Va'eira

The Right Match

לָקַח לוֹ מִבְּנוֹת פּוּטִיאֵל

Took for himself from the daughters of Putiel

(6:25)

Q A boy considered a proposal to meet a wonderful girl who comes from a prominent family. Her brothers are all paradigms in the community. At the same time, he was offered a *shidduch* with a girl who comes from a simple family, whose brothers are not particularly distinguished, but the girl herself could be a great help to him because of her great love of Torah and her reverence for *talmidei chachamim*. Whom should he meet?

A "And Elazar the son of Aharon took for himself from the daughters of Putiel, to be for him a wife."[9]

The *Ha'amek Davar* comments that the language "took for himself" is not a typical expression. There is also a

---

9. *Shemos* 6:25.

repetition in the verse: "took for himself ... to be for him." This teaches that although the daughter of Putiel was not from a prominent family, she still merited to have a son, Pinchas. This was because she was of exceptional assistance in the life of her husband. Elazar "took for himself" means that he realized that this woman was capable of building him into an exceptional person, and therefore he was not particular with regard to her ancestry.

According to this, if the proposed girl will decidedly be of great assistance to him, he should meet her, and if she is acceptable they will G-d-willing merit to have a son like Pinchas!

Measure for Measure I

וַאֲנִי אַקְשֶׁה אֶת לֵב פַּרְעֹה

But I shall harden Pharaoh's heart

(7:3)

 Yaakov was on his way to buy a lottery ticket, when he met his friend Shmuel. Yaakov realized that Shmuel was also going to buy a ticket, so he made him the following offer. Since the Gemara in *Bava Metzia*[10] states that the fortune of two people is better than that of one, it would be advantageous for both of them to buy their tickets with the intent that each ticket is for both of them. That way they will be partners and thus have a better chance of winning, and of course, in the event that the ticket wins, they will share the prize. Shmuel agreed, and each purchased a ticket and went on their way.

---

10. 105a.

After the drawing, Yaakov came to Shmuel to inform him that Shmuel's ticket had won, and that they should go together to collect their prize. Shmuel responded that he actually had not had Yaakov in mind when he bought his ticket, and therefore the entire prize belonged to him. Shmuel did not know that Yaakov had recorded their conversation and was shocked when Yaakov told him, that actually it had been Yaakov's ticket that has won, and that Shmuel had just decided his own fate. Since Shmuel had not had Yaakov in mind when he bought his ticket, Yaakov claimed that he did not have Shmuel in mind either, as the entire agreement had been only on the condition that they would each buy for both of them. Now Yaakov claimed that the entire prize belonged to him! Does it?

 The first issue that must be examined is if Yaakov and Shmuel's verbal agreement to buy tickets with each other in mind is binding, since they never reinforced their words with a "*kinyan.*"

The Gemara in *Bava Basra*[11] states that if brothers divided property by means of a lottery, once the lot has been chosen, the distribution is binding. The Gemara explains that since they decided that the lottery should determine the outcome, the pleasure experienced from the fact that they were willing to come to a mutual agreement is sufficient to finalize the agreement and make it binding. The *Rashba* explains that the same is true for any partners, and for any kind of merchandise as well. It would seem that in our case as well, their mutual agreement to have each other in mind would suffice to bind them to their words, to each buy tickets for both of them and to share the prize.

Now that it is clear that each of them was obligated to buy for the both of them, it must be determined if Shmuel is believed when he says that he did not honor his obligation to Yaakov. The

---

11. 10b.

S'dei Chemed[12] quotes the opinion of the majority of *Rishonim*, that one is not believed if he admits that he was wicked, or that he had engaged in dishonest behavior.

This concept is also expressed by the *Rema*.[13] "If someone gives his friend money and appoints him as an agent to purchase land or merchandise, and the agent used his own money to buy the land or merchandise for himself, his act is binding, although he had acted dishonestly (since he did not buy anything for the one who appointed him). If the agent bought the item with his own money, he may say afterward that he intended to buy it for himself. However, this is true only if he was appointed as an agent to buy an unspecified piece of property. If he was as an agent to buy a specific property, since it would be treachery to buy it for himself, he is not believed to say that he acted improperly. Certainly he bought for the one who sent him, and he may not change his mind afterward."

In our case, it would seem that Shmuel is not believed that he had not had Yaakov in mind when he bought the ticket, since that would be dishonest. If Yaakov's ticket would have won, Shmuel would certainly have asked him to share the prize, and had Shmuel not bought the ticket with intent for Yaakov too, he would have no right to do so. Therefore, it makes sense that Shmuel cannot claim that he bought his ticket only for himself.

Nevertheless, even if Shmuel is not believed, Yaakov may not have to divide the prize with him. Their entire agreement was predicated on the fact that they trust each other, to give each other the prize without any hassle. If Yaakov could only have gotten his share from Shmuel through a legal battle, Yaakov would never have bought his ticket with Shmuel in mind. וצ"ע.

However, even if we will conclude that Yaakov does not have to divide the prize with Shmuel, he should still give him part of it. The *S'dei Chemed*[14] records a case of a man who bought a lottery

---

12. Vol. I, page 21.
13. *Choshen Mishpat* 183:2.
14. Vol. II, page 190.

ticket, but instead of writing his own name on the ticket, he wrote the name of a very "lucky" person. The *S'dei Chemed* concludes that although there is no obligation to share the prize equally with the person whose name appears on the ticket, one should still grant him part of the prize, since the ticket won in his merit. In our case as well, Yaakov bought the ticket for himself and for Shmuel, and their collective fortune may have been what caused the ticket to win. For this reason, Yaakov should give part of the prize to Shmuel. [15]וצ״ע.

The Oldest Trick
in the Book

וַיִּבְאַשׁ הַיְאֹר
And the River became foul
(7:21)

Shmiel's wife devotedly cared for her elderly mother, who lived in a distant neighborhood. The travel time made the task all the more difficult, so Shmiel decided to

---

15. Editor's Note: Since there is no obligation to divide the prize because Yisrael in effect dissolved the partnership, there was in actuality no collective fortune, and therefore Yaakov may keep the entire prize for himself. However, since the case of the *S'dei Chemed* is similar, inasmuch as writing someone's name on a ticket does not give them any ownership on the ticket, and still he suggests that the ticket won in their merit, that is why Yaakov should consider giving part of the prize to Yisrael. When I asked Rav Zilberstein if I was correct, the *Rav* answered that had Yisrael been willing to share the prize, he would have deserved sharing Yaakov's prize as well. Therefore they still had a collective fortune. Even if subsequently Yisrael ruined his chance to share the prize, Yaakov still had the advantage of their collective fortune.

buy a house next to his mother-in-law. He could not find a suitable house that was available, so he approached his mother-in-law's neighbor Zevi, and offered to buy his house for more than its value. Zevi refused, saying that he was attached to his house and had no desire to move.[16]

The next day, Shmiel approached Zevi with the following offer. Since Zevi refused to sell his house, Shmiel would not pressure him, in order not to violate the tenth commandment, not to covet someone else's possessions. However, Shmiel asked if he could install a hook in Zevi's house on which to hang his things, as his mother-in-law would sometimes search his belongings, and Shmiel was interested in having a private place nearby to stash his things. He offered Zevi $10,000 for the rights to have such a hook in his house.

Zevi was overwhelmed by the offer, and happily agreed. They went to a lawyer, and drew up a contract stating that Shmiel could hang whatever he wanted on the hook, and Zevi could not object, nor could he touch Shmiel's belongings, and certainly not remove them. Failure to keep the terms of the contract would carry a $50,000 penalty.

The next day Shmiel hung a sack on his hook in Zevi's home, and left. Several days passed and Zevi's house began to reek. It did not take long to verify that the stench emanated from Shmiel's sack. Not wanting to break the terms of their contract, Zevi called Shmiel, and asked him to please take away the sack, as its stench was permeating the entire house. Shmiel answered

---

16. This story is printed in the name of the Baal Shem Tov as a parable of the *yetzer hara's* plan to uproot a person from his place in the World to Come. If the *yetzer hara* can cause a person to do even a small sin, it already gives him a foothold to sully the entire person, as one sin leads to another.

Even if the story is an allegory, the halachic discussion is real.

coldly that he was not curtailed from hanging odorous items on his hook, and that Zevi should please not disturb him again. When it became impossible to live under such conditions Zevi called Shmiel and offered to return the $10,000 in order to tear up their contract. Shmiel refused. He had no interest in relinquishing his rights. Alternatively, he offered to buy Zevi's house. Zevi had no choice at this point, and agreed to sell his house for the price that Shmiel had originally offered. Shmiel refused to pay such a high price, since he had already paid for the hook, and besides Zevi had no interest in living there anyway.

Can Zevi retract his sale of the hook since he did not realize Shmiel's true intent? Zevi thought that Shmiel just wanted a place to hang things. Had Zevi known that Shmiel would drive him out of his home he never would have agreed to sell him the hook. In addition, is Shmiel in violation of the tenth commandment, *"Lo Sachmod,"* since the sale of the house is really under duress?

Had Shmiel paid a reasonable price for the hook in Zevi's house, Zevi could have asked Shmiel to remove his aromatic sack. The Gemara in *Bava Basra*[17] states that one cannot acquire the right to make smoke or to have a lavatory adjacent to his friend's land if the latter is disturbed by the smell that pollutes his property. Even if the neighbor did not originally object when his friend started using his property for such activity, the neighbor does not lose the right to object to it afterward. If so, one could certainly object to his roommate using their common property for disturbing behavior.

In our case, when Shmiel paid an exorbitant sum for the rights to his hook, Zevi should have suspected that Shmiel was planning

---

17. 23a.

to use his rights for malevolent purposes. Perhaps in such a context, Zevi may not object to Shmiel's right to use his hook as he wishes. However, since such behavior was not clearly defined, it would seem that Shmiel does not have the right to use his hook to disturb Zevi's rights to live in his own home, and Zevi may remove the sack from his home.

Moreover, if Zevi actually sold his house to Shmiel due to the unliveable circumstances Shmiel has indeed violated the commandment of *Lo Sachmod*, as delineated in *Shulchan Aruch*.[18]

◆◆◆

Conditional Air

וְאֵשׁ מִתְלַקַּחַת בְּתוֹךְ הַבָּרָד

And fire flaming amid the hail

(9:24)

 The Katzes left Eretz Yisrael for the month of Nissan to spend Pesach with their family in Brooklyn. Their neighbor, Shmuel, was making *Sheva Berachos* on the first Shabbos in Nissan, and had the forethought to ask Mr. Katz if he minded hosting a young couple in his apartment for that Shabbos.

Mr. Katz good-naturedly agreed and left Shmuel the key.

When Mr. Katz turned the key in the lock of his apartment approximately one month later, he was hit with a rush of freezing cold air. It seems that the couple who enjoyed his hospitality that Shabbos, had left the

---

18. *Choshen Mishpat* 359:3.

air conditioner running for an entire month. When the electric bill for that month arrived in the mail, Mr. Katz invited the couple to pay the expensive bill that they had run up. The young guest brazenly claimed that he had received permission to turn on the air conditioner, and the fact that it stayed on indefinitely was merely a *gerama*[19] and therefore would not require him to pay. Who is right?

 It would seem that permission to turn on the air conditioner was given only on condition that it be turned off after use. If he never turned it off, then the guest had no permission to turn it on, and therefore, he should have to pay.

A proof can be brought from the *Darchei Teshuvah,*[20] who raises the following question. A *shochet* slaughtered his friend's animal, but neglected to check the animal's trachea and esophagus promptly. Subsequently they were misplaced, and as a result, the animal may not be eaten. Does the *shochet* have to pay for the animal because of his negligence, or is he innocent as his part in the loss was only causatory at best?

Perhaps it is similar to one who possesses information regarding someone's lawsuit, and does not come to testify. The witness is innocent as far as the court is concerned (although he has an obligation to Hashem) since he did not actively damage the person. Similarly, the *shochet's* damage was only passive. Nevertheless the *Darchei Teshuvah* concludes that the *shochet* actively damaged the animal, because to slaughter without checking the necessary organs is something that he had no permission to do.

In the same vein, one who opens a freezer to remove a container of ice cream and neglects to close the freezer door retroactively had no permission to open the freezer in the first place, and would be obligated to pay any damages he caused, due to the rule of *garmi.*[21]

---

19. See Glossary.
20. *Yoreh De'ah* 25 § 2.
21. See Glossary.

פרשת בא
Parashas Bo

The Absolute Truth

בִּנְעָרֵינוּ וּבִזְקֵנֵינוּ נֵלֵךְ
With our youngsters and with our elders shall we go
(10:9)

A teenage boy was sitting on a crowded bus when an elderly gentleman boarded. The boy offered the man his own seat, but the man refused. Should the boy lie and claim that he is alighting at the next stop so the man will feel comfortable taking the seat, or is lying not justified?

The Gemara says[22] that a poor man who is not willing to take *tzedakah* should be given the money as a loan, and afterward be told that he does not have to repay it. The *Shulchan Aruch*[23] rules this way as well, that a poor man who does not want to take *tzedakah* should be fooled and given the money as a present or as a loan. We may infer from this that if someone deserves something and is unwilling to take it, we may trick him

---

22. *Kesubos* 67b.
23. *Yoreh De'ah* 253:9.

into taking it. Since it is difficult for the elderly man to stand on the crowded bus, he should be given the seat, even if one must deceive him in order to accomplish this. Even if he does not have difficulty standing, it is a *chillul Hashem* not to stand up for him, and one may misrepresent the truth to enable him to sit. In reality this is not a misrepresentation of the truth, since the truth of the matter is that Hashem wants the older man to sit.

True Service

יְהִי כֵן ה׳ עִמָּכֶם

So be Hashem with you

(10:10)

 A father of several children wishes to travel to his *Rebbe* for the *Yamim Nora'im*. He is unsure if he should go by himself or take his children with him. His wife wholeheartedly agreed to let him go on his own. His concern is that although his children would certainly have a spiritually uplifting experience by accompanying him, if he will have to look after them, he will not be able to concentrate on his own *davening* as much as he would otherwise. What should he do?

 This question is discussed in very early sources. Moshe Rabbeinu told Pharaoh, "We will go with our young and our old, with our sons and our daughters, with our cattle and sheep, for it is our festival of Hashem." Pharaoh answered him, "May Hashem be with you when I send you and your children, behold that you are headed for evil."

The *Zayis Ra'anan*[24] questions what Pharaoh was saying. Was he trying to bless them? In addition, why did Pharaoh even agree to sending only the men?

The *Zayis Ra'anan* answers that one of the essential components in serving Hashem is to be calm and free of distraction, especially from little children, and especially if one is on the road. When both factors are present, i.e., being away from home with one's children, they will constantly be distracting him from focusing on the service of Hashem, since he must care for them. This is what Pharaoh wondered. Is it possible that Hashem will be with you when I send you with your children? The two things are a contradiction. To serve Hashem when you have your children with you is a terrible experience, because they will bother you day and night. Therefore Pharaoh suggested, "Just take the men, if you are interested in serving Hashem. If you insist on taking your children, it is a sure thing that your true intention is to escape from Egypt!"

Moshe differed with Pharaoh, "We will go with our children." True service of Hashem demands not only our personal observance, but also teaching and inspiring our children.

In our case as well, the father should go with his children. Although they will probably distract him, the merit of taking one's children to a place where they can absorb fear of Heaven will stand as a merit with which he can be exonerated in judgment.

The Kabbalist Rabbi Mutzafi, who *davened* with very deep concentration, would turn from time to time in the middle of his *davening* to his small son who stood at his side, and point with his finger to instruct him which parts of the *davening* to say.

---

24. The *Av Beis Din* of Kutna, *Divrei Aggadah* on *Parashas Bo*, in the back of Responsa *Zayis Ra'anan*.

Subtle Lighting

וַיְהִי חֹשֶׁךְ אֲפֵלָה

And there was a thick darkness

(10:22)

Meshulem rented a hotel room. When he got to his room late that night, he found that the light did not work. When he went to pay the next morning he demanded a discount, since a room without lighting should cost less. The owner of the hotel countered, "There was plenty of light from the street lamp outside your window. And if you wanted it off, you could draw the drapes! What difference does it make if I paid for the light, or if the city did?" Meshulem insisted that a normal hotel room has a light inside the room, although he conceded that street lamp provided adequate illumination. Should Meshulem pay less for his stay?

A similar incident occurred about a century ago, when watches were not yet common. Dovid rented a hotel room, and since he had an appointment the next morning with a government official, he rented a room with a clock. The room with a clock had a higher rate, which Dovid agreed to pay. Dovid never found the clock in the room, and when he went to settle his bill, he refused to pay the higher rate.

The owner asked Dovid, "Did you not see the clock tower, clearly visible from your window? Some rooms have a beautiful view. Your room had a view of a clock, and that room costs more."

Dovid responded, "I rented a room with a clock, the intention being that there should be a clock *in* the room. That room had no clock in it!" Is Dovid required to pay the higher rate?

Rav Elyashiv said that if a room with a view of a clock is worth more, then certainly he is required to pay for what he received. But if the reason for the higher rate was his agreement to pay more for a room with a clock, certainly his intention was a room that contained a clock inside.

As far as the light, since a room without a light is worth less, even though he could have used the light from outside, he should pay less. This is because a person wants to rent a room with a light inside, not an inferior room with which a person feels cheated.

Into the Fire

תַּשְׁבִּיתוּ שְּׂאֹר מִבָּתֵּיכֶם

You shall nullify the leaven from your homes
(12:15)

 After *bedikas chametz* Yosef's wife prepared all the bags of *chametz* to be taken out the next day to be burned. She accidentally included a bag of coconut cookies, thinking that they were *chametz*, when in reality they were indeed kosher for Pesach. The next day Yosef threw the bags into the fire and continued on his way. Hillel, who noticed the bag of cookies and recognized them as kosher for Pesach, quickly grabbed the bag out of the fire, with the help of a long stick. To whom do the cookies belong, to Yosef or to Hillel?

 It would seem that the cookies were *hefker*, and therefore should belong to Hillel. The Gemara[25] states that if an ox was accused of manslaughter and sentenced to death by

---

25. *Kereisos* 24a.

beis din, and it was discovered afterward that the testimony against the ox was false, the first one to grab the ox gets to keep it. The reason being that once the owner realizes that his ox has been given a death sentence, he relinquishes his ownership, thinking that the ox has no value. Even though the ox became *hefker* through a mistake, it is still considered *hefker*. The same should be true for the Pesach cookies.

However, *Tosafos* in *Pesachim*[26] states that an item made *hefker* in error does not become *hefker*. The *Mishpat Shalom*[27] answers the apparent contradiction between the Gemara and *Tosafos,* by explaining that the Gemara is not talking about *hefker*, as the owner did not declare that his ox should become ownerless. Rather, since he has no hope of being able to keep his ox, that itself gives others the right to obtain it. This is known as *yi'ush*. An example of *yi'ush* is when one gives up on recovering a lost item. Others may then take it for themselves if they find it. The *Maharam Schik*[28] explains that every *yi'ush* is by mistake. Had the owner known that someone would find his lost item, he never would have given up on its recovery, and still *yi'ush* is effective. This explains why the ox in effect remains *hefker*, as a result of the *yi'ush*.

In our case, Yosef had *yi'ush* because he thought the cookies were *chametz*, just as the owner of the convicted ox thought that his ox was sentenced to death. In addition, Yosef had *yi'ush* by putting his cookies into a fire that in seconds could have burned them completely. When Hillel removed them from the fire, it is like someone who saved something from a lion. It may be kept by the one who saved the item.[29]

---

26. 57a.
27. 194:2.
28. *Yoreh De'ah* 391.
29. *Shulchan Aruch, Choshen Mishpat* 259:7.

Whose Matzah Is It?

בָּעֶרֶב תֹּאכְלוּ מַצֹּת

In the evening shall you eat matzos

(12:18)

 The year was 1948. The place was the holy city of Yerushalayim. The city was under siege, and it was the night of the Pesach Seder. Matzos had been distributed in measured quantities to each family.

At one particular Seder, the father had just given each member of the family their portion of matzah when a soldier knocked on the door. The soldier had hurried away from his post for a few moments, and did not have the luxury of sitting at a Seder table. He asked the father if he could at least have a *kzayis* of matzah so that he, too, could fulfill the mitzvah of eating matzah on Pesach.

All eyes turned toward the youngest member of the family, who was not yet bar mitzvah. With the father's permission, the child gave the matzah to the soldier.[30]

Afterward, the question arose whether the soldier had actually fulfilled the mitzvah. The Gemara in *Maseches Succah*[31] states that although a halachic minor can acquire property when it is given to him by an adult, the minor cannot transfer property to others. Being that the matzah had already been given to the child, he could not transfer ownership to the soldier. Given that

---

30. Based on our discussion "Personal Responsibility" in *Parashas Vayeirah* (p. 57), the father's obligation of *chinuch* supersedes his obligation to the soldier. Our discussion here is only whether the soldier fulfills his obligation with this matzah.
31. 46b.

the Gemara in *Pesachim*[32] derives that matzah has to belong to those fulfilling the mitzvah, as is brought by the *Shulchan Aruch*[33] as well, could the soldier fulfill the mitzvah with the matzah the child gave him?

The *Beis Yosef*[34] quotes the *Roke'ach* as saying that when many people bake matzah in the same oven, they should declare that if anyone should happen to inadvertently switch matzos with them, he may keep it as a present. The *Magen Avraham* quotes this as the halachah. Accordingly, since the child acquired the matzah and cannot gift it to another, it would be problematic.

However, the *Maharit*[35] contends that a host does not intend that his guests should acquire their portion until they place it in their mouths. If the host would distribute portions, and subsequently take them back to give them to a woman for the purpose of acquiring her in marriage, it would be binding! Based on this ruling, the *Ateres Moshe*[36] rules that the father may indeed take his child's portion, and give it to someone else.

Rav Zilberstein offers that the *Maharit's* ruling seems to be the subject of disagreement between earlier authorities and therefore whether the soldier had actually fulfilled his obligation would remain in doubt.

--------◆◆◆--------

32. 38a.
33. *Orach Chaim* 454:4, *Mishnah Berurah* § 15.
34. *Orach Chaim* 454.
35. Vol. I, 150, cited in *Ba'er Heiteiv, Even HaEzer* 28 § 32
36. Vol. II, 167.

How Much Would You Give to Do a Mitzvah?

בָּעֶרֶב תֹּאכְלוּ מַצֹּת

In the evening shall you eat matzos

(12:18)

 It was the night of the Pesach Seder, and Yehudah was alone. To make matters worse, he did not have any matzah with him. The only way to get matzah would be to cross the courtyard to his neighbor's house. There was only one problem: a dog named Rex. Rex could be called vicious when he was in a good mood. Although there was no threat to Yehudah's life, Rex would probably take a bite or two from Yehudah's leg. Is Yehudah obligated to fulfill the mitzvah under such painful circumstances? Similarly, would a person be obligated to cross such a courtyard in order to do the mitzvah of repaying a loan?

 The *Tur*[37] writes that one is obligated to fulfill the mitzvah of drinking four cups of wine on Pesach night, even if by doing so he will suffer severe headaches. *R' Yehudah bar I'lai* suffered so, from Pesach until Shavuos, seven weeks later!

For other mitzvos as well, it seems that one would even have to allow himself to be hit in the process of their fulfillment! The

---

37. *Orach Chaim* 472:1.

Gemara in *Arachin*[38] asks: "Until what point is a person obligated to do the mitzvah of *tochachah*? Rav says, until his friend hits him! Rav Yaakov Kamenetsky[39] explained that this is a special dispensation regarding the mitzvah of giving *tochachah*, since once someone hits you, he will no longer listen to what you have to say. With other mitzvos, there is no such exemption. Lest one argue that with other mitzvos one would be exempt at an earlier stage than being hit, that cannot be, because the Gemara continues that Shmuel says that one must offer *tochachah* until his friend curses him. R' Yochanan says, until his friend gets angry at him. Would cursing or anger be reasons to exempt one from the mitzvah of *lulav* or *tzitzis*? It must be that only *tochachah* has a special exemption.

Especially if one would not be willing to spend one-fifth of his assets in order to avoid the pain, one would even have to suffer the pain in order to do the mitzvah. The pain would not be a reason to excuse him from the mitzvah, since one would be obligated to spend up to that much money to fulfill the mitzvah.[40] Therefore, the pain is an even smaller sacrifice, so why should he be excused?

The *Mishnah Berurah*[41] writes that one does not have to drink four cups of wine if it will cause him to be sick and commit him to bed, since the purpose of the mitzvah is to display freedom, and such an outcome would not be in accordance with the behavior of a freed man. One may infer from this that other mitzvos, which are not expressions of freedom, would be mandatory even if they would cause someone to be bedridden. Similarly, perhaps one would even have to suffer blows in order to do a mitzvah.

However, one could argue that a headache is a natural outcome of drinking wine, and is therefore included in the obligation to do the mitzvah. Being hit by someone is not a natural consequence of the mitzvah, and is perhaps beyond a person's call of duty.

In contrast it would seem that one would not have to suffer being

---

38. 15b.
39. *Emes LeYaakov, Parashas Vayeitzei.*
40. *Shulchan Aruch, Orach Chaim 651.*
41. 472 § 35.

bitten in order to repay a loan. Although the borrower accepted an obligation to repay, he did not obligate himself to be wounded. If so, we find an irony. One must repay a loan, even if the amount due is all he owns, whereas one's obligation to fulfill a positive commandment of the Torah would not require him to give away more than a fifth of his assets. On the other hand, as far as risking being bitten or beaten, a mitzvah is still obligatory, whereas repaying a loan is not.

The logic behind this is simple. The exemption of not having to pay more than one-fifth of one's assets for a mitzvah is a limitation of the obligation. A borrower has no such exemption since he has to pay back whatever he borrowed. As far as being bitten or beaten, the borrower only owes money, and not flesh. As the Chazon Ish[42] writes, "even though repaying a loan is a mitzvah, and *beis din* will force the lender to fulfill it, as is mentioned in *Kesubos,*[43] we do not force him to take a job in order to repay the loan. With regard to other positive mitzvos he must take a job if he must, in order to perform what is incumbent on him, and repaying a loan is an exception."

Leil Shimurim

לֵיל שִׁמֻּרִים הוּא

It was a night of anticipation

(12:42)

 Yonasan was entrusted with guarding his friend's expensive candelabra while the friend traveled to a neighboring town for the *Chag*. On Pesach night, after the Seder, Yonasan did not lock his door, as the *Magen Avraham*[44] states in the name of the *Maharil* that one should not lock his door with a heavy bolt on the night of the Seder. The reason for this is because it is *Leil Shimurim*, a special night that Hashem watches over our houses. That night, thieves came and stole the candelabra. Is Yonasan absolved of his responsibility for the valuables, since he observed the custom of the *Maharil*, or is he considered negligent for not locking his door in order to protect the item?

 This question was asked to Rav Elyashiv, who responded as follows: The custom cited by *Maharil* is great and exalted, and applies to everyone — for his own household and everything that concerns the person himself.

However, when one is entrusted with someone else's property, he has a halachic obligation to guard and protect that property. In this case, Yonasan would have had to ask his friend for permission to jeopardize the safety of the candlelabra by leaving his door unlocked. This is particularly so because thieves are well aware of this custom and are liable to take advantage of the opportunities it offers.

As long as Yonasan did not receive permission to do so, he remains obligated to watch his friend's property responsibly. One may not rely on a miracle to protect an item for which he undertook responsibility.

————— •◆• —————

---

44. 481 § 2.

There Is No Place Like Home

וְהִגַּדְתָּ לְבִנְךְ

And you shall tell your son

(13:8)

There was once a man whose children preceded him in entering the next world, and he was left with only one descendant, a grandson. The grandson lived with his widowed mother in a different city. With the coming of Pesach the grandfather knew that he would have to make a difficult decision. He would love to travel to his grandson, in order to tell him the story of the *Haggadah* at the Seder, but he knew that his wife would not be able to come with him. Although he knew that she would certainly agree that he could spend the Yom Tov away from her, he knew that she would also be sad that she would be left alone. What should he do?

The *sefer Vayaged Moshe*[45] suggests that perhaps there is a greater obligation to relate the story of the Exodus from Egypt to one's grandson than there is to relate it to other people, as it says in the *pasuk*,[46] "in order that you should tell the story to your son and your son's son, how I plagued the Egyptians." Even though one's grandson is not actually one's son[47] (and the mitzvah of *haggadah* is to tell one's son), with regard to the mitzvah to teach one's son Torah, the Torah found it necessary

---

45. 19:10.
46. *Shemos* 10:2.
47. See *Tosafos* in *Yevamos* 21b.

to specify that the mitzvah is to teach one's grandson as well. Since the *pasuk* records that one will tell the story to one's grandson, that is a greater fulfillment of the mitzvah than to tell other people. Even though the *pasuk* is not referring specifically to the night of the Seder, since the *Poskim* write that the entire year there is a mitzvah to remember the Exodus from Egypt, and on Pesach night the mitzvah is to tell the story, it appears that telling one's grandson is a special mitzvah. וצ"ע.

In the *Haggadah* of Rabbi Shlomo Zalman Auerbach, he writes in the name of the *Chasam Sofer* that the obligation of *haggadah* is to tell one's son. When the son will grow up and tell his son, that will fulfill the *pasuk* of, "in order that you should tell the story to your son and your son's son."

In this case, where the grandson does not have a living father, there is certainly reason for the grandfather to travel and relate to his grandson the story of the Jews leaving Mitzrayim.

However, since the Gemara in *Pesachim*[48] states that the mitzvah to be joyous on Yom Tov includes bringing joy to one's wife, it is logical that one should not leave one's wife alone. Even though the mitzvah of telling the story of the *Haggadah* to one's grandson is a *hiddur mitzvah*, it does not justify ignoring an absolute obligation to make his wife joyous on Yom Tov.

48. 116a.

פרשת בשלח
Parashas Beshalach

Buckle Your Seatbelt!

סוּס וְרֹכְבוֹ רָמָה

Having hurled horse with its rider

(15:1)

Avi drove his friend Yossi to work one day. On the way Avi was careless, and his car collided with an oncoming car. Avi emerged unscathed, but his friend Yossi was thrown forward and broke his nose. Had Yossi been wearing his seatbelt, nothing would have happened to him. Does Avi need to pay Yossi for his injury?

It would seem that since every passenger is required by law to buckle his seatbelt, Yossi is responsible for his own injury. However, according to international law the driver is also responsible that all passengers be buckled and if so, Avi may well be at fault for driving before insuring that all passengers had fastened their seatbelts. Especially since driving requires a license and the law stipulates that one not drive with passengers who are not seatbelted, Avi had no permission to drive!

On the other hand, even though Avi is certainly responsible for his actions, Yossi still had an obligation to protect himself.

The *Yerushalmi*[49] states that two people who went to sleep next to each other are responsible for any damage they cause each other in the course of their sleep. One may ask, why should either of them be accountable? If each one knowingly went to sleep adjacent to his friend, he was certainly aware that his friend may flail his arms while asleep, and if so each one should be responsible for his own well being. Could this prove that the accountability rests on the one who actually harmed his friend, and not on the one who placed himself in a situation where he could possibly be hurt?

In truth, the *Yerushalmi* and our case are not alike. Even though it is possible for a person to be hurt while lying next to a sleeping person, it is not very likely. Therefore, one who did so is not considered negligent. In contrast, one who travels in a car without fastening his seatbelt is considered negligent since he did not obey the law. Therefore Yossi is responsible for his own mishap.

Determining Your Budget

זֶה אֵ־לִי וְאַנְוֵהוּ

This is my G-d and I will build Him a sanctuary

(15:2)

 A person has the opportunity to buy a beautiful set of *lulav* and *esrog*. Alternatively, he could buy a set that is certainly kosher, yet not "*mehudar*," and the money he

---

49. *Bava Kamma* 2:8.

saves by buying the less beautiful set could be distributed to the poor. Which set should he purchase?

 First we must determine if the obligation to beautify the mitzvos is *mi'd'Oraisa* or *mi'd'Rabbanan*. The *Ra'avad* in *Succah*[50] implies that it is indeed a Torah-based concept. However the *Ritva*[51] implies that it is in fact of Rabbinic origin. *Tosafos* in *Menachos*[52] agrees with this view. According to this opinion, it seems that it would be better to save the additional money to give to the poor, as the *Rambam* adjoins that there is no greater joy than to gladden the hearts of the poor, orphans, and widows etc.[53]

Rabbi Yechezkel Abramsky once asked a close acquaintance to buy him *tzitzis* strings. The latter mentioned that there were two kinds available. Both were strictly kosher, but one of them was exceptional, and its cost was three times as much. Rav Yechezkel immediately gave him the amount for the expensive strings, but instructed him to buy the less expensive strings, and distribute the difference to *tzedakah*.

This story does not have bearing on our case, since in the case of the *tzitzis* both strings were beautiful, just one of them was exceptional. In our case, the less expensive *esrog* was not beautiful at all, and therefore one will not have fulfilled the obligation to beautify a mitzvah.

If a person feels that for his service to Hashem, he needs a beautiful *esrog* because this will elevate his *davening* and his happiness on Yom Tov, then his own needs take precedence. If, however, his *tzedakah* is as valuable to him as is his *esrog*, it would be preferable to give his money to the poor.

---

50. 11b.
51. Ad loc.
52. 41b.
53. *Hilchos Yom Tov* and *Hilchos Megillah*.

Mitzvah Accessories

זֶה אֵ-לִי וְאַנְוֵהוּ

This is my G-d and I will build Him a Sanctuary

(15:2)

 Gershon accepted upon himself to perform the mitzvah of *esrog* in accordance with all of its details. Does this require that he purchase a silver esrog box, or is the box not considered an enhancement of the mitzvah.

 The Gemara in *Succah*[54] relates that they would pick *aravos* for the *Beis HaMikdash* before Shabbos and put them in golden water jugs so that they should not wither. The *Mishnah Berurah*[55] explains that although placing the willows in water to keep them from withering was not part of the mitzvah, it was done nevertheless in order to beautify the mitzvah. We may derive from the fact that they used golden jugs for this purpose, that even though it was not a necessary part of the mitzvah, there is a point in beautifying even an accessory to an object of a mitzvah.

The *Mekor Chaim*[56] writes that one should have an attractive bag for his *tallis* and *tefillin*, as this is also included in beautification of mitzvos. It would seem that an *esrog* holder should also be beautiful for this reason. The *Sefer Chassidim*[57] comments regarding the *pasuk "Kabed es Hashem mehon'cha"*: If you buy a chest in which to keep your gold and silver, it would be more worthwhile to buy a chest to store your *sefarim* and your *tefillin*!

From here we see the significance of buying a beautiful bookcase for one's *sefarim* as well as other beautiful mitzvah containers.

---

54. 45a.
55. 664 §18.
56. (written by the *Chavos Ya'ir*) 28:2.
57. 12a.

Although there is certainly no obligation to invest in a beautiful *esrog* box, there certainly is significance in having one, in order to adorn the mitzvah article.

———◆———

In Honor of Shabbos

וְהֵכִינוּ אֵת אֲשֶׁר יָבִיאוּ

When they prepare what they bring

(16:5)

 Sarah is a teenage *baalas teshuvah*. Her parents are still distant from *Yiddishkeit*. Nevertheless, Sarah spends Shabbos at home with her parents, who basically tolerate their daughter's new practices.

One week Sarah learned that one may not wash the dishes on Shabbos if the dishes are not needed again on Shabbos, and the sole purpose in washing them is only to use them during the week. The reason for this is because there is a prohibition to prepare on Shabbos for after Shabbos.[58] However, Sarah knows that if she will not wash the dishes after lunch, her mother will wash them in the dishwasher, causing her mother to desecrate Shabbos. May Sarah wash the dishes (a violation of a Rabbinic decree of preparation for the week) in order to prevent her mother from using the dishwasher (a violation of Shabbos *mi'd'Oraisa*)?

 Sarah may wash the dishes on Shabbos since she is not doing so in order to prepare for the week, which would be prohibited because it is preparing for after Shabbos;

---

58. See *Shulchan Aruch, Orach Chaim* 323:6.

rather, she is doing so in order to preserve the honor of Shabbos. Not only could Sarah do so to prevent her mother from activating the dishwasher, but even if the only problem was that her parents would be upset at her, it would be permitted as well since her intention is not to prepare for tomorrow, but to maintain the peace today, and her dishwashing is therefore not merely an act of preparation.

In addition, Sarah's refusal to wash the dishes may cause her mother to be intolerant of Sarah and her religion, making the mother guilty of *sinas chinam*,[59] and therefore Sarah is not merely preparing for tomorrow, but preserving *shalom bayis* today.

---

59. See *Chazon Ish, Shevi'is* 12:9.

פרשת יתרו
Parashas Yisro

High-Volume Service

וַיְהִי קוֹל הַשּׁפָר הוֹלֵךְ וְחָזֵק מְאֹד

The sound of the shofar grew continually much stronger

(19:19)

One of the members of the *kollel* has a loud, booming voice, and he uses it while learning (when he does not have a study partner) in a way that is impossible to ignore. His high profile disturbs the concentration of the other members of the *kollel*, yet he claims that he cannot learn any other way. He is a valuable asset to the *kollel*, as he learns constantly without wasting a second. Yet the other members are unsure if he has a right to learn his best at the expense of others.

The *Shulchan Aruch*[60] rules that one may not *daven Shemoneh Esrei* out loud lest he disturb others. The *Beur Halachah* adds that if one cannot concentrate when he *davens* quietly, he should *daven* at home. It is clearly implied

---

60. *Orach Chaim* 101:2.

that one may not differ from standard behavior at the expense of others.

In addition, the Mishnah in *Yoma*[61] states that the Kohen Gadol would pray only a brief *tefillah* before leaving the *Kodesh HaKodashim* on Yom Kippur, in order that the people waiting outside should not be apprehensive that something had happened to him. One may infer from this practice that one needs to curb his personal service to Hashem, in order not to cause discomfort to others.

One of the *gedolei hador* said that one cannot compare learning Torah to *davening Shemoneh Esrei*. *Shemoneh Esrei* is meant to be said quietly, as we learn from Channah,[62] who *davened* with her lips, but her voice could not be heard. A special allowance is made for one who cannot concentrate while praying quietly, to *daven* more loudly, on condition that he does not disturb others. This is not necessarily the case when it comes to learning Torah, which is supposed to be learned out loud,[63] and is therefore not necessarily bound by this condition.

On the other hand, even though Rav Chaim Kanievsky testified that the Chazon Ish ruled that one who learns out loud at night cannot be prevented from doing so by neighbors whose sleep is being disturbed as a result, in our case, where other people are also trying to learn, perhaps he would still have to lower his voice even though it will detrimentally affect his learning. וצ״ע.

---------◆---------

61. 53b.
62. *Berachos* 31a.
63. See *Eruvin* 54a.

A Difficult Mitzvah

כַּבֵּד אֶת אָבִיךָ

Honor your father

(20:12)

 Pinny is a devoted son and would love to take care of his elderly father in his home. His father has Alzheimer's disease, and does not have control of his faculties. Many times his father behaves irrationally, and Pinny cannot contain his own disrespectful outbursts. Pinny wants to know if it would be better to put his father in a nursing home in order to avoid showing his father any disrespect, or if it is better for him to keep his father at home, where he will receive better care. Should Pinny keep his father home, even though it is clear to Pinny that he will not be able to avoid yelling at his father from time to time?

 It would seem that since it is best for the father's care to remain in the home of his son, that is certainly the will of the Torah, even though occasionally the father will be pained by his son. It is similar to one who owes his friend a debt, and knows that if he will repay his debt he will not be able to keep himself from damaging that person's property. Would that excuse him from repaying his debt? So too, honoring one's parents is like one who is repaying a debt; the son has a debt to his father to keep him in his home, since it is a possible option. Even if doing so will cause the son to sin, that does not excuse the son from hosting his father.

Certainly the son should *daven* to Hashem that he should be able to control himself, but it is probable that even if he slips occasionally, Hashem will forgive him, since at times it may be beyond human capability not to react in such a way.

True Honor

כַּבֵּד אֶת אָבִיךָ

Honor your father

(20:12)

The Gemara in *Kiddushin*[64] relates that someone asked R' Eliezer, "If my father asks me to bring him a cup of water, and my mother asks me for a cup of water, to which parent should I listen first?" R' Eliezer answered, "Set aside the honor of your mother, and do your father's bidding first, for both you and your mother are obligated to honor your father (because he is her husband)."

The son of a married couple, who held each other in the highest esteem, found himself in a dilemma. The father asked the son to bring his mother a cup of water. At the same time, the mother asked the son to bring his father a cup of water. Whose request should he honor first?

The *Pischei Teshuvah*[65] is explicit that the Gemara is only relevant regarding acts that a woman must do for her husband. Other acts that a woman is not obligated to do for her husband are not included in the rule of "you and your mother are obligated to honor your father." In such a case a father and a mother would be equal, and the son could choose

---

64. 31a.
65. *Yoreh De'ah* 240 § 9.

between them. This is why the Gemara chose a case of bringing a drink, which a wife does for her husband[66] even if they have several servants. The *Pischei Teshuvah* concludes that the halachah is not clear in this matter.

Rav Elyashiv commented on the *Pischei Teshuvah* from the words of the *Rambam*.[67] Although the *Rambam* states explicitly that a man must honor his wife more than he does himself, the *Rambam* also says that a woman's obligation to honor her husband is even more than her husband's obligation to honor her. The *Maggid Mishneh* explains that the *Rambam's* source is the Gemara that says, "you and your mother are obligated to honor your father." From that fact that the *Rambam* learns from this Gemara a general rule in affording honor, we see that he must have understood that the Gemara is referring to a general obligation to give honor, and not specifically to particular tasks, like giving one's husband a drink. Thus, a woman's obligation to honor her husband is always greater than her husband's obligation to honor her, unlike the understanding of the *Pischei Teshuvah*.

Rav Chaim Kanievsky said that in our case he should listen to his father, and give his mother a drink first. To fulfill a person's desire gives him honor. Therefore his father's will should be done first.

The *Yerushalmi* in *Pe'ah*[68] relates that when R' Yishmael would come home from yeshivah, his mother would wash his feet with water and drink the water! When R' Yishmael refused to let his mother maintain this practice, she complained to his colleagues that her son refuses to honor her. Our Rabbis told R' Yishmael "Since that is her will, that is how you are meant to honor her."

———◆———

66. *Even HaEzer* 80.
67. *Hilchos Ishus* 15:19.
68. 1:1.

The Best Seder

כַּבֵּד אֶת אָבִיךָ וְאֶת אִמֶּךָ

Honor your father and mother

(20:12)

 Joseph is a *baal teshuvah* who learns in a yeshivah. His family has not yet followed his lead. Several weeks before Pesach, Joseph's *Rosh Yeshivah* approached him and invited him to attend the *Rosh Yeshivah's* Pesach Seder. Joseph was honored by the invitation and asked his parents for permission. His parents were insulted by the thought. They strongly felt that Pesach is a time that the whole family spends together.

Joseph was torn. On the one hand, he could gain so much by spending the Seder with the *Rosh Yeshivah* and his family. On the other hand, doing so would upset his parents. Perhaps it would be better to stay with his family, and honor his parent's wishes. He might even be able to bring them closer to *Yiddishkeit*. What should he do?

 The Gemara in *Bava Metzia*[69] speaks of a case of two people who were traveling in the desert, and only one of them had a bottle of water. If they share the water, both will die of dehydration. If the one with the bottle will reserve all of the water for himself, he will be able to survive until he reaches civilization. R' Akiva taught that one's own life has precedence over the life of his friend, and he should keep the water for himself.

The *Sha'arei Teshuvah*[70] writes that this holds true in relation to one's spiritual life as well. If for physical existence it is true, how

---

69. 62a.
70. *Orach Chaim* 482 § 2.

much more so it is true regarding one's spiritual existence. Even though we find that one may not fool one's friend to take something away from him, that applies only to property. In regard to mitzvos, at least in a case where your friend has not yet acquired them, one may do his best to do the mitzvah himself. Each person is responsible to build himself spiritually and do the mitzvos.

Accordingly, Joseph is responsible to build himself spiritually, and his spiritual life has precedence over the spirituality of his parents. Therefore he does not have to sacrifice a Seder with his *Rosh Yeshivah* for their benefit. His parents also have to honor Hashem and let their son serve Him to the best of his ability. Spending the Seder with them is not the highest form of *kibbud av va'eim*, since they are not asking him to feed them,[71] but to spend time with them.

Joseph has to make an accounting as to where he will accomplish more mitzvos. If the Seder in his house is a farce, he should certainly go to the *Rosh Yeshivah's* house. If, however, he could fulfill *kibbud av va'eim* and also possibly draw them closer to Torah and mitzvos, and his parents are interested to have a real Seder and to hear their son's words of Torah, Joseph should attend his parents' Seder. Even though he will not have the same inspirational experience, the mitzvah of *kibbud av va'eim* itself is very great, even if one cannot see how much he really gains from it spiritually.

---

71. See *Shulchan Aruch, Yoreh De'ah* 240:4.

פרשת משפטים
Parashas Mishpatim

The Best Things in Life Are Free

וְיָצְאָה חִנָּם אֵין כָּסֶף

She shall leave free of charge, without payment

(21:11)

 A first grader, accompanied by her mother, came into a private dental clinic. Apparently, her parents, being new immigrants, were unaware that the child was entitled to free dental care available through her school at a clinic that was paid for by the government. Does the dentist have to tell the parents that they could use the government services to which they are entitled, even though by informing them of this, he will lose their business?

 The dentist has an obligation to tell the parents for two reasons. 1) The Torah instructs us, "Love your neighbor as you love yourself." One of the ways to do that is to do kindness with others and to advise them properly. It is similar to returning a lost object, since they do not even know of the privileges to which they are entitled.

2) Perhaps, since the same treatments are available to them for free, it would be unfair for them to have to pay. This would be a violation of "*o'na'ah*" (overcharging).[72] It is not fair to charge for something that is available gratis. Only if the treatment in the dentist's clinic is superior to that which is provided by the government, could the clinic charge for its services.

If the dentist is only an employee, and by informing the parents he will jeopardize his job, he would not have to tell them, since his personal loss takes precedence over their's.

The Man Who Cried, "Ambulance!"

וְהָאֱלֹקִים אִנָּה לְיָדוֹ
And G-d had caused it to come to his hand
(21:13)

 A. Elderly Mr. Klein would complain to his wife many a time that he did not feel well, and he would ask her to call an ambulance. Each time the complaint was not justified, and the ambulance was summoned unnecessarily.

This past Tuesday, he asked his wife to call an ambulance, and she thought that this was just another false alarm. He appeared to be in good condition, so

---

72. *Vayikra* 25:14.

she decided to spare the expense of calling the ambulance, and wasting the time and trying the patience of the paramedics. A short while later she discovered her husband lying lifeless on the floor. She frantically called an ambulance, but it was too late.

Mrs. Klein is plagued by pangs of guilt. She wants to know if she needs atonement for not heeding her husband's request to call an ambulance, or if she was correct in her behavior, since she knew that many times her hypochondriac husband's complaints were for naught.

B. Dr. Zweig knows that his patient is a hypochondriac, and the patient calls the doctor many times to come to the hospital unnecessarily. May Dr. Zweig go to the hospital even on Shabbos or Yom Kippur when this patient calls him?

 The *Beur Halachah*[73] writes, "A sick person who claims that one of his organs is in need of medicine is to be listened to, as a heart knows its own pain. Even if a doctor will claim that the patient is not ill, we do not listen to the doctor, because the patient knows his own pain." Similarly, the *Shulchan Aruch*[74] writes, concerning eating on Yom Kippur: "If a sick person claims that he must eat, even if 100 doctors claim that he does not have to eat, we listen to the sick man because he knows his own pain."

Therefore, there is reason to say that every time a sick person requests an ambulance, we must heed his request. Even if we have evidence from past experience that his complaints are not to be taken seriously, we cannot ignore his plea. When it is a matter of life and death, we must be suspect of even a remote possibility of danger.

The Gemara in *Sanhedrin*[75] states that a man who is being led to his execution by *beis din* is to be returned to court if he claims

---

73. 328: "*HaRofeh.*"
74. *Orach Chaim* 618:1.
75. 42b.

that he has a new defense for his case. This is so even if he has to be returned many times. This shows that even if he already claimed several times to have a new defense, and his defense was rejected, *beis din* is still hopeful that maybe this time he will be exonerated. Accordingly, it would seem that Mrs. Klein should have acceded to her husband's request despite his history of "false alarms."

However, when this question was posed to Rav Elyashiv, he responded that the sick man's wife certainly knew her husband well and was proficient in all aspects of his illness. If she was convinced that her husband was overreacting, and that was her reason for not summoning an ambulance, she may rely on her experience to spare the expense and the bother of calling an ambulance. If as a result her husband died, it was Hashem's will, and she is not to be blamed. It is not similar to the case in *Sanhedrin*, because the defendant has to claim to have a new defense every time. In our case, the complaint was the same as always. If the husband would have claimed to have new symptoms, then she would have to listen to him. If, however, she was not completely convinced that her husband was not in danger, and was only hesitant to call an ambulance because of the frequency of the calls, then she would need atonement for her laxity.

Similarly, if a doctor is convinced that the patient is calling for his usual condition of hypochondria, the doctor would not have to desecrate Shabbos to visit the patient. On Yom Kippur perhaps the doctor should be more forthcoming, since the fast could have a detrimental effect on the patient's condition.

———◆◆◆———

Medical Expenses I

וְרַפֹּא יְרַפֵּא

And he shall provide for healing

(21:19)

A woman gave birth prematurely during an international flight. The pilot made an emergency landing in the closest country, where a medical team met the plane and took the mother and her baby to the hospital. The baby was placed in an incubator, and his life was saved. The entire affair cost the airline company 30,000 pounds sterling. Normally the insurance company of the traveler or the airline would pay for such an event, but in this case, the insurance company argued that they would not cover the expense. Who is responsible to cover the cost — the parents or the airline?

The *Rosh*[76] writes that one who was saved from drowning must pay the expenses of the one who saved him. In a case where a person has the means, no one else is obligated to pay to save his life. According to this, it would seem that the baby's parents must foot the bill.

If, however, the baby had not survived, it would seem that the parents would not have to pay, since they did not benefit from the airline's efforts.

In truth, even in such an event there is still reason to obligate the parents, based on the responsa of the *Rosh*.[77]

There was an instance where a man's relatives went to great expense in the effort to save his life, and they were unsuccessful.

---

76. *Sanhedrin* 8:1.
77. 85:2.

They asked the *Rosh* if they were entitled to be repaid from the man's estate, or since the man had not asked them to spend money on his account, it would not be possible to retrieve their expenses.

The *Rosh* responded that there was no reason for them not to be repaid. It is a known custom that when a person falls ill and is unable to care for himself, that his relative intercedes on his behalf. Even if a non-relative had attempted to heal someone dangerously ill, they would be entitled to reclaim their expenses, as they are involved in saving a life. One who does such with zeal is to be praised.

In our case as well, perhaps the baby's parents are obligated to pay, for if they refuse, the airline may not be willing in the future to make emergency landings in order to save lives!

However, since in our case the insurance company usually pays for such events, the airlines would continue to make such landings and it is therefore not similar to the case of the *Rosh*. Thus, the parents would not have to pay. ‏וצ״ע.

Medical Expenses II

וְרַפֹּא יְרַפֵּא

And he shall provide for healing

(21:19)

Chaim went beyond the call of duty in his drinking on Purim. He was found lying on the sidewalk. People tried to wake him up, but they were unsuccessful. They did not know if he was very drunk, or was the victim of alcohol poisoning. They tried pushing him and pricking him with needles, but they could not elicit a response.

Someone decided to call an ambulance, and Chaim

was taken to the hospital. The hospital ran the necessary tests to verify his condition, and Chaim awoke the next day in a hospital gown, lying in a hospital bed. He asked why he had been brought to the hospital, and was told that he had been found by concerned citizens who did him the favor of calling an ambulance. The next thing he knew, Chaim was presented with an exorbitant hospital bill. Being an American tourist, he had no Israeli insurance. He claimed that he had not requested hospitalization, and refused to pay the bill. He insisted that the people who called the ambulance should pay the bill. What is the halachah?

 According to the *Rosh*, [78] since it is a standard procedure that when someone is found unconscious and is in possible danger, that people will call an ambulance to bring him to the hospital, everyone knows that a person would want people to help him if he were ever found in such circumstances. Therefore, Chaim needs to pay.

Dangerous Shame

אִם בַּמַּחְתֶּרֶת יִמָּצֵא הַגַּנָּב

If the thief is discovered while tunneling in

(22:1)

 Don has very firm suspicions that his neighbor has been stealing from him, and would like to confirm his suspicions by searching the neighbor's house. However,

---

78. Responsa 85:2; see previous question.

it is clear to Don that if his neighbor is caught, he will be forced to leave the community due to the shame he will suffer, and as a result he may abandon his *Yiddishkeit*. Should Don put an end to his neighbor's career as a thief, or should he overlook it in order to preserve his neighbor's career as a Jew?[79]

 There are two compelling reasons to catch the thief: to return the property of the victim, and to benefit the thief by preventing him from perpetrating additional crimes.

If being caught will cause the thief to abandon his *Yiddishkeit*, it may not be beneficial to him to be caught. If the victim of the thievery is willing to forgive the neighbor for his property which is in the thief's possession, he is certainly doing a kindness beyond the call of duty. However, he should find a way to inform his neighbor that he is under suspicion and that he should desist immediately from any dishonest activity.

A proof to the above can be found in *Bava Metzia*.[80] Mar Zutra Chassid had a silver goblet stolen from the inn in which he was staying. He saw one of his students wash his hands and dry them on another's cloak. Mar Zutra proclaimed, "This is the one who took the goblet, since we see he has no regard for his friend's property." The student was tied up, and confessed to the crime.[81]

Rashi comments that the goblet had been the property of the hotel owner. What caused *Rashi* to mention this detail? The *Ben Yehoyada* explains that if a student is caught stealing from his *Rebbi*, the shame is so great that one has to be fearful of the consequences. Had the goblet belonged to Mar Zutra, he certainly would not have attempted to catch his student, lest the student leave his faith as a result. However, since the silver cup belonged

---

79. Don is not *obligated* to forfeit his money lest his friend leave the fold. That is his friend's decision, not Don's. The question is: What should Don do?
80. 24a.
81. *Chofetz Chaim, Hil. Lashon Hara* 7:13, explains that Mar Zutra, as head of the *Beis Din*, was allowed to have the student tied up.

to the hotel owner, and all of the students were under suspicion, it was a situation of *chillul Hashem*. Mar Zutra had no choice but to reveal the thief and return the stolen property, since the possibility of *chillul Hashem* was a more serious concern than the possibility of the student's spiritual downfall.

One may infer from this that as long as there is no issue of *chillul Hashem*, he may be allowed to determine if his neighbor is a thief, but it is praiseworthy not to do so. וצ"ע.

False Security

כִּי יִתֵּן אִישׁ אֶל רֵעֵהוּ

If a man shall give his fellow
(22:9)

 Asher was going on a two-week vacation, and was relieved that his friend Naftali agreed to watch Asher's family jewelry. Even though Asher would have to pay to secure Naftali's services, it would give Asher the peace of mind he needed to enjoy his vacation. While Asher was away, Naftali left the jewelry in his home without watching it properly. Nevertheless, Divine Providence ensured that no harm should befall the precious items. When Asher returned, Naftali returned his jewelry. Does Naftali deserve to be paid for his services?

On the one hand, Naftali did not watch the jewelry as he was supposed to. Had Asher known how Naftali would act he never would have hired him. On the other hand, Naftali would have had to pay had the jewelry been stolen. Perhaps the fact that Naftali took responsibility for the jewels is enough to entitle him to be paid.

 The Torah details the laws of a hired watchman, including his liability for theft or loss. Rabbi Akiva Eiger[82] ponders whether he receives payment for watching, and the liability is only a result, or if he receives payment because he accepts the responsibility to pay for theft or loss. The distinction between the two possibilities would make a difference in our case. If payment is for the acceptance of liability, Naftali deserves to be paid because if the jewelry would have been lost or stolen, Naftali would have had to pay for it. If, however, the liability is only a result of payment, but the payment is for actually watching the object, then since Naftali did not watch the object he does not deserve to be paid.[83]

Although one may not be paid for doing even permissible work on Shabbos, the *Shulchan Aruch*[84] rules that if one was hired as a watchman (which does not involve any violations of Shabbos) on a weekly basis, he may be paid for Shabbos as well. The *Mishnah Berurah*[85] explains that he must also watch the items on Shabbos, and if they were ruined on Shabbos the watchman would be liable. The *Mishnah Berurah* concludes that if he did not do his job on Shabbos, even if nothing went wrong, the watchman's pay could be reduced. It is clear that the *Mishnah Berurah* understood that the watchman's payment is in return for his efforts. Thus, Asher does not have to pay Naftali.

---

82. *Derush VeChiddush, Parashas Mishpatim.*
83. Editor's Note: Even though according to this side of the issue Naftali would not be paid, he would still have to sustain the liability since he accepted it along with the opportunity for payment. Although he may forgo his own payment, he cannot relinquish his responsibility. This is true every time an object is stolen or lost. The watchman cannot forgo his payment in order to shirk his responsibility to pay for the theft or loss.
84. *Orach Chaim 306:4.*
85. § 18.

In Absence of X-Ray Vision

כָּל אַלְמָנָה וְיָתוֹם לֹא תְעַנּוּן

You shall not cause pain to any widow or orphan

(22:21)

Mrs. Goldring was an elderly widow who lived alone. Some kind friends invited her to be their guest for the first days of Pesach so she would not have to make the Seder by herself. On Erev Pesach, she packed a suitcase and left her apartment.

Later that day, one of her neighbors was passing by her door and smelled something burning in her apartment. He knew that she was not home, and that something was wrong, but he did not know exactly what. Had Mrs. Goldring left something cooking on the stove? Then it would suffice to shut off her gas from the main valve. But perhaps she had an electrical problem that could start a fire? To be safe, he shut off her gas and her electricity from outside her apartment.

On Chol HaMoed, Mrs. Goldring returned home to find that all of the food that she had prepared for the remainder of the holiday had spoiled in the refrigerator, since the electricity had been shut off. The chicken and the fish, as well as the milk products, were all deposited in the nearest trash receptacle. Does the neighbor have to pay for the spoiled food, since in the end it was discovered that a pot had burned on the stove, and there was nothing wrong with the electricity?

A It would have been proper for the neighbor to consult with other people as to whether he should turn off her electricity. Perhaps there were other ways to prevent the danger and the damage. Maybe someone had Mrs. Goldring's phone number or the phone number of a relative who knew how to locate her and they could have contacted her and she could have said, "Oh, yes, I left a pot on the stove."

Nevertheless, given the lateness of the hour, on the afternoon of Erev Pesach, and the difficulty involved in calling an electrician to offer an opinion, as well as the impossibility of entering the apartment, there is a mitzvah of preserving property (*hashavas aveidah*) and preventing a dangerous situation. In such a case, it would have been proper to gather three people to estimate the possibility of danger, and then they would have done the mitzvah of returning property under the auspices of a *beis din* (i.e., shutting off her electricity).

Even though this was not done, and the neighbor acted on his own accord, he does not have to pay, especially since he only caused the damage to occur on its own,[86] as the chickens did not spoil right away.[87] Mrs. Goldring is also partially responsible for not leaving a contact phone number in case of emergency.

However, if one would go beyond one's obligation and replace the widow's loss, the Father of all orphans, and the Judge of all widows, will certainly return his favor with a just reward.

---

86. See Glossary for an explanation of *gerama*.
87. Since he did not intend to cause damage, he has no obligation to pay even *b'dinei Shamayim* (see Glossary), as noted in *Meiri* at the beginning of *Perek HaKoness*.

Check Changing

אִם כֶּסֶף תַּלְוֶה אֶת עַמִּי

When you lend money to My people
(22:24)

 The banks in Israel will honor a check for six months from the date written on the check. After that, the date must be changed and signed by the owner of the check. A certain creditor had been chasing a debtor for a long time to get him to repay an outstanding loan. Finally the creditor was able to collect a check from the debtor. It was dated a few months earlier. The creditor delayed depositing the check until after the latest date possible to cash it. To get the debtor to change the date would be a laborious task. By merely adding a digit to the check, the banks will honor it. (e.g. making a "2" into a "12"). May the creditor do so?

 Generally, one may not change the date on someone else's check, for two reasons. 1) One may not forge the signature of his friends, as doing so is a violation of "*Mi'dvar sheker tirchak,*"[88] the mitzvah to distance oneself from falsehood. 2) It may be that his friend is aware that the check has expired and therefore has written other checks, relying on the fact that the lapsed check is invalid. By changing the date and cashing the check, he may cause the other checks to bounce.

However, in our case, the check was given to repay a loan. Even though ideally one should approach the debtor to ask him to extend the check, if doing so would be difficult, and the debtor will try to postpone the payment as he has done in the past, then if the

---

88. *Shemos* 23:7.

check can be changed without requiring a signature, the creditor may add a digit to the check. In this instance it is said that "one who takes a loan is subservient to his lender."[89]

━━━━◆◆◆◆━━━━

Being Holy at Someone Else's Expense

טְרֵפָה לֹא תֹאכֵלוּ

You shall not eat flesh
(22:30)

 The **Shulchan Aruch**[90] rules that one is not required to check an animal for any physiological defects that might render it a *tereifah* unless one has reason to believe that an area is unsound. (A *"tereifah"* is an animal that has a bodily defect or wound that halachah views as making it unable to live for a period of twelve months, and which may not be eaten by Jews even if slaughtered in accordance with halachah.) The exception to this rule is the animal's lungs, which must be checked for adhesions. [The *Shulchan Aruch* also rules[91] that if one sold an animal for the purpose of slaughtering, and the animal was found to be a *tereifah*, the transaction is a *mekach ta'us*, and the money must be returned.]

Rabbi Jacobson bought a slaughtered animal and, being an exceedingly scrupulous individual, he checked

---

89. *Mishlei* 22:7.
90. *Yoreh De'ah* 39:1.
91. *Choshen Mishpat* 232:11.

parts of the body that one is not required to check in order to verify that the animal was indeed not a *tereifah*. Lo and behold, he discovered that it actually was a *tereifah*. He tried to return the animal to the butcher who sold it to him, but the butcher claimed that Rabbi Jacobson checked the animal more than was the norm. According to halachah the animal was fit to be eaten.[92] By checking it unnecessarily, he caused the damage to himself! Who is correct?

 The *Darchei Teshuvah*[93] quotes the *Pri To'ar* as saying, that if one wants to be stringent on himself and check for additional *tereifos*, this is not called doing more than is required; rather, he is being extracautious to safeguard the purity of his soul. According to this opinion, the transaction should be null and void, and the butcher would have to return the money.

However, it is possible that Rabbi Jacobson would still have to pay for the animal. The *Tevu'as Shor*[94] comments on the Gemara in *Chullin*,[95] concerning a needle that was found in the cow's stomach. This in itself would not render the animal a *tereifah*, as long as the needle did not pierce the stomach. Rebbi inverted the stomach to check if the needle had pierced it. The *Poskim* discuss if one is required to do so, or if Rebbi did so by accident. The *Tevu'as Shor* refutes the argument that Rebbi did so unintentionally, for why would Rebbi cause the owner of the cow to lose a cow. Once the animal was deemed kosher because the needle had only been found on one side, Rebbi should have been careful not to look at the other side, which could possibly jeopardize the kosher status of the animal.

---

92. The *Panim Me'iros* (cited in *Pischei Teshuvah, Yoreh De'ah* 29 §1) writes that one who ate a chicken that was subsequently found to have had one of the defects that render it a *tereifah*, but which one is not obligated to check, does not require a *kapparah* (atonement).
93. *Yoreh De'ah* 39:1.
94. Ibid. 48:13.
95. 51a.

The *Tevu'as Shor* seems to clearly state that although one may check the animal's other organs if he wants to, he may do so only at his own expense, but not if this causes a loss to others. In our case, Rabbi Jacobson is causing a loss to the butcher by checking beyond what is required.

However, practically speaking, the transaction is still null and void. The *Shulchan Aruch*[96] writes of a man who sold an animal to his friend for slaughter, and upon slaughter the animal was found to be a *tereifah*. If it is clear that the defect existed at the time of the sale, e.g. its stomach was punctured, the sale is void, and the money must be returned.

A puncture in the stomach is an example of something that does not require checking, yet it is clear that if one did check, and found it to be problematic, it invalidates the sale. It is highly unlikely that the *Shulchan Aruch* is only discussing a case where it was checked accidentally.

Majority Rules

אַחֲרֵי רַבִּים לְהַטֹּת
Yield to the majority
(23:2)

 At a tenants' meeting at Choshen Mishpat Street 61, the majority of the neighbors approved the resolution that the building's elevator not be used for construction purposes. The elevator's use is to be restricted to carrying people, and not building supplies, in order to prevent damage to the elevator. One of the tenants wants to

---

96. *Choshen Mishpat* loc. cit.

use the elevator while he does construction, and claims that he is not bound by his neighbors' decision. Since he is a partner in the elevator, as he also paid for its installation, he maintains that they cannot curtail the use of his property. Is he correct?

 The *Rema*[97] writes, "For any communal need that is the subject of disagreement, all homeowners who pay taxes should be gathered. They should accept upon themselves to offer their opinion *l'sheim Shamayim* (for the sake of Heaven), and the majority opinion is to be followed … One who refuses to offer his opinion has declined his right to do so, and the majority opinion is still binding."

If the neighbor had not been invited to the meeting, the *Pischei Teshuvah*[98] says that the majority cannot force the minority to be bound by their decision. The *Rashba*[99] goes further and states that the opinion of the majority is only valid if they came to a conclusion after everyone had a chance to deliberate and discuss the issue.

The *Chasam Sofer*[100] was asked about a city that numbered 100 families. A meeting was called to decide a tax issue, and only 30 men attended. The *Chasam Sofer* writes that the 30 men present can decide for all 100 families. Since everyone knew about the meeting, anyone who did not come has empowered those who did, to decide for him. In any event, that is certainly the custom, since without such understanding, nothing could ever be decided or accomplished.

Therefore, in our case, the majority of the tenants can force their neighbor not to use the elevator to carry building materials, especially since such use clearly damages the communal property, and such is the accepted custom in most places.

---

97. *Choshen Mishpat* 163:1.
98. 163 § 1.
99. Responsa Vol. III, 104.
100. *Choshen Mishpat* 116.

Israeli Healthcare

הָשֵׁב תְּשִׁיבֶנּוּ לוֹ

You shall return it to him repeatedly
(23:4)

 Dr. Raphael Mintz did his medical residency in Sha'arei Marpeh Hospital, and continued to consult with the staff there, even after he opened his own practice. Today he is an orthopedic consultant for a medical group, and he refers many patients to Sha'arei Marpeh. However, for operations on hands and knees he refers his patients to a different hospital where they have excellent surgeons skilled in those particular procedures. Sha'arei Marpeh also has a good staff, with a good track record; however, the other hospital has a better one.

One day the doctors in Sha'arei Marpeh discovered that Dr. Mintz was sending patients to their competing hospital, and decided to stop providing him with information for his medical research. Dr. Mintz is troubled: Should he stop referring patients to the other hospital in order to continue benefiting from support from Sha'arei Marpeh?

 It would be wrong for Dr. Mintz to compromise the care provided for his patients out of gratitude to the hospital where he learned. However, Dr. Mintz does not have to compromise his career for the sake of his patients since his own loss takes precedence to that of his patients. The obligation to heal people is learned from the mitzvah to return lost property,[101] and a person's own property has priority over anyone else's property.[102] This is especially true, since, in our case, the advice Dr. Mintz receives from Sha'arei Marpeh is to the advantage of his patients.

Although the patient may claim that he pays money to receive the best medical care, the standard national insurance does not promise to give the best care, only appropriate care, nor would the pursuit of "better" care be halachically required.

If there would be a life-threatening situation, the doctor would have to refer the patient to the appropriate hospital to save his life, regardless of the negative ramifications to himself.

<hr />

The Whole Truth

מִדְּבַר שֶׁקֶר תִּרְחָק
Distance yourself from a false word
(23:7)

 At the *levayah* of Reb Yisrael Yaakov Flam, a *Rosh Yeshivah* told the following story. The *Rosh Yeshivah* had come to Rabbi Flam and informed him that his yeshivah did not have a *Sefer Torah*; perhaps he would like to contribute toward writing one. Rabbi Flam countered with the following proposal: "If the *Rosh Yeshivah* can find someone to donate half the cost of a *Sefer Torah*, I will gladly donate the other half!" The *Rosh Yeshivah* indeed found someone who was willing to contribute

---

101. *Sanhedrin 73a.*
102. *Bava Metzia 33a.*

half, but on condition that only his name would appear on it, so it would seem that he had donated the entire cost of the *Sefer Torah*! When the *Rosh Yeshivah* told this to Rabbi Flam, the latter was thrilled. "This is what I intended," he said, "to pay for half the *Sefer*, and my name should not appear on it!"

Let us consider, is it proper that a Torah scroll, that contains the commandment to distance oneself from dishonesty, should itself be a misrepresentation of the truth, by giving the impression that it was written with funds of a single donor, when really it was commisioned by two partners?

 It would seem that if one partner agreed to remain anonymous, there is no deceit. The Gemara[103] teaches that one who started a mitzvah that was subsequently completed by someone else is considered by the Torah as if the entire act was done by the one who brought it to completion. Therefore, since the initiator did not complete his act by donating the entire sum needed, there is no compromise of the truth to attribute the writing of the *Sefer* to the one who facilitated the completion of the project.

---

103. *Sotah* 13b.

פרשת תרומה
Parashas Terumah

A Modern-day Holdup

וְיִקְחוּ לִי תְּרוּמָה
And let them take for Me a portion
(25:2)

 A fund-raiser solicited a donation from a wealthy philanthropist, and received a check for $1,000 to benefit his organization, which promoted Torah study. The collector refused such a " paltry" sum, and was offered a check for $3,000, which was also rejected. The wealthy man realized he could not get rid of the high-handed collector, and asked him to name his price. The solicitor asked for no less than $100,000. The wealthy man wrote a check for $100,000 and sent the collector on his way. The next day when he tried to cash the check, the bank teller told him that the funds in the account were insufficient. Somehow, the collector found out how much money was missing, deposited the difference, and was able to cash the check!

When the wealthy man found out, he began to yell that he never intended to give so much money and had only written the check because he knew the bank would never honor it, since there were insufficient funds. His intention was to fool the collector, but the collector had the last laugh. Does the wealthy man have a chance to recover his money?

 It would seem that since the check was written and signed properly, even though the check was supposed to bounce, it is still a legal document with which the collector could go to court and collect its value. In addition, the wealthy man might have to give the collector the difference that he needed to deposit in order to draw the value of the check!

However, in our case the collector should probably have to return the money. The Gemara in *Bava Basra*[104] states that a gift given under duress is void. The *S'ma*[105] explains that not only physical duress, but even emotional duress will invalidate the gift. This is stated explicitly in the *Shulchan Aruch HaRav,*[106] that a gift must be given wholeheartedly.

In our case the collector knew that the check was given only in order to end the uncomfortable meeting, and any money that changed hands is robbery on the collector's part (with the exception of $1,000 that was originally offered). וצ״ע.

---

104. 40b.
105. *Choshen Mishpat* 242 §A.
106. Monetary Damages 18.

Unnecessary Money

מֵאֵת כָּל אִישׁ אֲשֶׁר יִדְּבֶנּוּ לִבּוֹ

From every man whose heart motivates him

(25:2)

Q A *shadchan* proposed a match between a young man and a young lady. When the boy's father asked what the other side was willing to contribute, the *shadchan* informed him that they had offered $70,000. The children met and they agreed to marry. When the parents met, the boy's father mentioned the commitment for $70,000. The girl's father was shocked. He claimed that he had agreed to give only $40,000. The *shadchan* had made a mistake. The boy's father said that if that was the case, the *shidduch* was not meant to be, and returned home.

A concerned Jew heard the story, and decided that for such a sum, the *shidduch* should not be stopped, and agreed to give $30,000 of his own, toward the dowry.

In the interim, the boy's father visited his *Rebbe* and told him the whole story. His *Rebbe* rebuked him, and told him that one does not stop a *shidduch* over $30,000. The father was shaken by the *Rebbe's* words, and returned to the *shadchan* to finalize the *shidduch*.

Does the generous individual who agreed to contribute $30,000 for the sake of the couple have to honor his pledge? He had agreed to give the money only if the *shidduch* was contingent on it. Now that things worked out without his involvement, is he freed of his obligation?

A This is probably similar to the ruling in *Shulchan Aruch*[107] that states that if money was collected to redeem a captive, and the captive died before he could be redeemed, some say the money belongs to the heirs, and some say that it does not. In our times, the *Shulchan Aruch* concludes, the second opinion is to be followed, as it was not with that intention that the money was donated. The *Rema* adds that the same is true about money that was collected to marry off an orphan and the orphan died.

It would seem that our case is similar, as the donor's sole intention was to ensure that the *shidduch* be concluded. In light of the new circumstances, his donation is no longer required.

In truth, there is a difference. In the case of the *Shulchan Aruch*, the money is completely superfluous, as the beneficiary of the collection is no longer alive. In our case, the beneficiaries of the donation could use the money very well, even though their marriage is not dependent on it. It could be that the man's pledge is still in force, and therefore he should be "*matir* his *neder*."[108]

The *Imrei Yosher*[109] records the incident of a group of men who commissioned the writing of a *Sefer Torah*. When it was finished, they made an accounting, and found that they had 80 ruble left from their expenses. One of the men pledged another 70 ruble in order to buy silver ornaments for the *Sefer Torah*, which cost 150 ruble. Later, they discovered that they actually had 120 ruble left, and the man who made the pledge wanted to reduce his contribution to 30 ruble. The *Imrei Yosher* ruled that the man may do so, as his vow was based on an error. In the case of the *Imrei Yosher* as well, the extra money was not necessary, which is not so in our case.

---

107. *Yoreh De'ah* 253:6.
108. Committing money to charity constitutes a *neder*.
109. Vol II, 148.

Undue Dues

וְיִקְחוּ לִי תְּרוּמָה

And let them take for Me a portion

(25:2)

 The members in charge of the shul's *Ma'os Chitim*[110] campaign pressured Levi to give a very generous donation, which was much more than he was obligated or wanted to donate. When they refused to take "no" for an answer, and Levi understood that he could not get away, he decided to give them what they sought. He wrote a check for the amount they wanted, that could only be deposited into the shul's account. Instead of signing his name, he made a scribble, and sent them on their way. The result was that the check was refused. Did Levi do the right thing?

 If the fund-raisers acted improperly, and demanded money that they were not entitled to, one may certainly treat them in kind. The Gemara in *Bava Basra*[111] learns that the *pasuk* that Hashem will call to accounting all those who oppressed others, refers even to those who collect *tzedakah*. One is certainly allowed to free himself from their pressure.

---

110. *Tzedakah* for Pesach needs.
111. 8b.

The Dye Is Cast

וּתְכֵלֶת וְאַרְגָּמָן וְתוֹלַעַת שָׁנִי

And turquoise, purple, and scarlet wool

(25:4)

 A philanthropist suspected that one of his attendants was taking money from his pockets, so he went to the Chazon Ish to ask for advice. The Chazon Ish suggested that the man smear his pockets with ink, so that if anyone will try to remove something from the colored pockets, it will be discovered very quickly.

Could one do this on Erev Shabbos when it is likely that he will cause the thief to dye his hands on Shabbos?

 It should be permissible. The *Mishnah Berurah*[112] rules that a man who is not accustomed to coloring himself (as opposed to women who wear makeup) would be allowed to put a dye on his skin on Shabbos, as we find that one may eat berries on Shabbos even though they stain the skin.

In addition, it is not the custom of people to dye skin with ink, and the *Mishnah Berurah*[113] explains the reason that eating berries is permissible is because it is not the way that people dye (human) skin.

In our case, where the thief has no inkling that he is inking himself, it should certainly be permissible.

We could also add that the *Radvaz*[114] permits eating berries because the stains are considered dirtying one's self, not dyeing.

On the other hand, the cases are not really identical. One who eats berries has no intention at all to color himself. In our case,

---

112. 303:79.
113. 320: 58.
114. Cited in *Mishnah Berurah*.

the one who smeared his pocket with ink is interested in dyeing the thief's hand. Therefore we must consider what the halachah is when the one committing the act has no intention to do so, but the one for whom the act is being done does have intent.

The *Pri Megadim*[115] considers such a question, if one may brush dirt off his friend's coat on Shabbos,[116] when to the one brushing, the dirt is insignificant, even though the owner of the coat, who is more finicky, does consider the dirt to be significant. Do we look at the one who is doing the act, or the one for whom the act is being done? Our case has even more reason to be lenient since the one committing the act (the thief) is dyeing his own hands, without any intent, and the owner of the pocket is not doing any action to apply the dye on Shabbos.

Another reason it should be permissible is based on the *Chasam Sofer's* comments on *Kesubos.*[117] He explains that dyeing, which is forbidden on Shabbos, is forbidden only when the coloring is for the sake of that which is being colored. However, when one dyes a napkin as a result of wiping one's mouth, without being interested in the napkin being colored, it is considered dirtying, and not dyeing. So, too, in our case, no one is interested in the thief's hands being colored. The intention is only to catch a thief.

---

115. *Orach Chaim* 302.
116. The *Rema* rules that one should be careful not to brush dirt that he finds annoying from his clothing on Shabbos, in order not to "launder" his clothing, which is forbidden on Shabbos.
117. 5b.

Priorities

וְעָשׂוּ לִי מִקְדָּשׁ

They shall make a Sanctuary for Me

(25:8)

A man passed away, leaving a son who held a prominent position in a large corporation. The son was not yet religious, and although he had never previously attended services, he came to shul to say *Kaddish* for his father. People respected his loyalty to his father, and the fact that he was willing to say *Kaddish* in spite of his lack of affiliation. The son would come at the end of *davening* to say the *Kaddish*, without having *davened*, and without putting on *tefillin*.

A *talmid chacham* who witnessed this scene day after day approached the son, and told him that certainly his coming to shul was a source of merit and joy for his father's soul, but that it was the son's obligation to don *tefillin* and say *Shema* as well.

The son responded that he was very busy, and did not have the time to do both. Either he could put on *tefillin* and say *Shema* at home, or he could come to shul to say *Kaddish*, but without *Shema* and *tefillin*.

What should he advise the son to do: to come to shul and say *Kaddish* or to do the mitzvos at home? Perhaps coming to shul might cause the son to do *teshuvah*. Which has priority?

This question was posed to Rav Elyashiv, who answered that it is obvious that saying *Shema* and laying *tefillin* are preferable to saying *Kaddish*. Although his *Kaddish*

is a sanctification of Hashem's Name, we do not have the authority to make calculations about whether is more beneficial to forgo obligatory mitzvos like *Shema* and *tefillin; Kaddish* in contrast is not a Torah commandment.

However, if it is *likely* that shul attendance will cause a spirit of purity to enter him, then it would have to be weighed if perhaps that would be preferable.

פרשת תצוה
Parashas Tetzaveh

Defective Merchandise I

וְנָתַתָּ אֶל חֹשֶׁן הַמִּשְׁפָּט
Into the Breastplate of Judgment shall you place
(28:30)

Ari purchased a new velvet sleeper couch in honor of his father's visit. Five minutes after the delivery men drove off, he discovered a hole in the upholstery and decided that it must be returned to the store. By this time, it was already night and the store had already closed. Since he had given his old couch away, he had "no choice" but to let his father sleep on the new couch that was to be returned the next day. Can Ari still return the couch even after his father used it?

The *Shulchan Aruch*[118] rules that one who purchased an item and found it to be defective may return the item even several years later, provided that he did not use

---

118. *Choshen Mishpat* 332:2.

the item subsequent to his discovery of the defect. However, if he indeed used it, he has conceded his right to return the item.

By using the couch, Ari lost his right to return it. Perhaps an argument could be made in Ari's favor that he had no intention to concede his right to return the item; he used the couch under duress since he had nowhere else for his father to sleep. The *Pischei Teshuvah*[119] mentions a case where a man bought a horse and traveled halfway to his city before noticing a defect in the horse. He rules that the man may continue his journey with the horse and still retain the right to return it, since he is only continuing to use the horse as he has no other choice. Otherwise, the man himself would have to haul his wagon containing all of his belongings back to the city!

However, there is a difference between these cases. It is not imperative for Ari to let his father sleep on the couch. His father could have used Ari's bed, and Ari could have slept on the floor. The case of the defective horse is not completely similar, since the man could not carry the horse and wagon back to the city, and truly had no alternative. Ari may therefore no longer return the couch to the store.

———◆◆◆———

Defective Merchandise II

וְנָתַתָּ אֶל חֹשֶׁן הַמִּשְׁפָּט

Into the Breastplate of Judgment shall you place
(28:30)

 Mrs. Levy was pleased to use her new *Machzor* for Yom Kippur during her first year of marriage. In the middle of *davening* she was distressed to find several blank

119. Ad loc. §1.

pages in the middle of the *Machzor*. She continued to use the *Machzor* for the remainder of the day. May she exchange it even though she continued to use it?

 The same question could be asked *"lehavdil"*: One who found a defect in a pair of shoes, may he continue to wear the shoes until he arrives at the store to return them?

It would seem that one may indeed return them, and one has not compromised his position by continuing to wear them, since one is not expected to walk barefoot to the shoestore! This is similar to the case of the horse that was found defective while on the road. (See previous question, Defective Merchandise I.)

In the case of the *Machzor* there is even more of a reason to allow its return. First, Mrs. Levy does not have another *Machzor* to use. Even though she might have been able to share with the woman next to her, she still *davens* best using her own. Secondly, an argument could be presented that a *Machzor* that is missing 20 pages is not just a defective *Machzor*, but an incomplete *Machzor*. This differentiation is significant: Whereas one could overlook a defect in an item, in order to use it, even the buyer's use of an incomplete item would not excuse the supplier from supplying the rest of the item. Mrs. Levy is still entitled to the additional pages needed to complete her *Machzor*.

In addition, since the storeowner will return the *Machzor* to the publisher, and the expense of rebinding the *Machzor* is generally not cost efficient, it can be assumed that the *Machzor* is destined for *genizah* — unlike the couch in the previous question, which will likely be repaired and resold. Since no one will lose if Mrs. Levy uses the *Machzor*, she may do so, and return it after Yom Tov.

Peace Plan

וְהָיוּ עַל לֵב אַהֲרֹן

And they shall be on Aaron's heart
(28:30)

To say that Moishie and Kivi did not get along with each other would be an understatement. It greatly pained their friend Velvel that there was so much animosity between them. Velvel decided to follow in the footsteps of Aharon HaKohen, and bring peace to the long-time rivals. Velvel bought an expensive *Mishloach Manos* and had it delivered to Moishie's house. He included a card that indicated that the sender had been none other than Kivi. Moishie was shocked, yet touched that Kivi had decided to "bury the hatchet." Moishie assembled his own fancy *Mishloach Manos* and sent it off to Kivi. That afternoon Moishie and Kivi met and made peace between themselves. Velvel wants to know if he fulfilled the mitzvah of *Mishloach Manos* when he sent the *Mishloach Manos* to Moishie, as the *K'sav Sofer*[120] writes that one cannot fulfill the mitzvah by sending *Mishloach Manos* anonymously.

It is likely that Velvel did do the mitzvah. The reason why the *K'sav Sofer* says that one must identify the sender of the *Mishloach Manos* is because the *Manos HaLevi* writes[121] that the reason for the mitzvah is to promote friendship and brotherhood, and one does not accomplish this goal when it is not known who sent the *Mishloach Manos*. In our case, Velvel

---

120. Responsa 141.
121. *Megillas Esther* 9:19.

certainly promoted friendship and brotherhood between his two friends.

On the other hand, it is just as likely that Velvel, although he accomplished the mitzvah of bringing peace between man and his fellow man, has not done the mitzvah of *Mishloach Manos*, since *Mishloach Manos* is meant to increase the peace between the sender and his friend, and not just in the world. ‏וצ״ע‎.

פרשת כי תשא
Parashas Ki Sisa

Rare Photos

וּשְׁמַרְתֶּם אֶת הַשַּׁבָּת
You shall observe the Sabbath
(31:14)

A certain Jewish hospital has 24-hour surveillance from security cameras to deter mistreatment of the patients by the staff. They operate seven days a week since it is a matter of *pikuach nefesh.*

In the hospital's shul, one of the patients celebrated his Bar Mitzvah. Could he ask the hospital for a video of the event as a souvenir, since the cameras were working anyway to prevent a life-threatening situation?

It is a *chillul Hashem* to view pictures that were taken on Shabbos, and one may therefore not copy film that was used to take pictures on Shabbos. If they had in mind before the event to use these pictures, the *chillul Hashem* would be even greater.

Minimizing the Damage

וּשְׁמַרְתֶּם אֶת הַשַּׁבָּת

You shall observe the Sabbath

(31:14)

 Boruch Zev would like to visit his neighbor, Mr. Brown, to attempt to bring him and his family closer to their Jewish heritage. Mr. Brown is only available to accept visitors on Shabbos night. Boruch Zev knows that if he will knock on Mr. Brown's door, Mr. Brown will turn on his outside light to see who is knocking. When he sees Boruch Zev, he will turn off the computer in his living room in honor of his guest, and turn it on again when Boruch Zev leaves. May Boruch Zev visit Mr. Brown under such circumstances, since there is a possibility that by visiting him he may influence Mr. Brown into becoming a *baal teshuvah*?

 The *Shulchan Aruch* rules[122] that one who was informed that his daughter was taken out of his house on Shabbos, with the goal of uprooting her faith from her, has a mitzvah to set out immediately in an attempt to rescue her. The *Mishnah Berurah* adds that this is so even if it involves engaging in *melachah*, because if G-d forbid his daughter will leave her religion, she will desecrate the Shabbos and worship false gods her entire life. If he will desecrate one Shabbos to prevent this tragedy, it will be a minuscule transgression in comparison.

---

122. *Orach Chaim* 306:14.

According to this, even if the person they are trying to save will do an *aveirah* in the rescue process, it should be permissible even if it is the rescuer's fault, since they may be saving the rest of that person's life. Imagine if Noach would see Berel amputating his hand, and Noach could convince Berel to cut off just one finger. Would we forbid Noach from intervening because he is giving bad advice? Certainly it is better to cut off just one finger rather than the whole hand. Similarly, it is far better that Mr. Brown desecrate the Shabbos a few times, if doing so may save him thousands upon thousands of transgressions.

When Rav Zilberstein presented this approach to Rav Elyashiv, Rav Elyashiv rejected it. He clearly stated that an *aveirah* cannot produce a mitzvah. If it is definite that the visit will cause someone to shut off an electrical appliance or turn on a light, even though he will desecrate the Shabbos many other times for his own reasons, it is still not permissible for one to visit this person and cause new *chillul* Shabbos on the visitor's account. Similarly, one may not invite a guest for a Shabbos *seudah*, or even the Pesach Seder, if he knows that it will involve his guest driving on Shabbos.

It is not comparable to the case of Berel, who has already decided to cut off his hand, and Noach is only minimizing the damage. In our case Boruch Zev is causing additional sinning in the interim. It is also not similar to the story of Rabbi Yisrael Salanter who taught businessmen who were not Shabbos observant, to write with their left hands instead of their right hands on Shabbos, so that any writing they did on Shabbos would not be a Biblical transgression of Shabbos.[123] These businessmen were going to write in any event, and his advice was strictly to minimize their transgressions. The example of the man following his daughter is also not applicable, since in that case the father is fulfilling his obligation. That is not the case of Mr. Brown, who is doing *melachah* without justifiable cause.

---

123. See *Shabbos* 103a.

It's for the Kids

וְשָׁמְרוּ בְּנֵי יִשְׂרָאֵל

The Children of Israel shall observe

(31:16)

 In Congregation *Eitz Chaim* there are some people who are not very well versed in the area of halachah. Mr. Shulman is making an *aufruf* for his son, and was bothered by the following question.

Should one refrain from upholding the custom of throwing candies at a *chassan* who is called to the Torah at his *aufruf* in order to prevent those who do not know any better from eating before *Kiddush*? (The *Shulchan Aruch* rules that one may not eat before the daytime *Kiddush*, just as much as one may not eat before *Kiddush* at night.)[124] By throwing candies, one is providing food in shul that may be eaten before *Kiddush*. Maybe doing so is a violation of *lifnei iver*?

 There is no obligation to refrain from throwing candies (which is done as a good omen for the marriage) because of unlearned people. It makes sense that there is no *lifnei iver*, as explained by the *Maharil Diskin*,[125] for one does not have to suffer a financial loss in order that another person not violate a prohibition. Similarly, one does not have to forgo a good omen because of another's ignorance.

---

124. *Orach Chaim* 289:1.
125. *Kuntrus Acharon* 145.

In addition, the *Ra'avad*[126] is of the opinion that one may eat before the daytime *Kiddush*, and one may rely on this opinion under difficult circumstances.[127]

In this instance, however, it may be that withholding the temptation for people to eat before *Kiddush* would be a better omen for the *chassan* than throwing candies.

Phone Home

וְשָׁמְרוּ בְנֵי יִשְׂרָאֵל אֶת הַשַּׁבָּת

The Children of Israel shall observe the Sabbath

(31:16)

Mr. Schmidt met a not-yet-religious teenage boy in shul on Friday night. The boy was interested in experiencing a Shabbos *seudah* and Mr. Schmidt was happy to invite him. Mr. Schmidt asked him to please sleep over so he should not have to drive home on Shabbos. The boy agreed, but he said that he would have to phone his mother so she would not be worried about his not coming home.

Should Mr. Schmidt invite him for the whole Shabbos, thereby preventing the boy from further desecration of Shabbos, even though by doing so he is making the boy call home, which he would not have otherwise done?

It would seem that Mr. Schmidt may invite him to save him from multiple transgressions of Shabbos. Even though Mr. Schmidt is causing him to call home, the

---

126. *Hilchos Shabbos,* Chapter 29.
127. See *Magen Avraham* 289 §4, brought in the *Mishnah Berurah* §10, *Sha'ar HaTziyun* § 6.

phone call could be made in an unusual manner, rendering it a Rabbinic transgression, as opposed to a Biblical one. Even though he is causing the mother to transgress as well, by answering the phone, if the mother does not receive a phone call, she will call the police and others in search of her son, so this is actually not an additional transgression.

━━━━━━━◆━━━━━━━

It's a Living

וְשָׁמְרוּ בְנֵי יִשְׂרָאֵל אֶת הַשַּׁבָּת

The Children of Israel shall observe the Sabbath

(31:16)

 An ambulance driver in Israel was under financial strain. He knows that if he offers to drive the ambulance on Shabbos he will be paid extra. Is he allowed to take Shabbos duty, which is permissible for *pikuach nefesh*, simply for the sake of making extra money, or is that a desecration of Shabbos?

 There is no desecration of Shabbos in driving an ambulance in the course of duty, since it is necessary to save lives. As such, he is allowed to be paid, as it is stated in *Mishnah Berurah*[128] that a midwife may take money for services provided on Shabbos. *Mahari Bruna* explains that the reason for this is because her work is necessary to save lives, and if she would not be paid, she might not come. The *Minchas* Shabbos[129] qualifies that if she would not be paid, she may be lax in coming, which is also something that must be avoided.

---

128. 306:24.
129. 90 § 19.

The issue in our case is that the driver's sole intent to drive specifically on Shabbos is for the money involved. The *Sha'ar HaTziyun*[130] brings a difference of opinion in a case where one is allowed to break a door in order to free a child, if he is allowed to have intent to use the pieces of wood afterward. Some say that even though he intends to use the boards that he produced by breaking the door apart, it is still a praiseworthy deed. Others say he may not intend to use the boards.

Our case is different. Breaking a door is not a Torah desecration of Shabbos unless one intended to use the boards. The intent transforms breaking the door to a positive act, and thereby it becomes a Torah violation of Shabbos. Therefore, according to some opinions that intent would be prohibited. Driving an ambulance, though, is in essence a violation of Shabbos, and yet it is permitted in order to save lives. Intending to drive on Shabbos in order to earn money does not make the violation any worse. He is allowed to be paid to ensure that he will work efficiently. Therefore he would be permitted to drive on Shabbos to save lives, even though his motivation is a financial one.[131]

---

130. 328:17.

131. A *talmid chacham* questioned me regarding the difference between the ambulance driver, who is allowed to drive on Shabbos, and the Bar Mitzvah boy who celebrated his Bar Mitzvah in the hospital's shul and was not permitted to have the pictures, which were taken on Shabbos, (as was discussed earlier in this Parashah). In both cases Shabbos is being "violated" for the sake of saving lives, yet the driver may benefit from his Shabbos violation and the boy may not. Why is this so?

I suggested that perhaps the driver is being paid for his performance of the mitzvah of saving lives. It is necessary to pay him so that he will fulfill his duty to the best of his ability. In the case of the Bar Mitzvah boy, however, while the surveillance cameras in the hospital must operate in order to protect the lives of the patients, the photos of the Bar Mitzvah are in no way connected to saving lives. Those images are only coincidental to the protection of others, and thus there is no leniency to allow benefiting from them.

Rav Zilberstein agreed that my answer is indeed correct.

פרשת ויקהל
Parashas Vayakheil

A Diagnosis in Honor of Shabbos

שֵׁשֶׁת יָמִים תֵּעָשֶׂה מְלָאכָה

On six days, work may be done

(35:2)

 Mr. Green visited Dr. Pollack on Friday afternoon and requested a note with a diagnosis of a migraine headache. Even though the diagnosis would not be truthful, Mr. Green needed the note because his employer insisted that Mr. Green work on Shabbos, and the only way he could keep his job would be if he brought such a note from his doctor. May Dr. Pollack write the note for Mr. Green?

 A worker who takes a day off under the pretense of sickness is guilty of stealing if he will be paid for a sick day. Any doctor who would write a false diagnosis under such circumstances would be an accessory to the crime.

In this scenario, Mr. Green needs a note because of Shabbos. Since his boss is a Jew, albeit a non-observant one, Shabbos is a day on which he cannot compel Mr. Green to work, and any demand that he do so is not halachically binding. One would therefore think that it would be permissible for Dr. Pollack to write such a note, and excuse Mr. Green from working on Shabbos.

However, when this question was posed to Rav Elyashiv, he maintained that the doctor should not write such a note: "We do not do mitzvos through deceit!" In the end, the doctor will be caught, and it will cause a desecration of Hashem's Name. Rather, Mr. Green should approach his superiors and tell them clearly that he can only continue to work for them if they do not require him to work on Shabbos. Even if this will cause them to terminate his employment; Hashem will certainly reward him fully for his determination.

Fare Is Fair

שֵׁשֶׁת יָמִים תֵּעָשֶׂה מְלָאכָה
On six days, work may be done
(35:2)

 One Erev Shabbos, the last bus from Yerushalayim to Bnei Brak was severely delayed in leaving the Yerushalayim Central Bus Station. The passengers calculated the time of the trip and understood that they would nevertheless have more than enough time to reach their destinations. They did not realize that the bus driver was a Yerushalayim resident, and also needed to get home for Shabbos.

At the entrance to Bnei Brak, the driver stopped the bus, and asked all the passengers to alight. He informed them that he was also a *shomer* Shabbos, and if he would finish his route along the streets of Bnei Brak, he would be forced to desecrate the Shabbos on his return to Yerushalayim. Since they could all walk home from the bus stop, he felt that his request was reasonable. He added that he had not wanted to drive the bus out of Yerushalayim, but had been forced to do so by his superiors. Therefore, he begged all of the passengers to understand his position, and allow him to keep the Shabbos.

The passengers understood, and left the bus. Those who had closer destinations made their way by foot, and those with further destinations continued by taxi.

Could the passengers ask the driver to pay for their taxis from the entrance of Bnei Brak?

 The passengers cannot request compensation from the driver, because they are obligated through *"Arvus"*[132] to allow the driver to return to Yerushalayim. (The driver's spending Shabbos in Bnei Brak when his family is in Yerushalayim is not a practical option.)

The driver did not earn a profit by making the trip, as he is paid a monthly wage, and therefore they cannot ask him to reimburse them for having to shorten their trip. They should have known when they got on the bus that they might not be able to travel through Bnei Brak . They cannot even ask the bus company to compensate them, because they placed themselves, albeit unknowingly, into the situation.

This is a lesson for anyone traveling before Shabbos, to leave early enough for the driver to return home for Shabbos, or to use a non-Jewish driver.

------ ◆ ------

---

132. See Glossary.

A Living Torah

לֹא תְבַעֲרוּ אֵשׁ בְּכֹל מֹשְׁבֹתֵיכֶם

You shall not kindle fire in any of your dwellings

(35:3)

 The *Shulchan Aruch*[133] rules, "In our time, one must save any Torah literature from a fire (on Shabbos, and without extinguishing the fire).

The *Mishnah Berurah*[134] comments that *Torah Shebichsav* has precedence to *Torah Shebe'al Peh*.

Rabbi Gross has dedicated his life to elucidating the writings of the Vilna Gaon. He was close to publishing his work, when one Shabbos the candle fell onto the table, and set the dining room on fire. The fire spread quickly, and the *Rav* was torn whether to save his writings from his study, that he had worked on for years, or the *Megillas Esther* that was in his living room. He could only save one of them. Do his writings take precedence over *Torah Shebichsav*, since they are irreplaceable?

 The *Aderes*[135] ruled in such a case that it may be a case of *safek pikuach nefesh*. Since the author toiled with such effort to produce the manuscripts, he could fall sick from the depression ensuing, knowing that his work was consumed. This happened to Rav Charlap, the Chief Rabbi in Bialystok, when his writings were obliterated. He died shortly afterward from a broken heart. If, however, the manuscripts belonged to others to whom there would be no danger to their lives, there would still be room for doubt.

---

133. See details in *Orach Chaim 334*.
134. Ad loc.
135. *Kuntrus Oveir Orach*.

פרשת פקודי
Parashas Pekudei

It Pays to Be Nice

אֵלֶּה פְקוּדֵי הַמִּשְׁכָּן

These are the reckonings of the Tabernacle

(38:21)

 Little Boruch was given a gift of 100 shekels to buy a toy. His mother saw a sturdy truck which she thought her son would enjoy. The sticker on the package read "80 shekels." She purchased it, and the boy ripped open the packaging and began playing with it.

The mother told her neighbor about the toy she bought for 80 shekels, and her friend decided to buy one for her son. When she got to the store she saw the same toy being sold for 300 shekels. She questioned the saleslady, "My friend bought this here yesterday for 80 shekels, and now it's 300 shekel!?" The saleslady replied, "There must have been a mistake." The neighbor reported the error to Boruch's mother. The mother returned to the store immediately, and the saleslady asked her to add 220 shekels to pay for the toy. The mother exclaimed, "I do not have that kind of money to spend on a toy. I can only pay 100 shekels. I will return the toy instead, and I'll take back my money!"

The saleslady answered, "I cannot take the toy back, since the packaging has been torn. The store manager will accuse me falsely of being negligent by sticking the wrong price on the toy, and I will lose my job for no good reason. Take the toy home and do not say anything!"

Boruch's mother believes the saleslady, but now she wants to know, how can she keep a 300-shekel toy, when she only paid 80 shekels?

 There is basis to be lenient to allow Boruch's mother to keep the toy for the amount she paid, since she paid the price marked on the toy, and she was not interested in buying a more expensive toy. She does not have the option of returning the toy, since this will cause an injustice to the saleslady. Therefore the debt to the storeowner is null and void.

The Gemara states,[136] "One who is traveling with money and sees a robber approaching may not use that money to redeem 'ma'aser sheni'[137] fruits that are in his house. *Rashi* explains that since his money is about to be lost, it is as if he does not own it anymore.

In our case, since the toy cannot be returned, the storeowner's rights to the toy are forfeited.[138]

However, what Boruch's mother should do is to add the 20 shekels she was willing to pay, and save up until she has another 200 shekels to make up the difference in order to do the mitzvah of *hashavas aveidah*. If she uses her *ma'aser* money for mitzvos, it

---

136. *Bava Kamma* 115b.

137. During the first, second, fourth, and fifth years of the *shemittah* cycle, one must separate one-tenth of his produce grown in Israel. During the time of the *Beis HaMikdash,* the fruits were eaten in Yerushalayim or the sanctity was transferred from the fruits to coins to be taken to Yerushalayim and spent on food.

138. It is possible that the one who affixed the wrong price would be responsible under "*grama.*"

would seem that she could take this money from *ma'aser* since by law she does not have to pay at all since she did not want such an expensive toy,[139] and she is doing "*hashavas aveidah*" to the storeowner, who will otherwise lose income from the sale of the toy. וצ"ע.

Whose Mitzvah Is It?

אֵלֶּה פְקוּדֵי

These are the reckonings

(38:21)

Rafi delivered the *Daf Yomi shiur* in his shul for many years. The shul members held him in high esteem. One day, he decided to open a *gemach* named after his father. He asked the shul's members to donate to the fund, and they responded generously. Rafi served as the sole treasurer, and each year he would publicize a report of the *gemach's* activity. As time went on, Rafi decided to have two people join him in running the *gemach*.

Ten years later, Rafi expressed his wish to have his son join the management of the *gemach*, but he changed his mind when he realized that it was not appropriate for a father and son to manage communal funds together.

Five years later, Rafi wanted to resign from his position in the *gemach* and appoint his son in his place, but the other two managers, as well as several shul members, objected. They felt that if Rafi resigned, it would

---

139. See *Rema, Yoreh De'ah* 249:1, and the *Taz* there.

only be fair to call for an election of a new head of the *gemach*. They claimed that the *gemach* belonged to the shul, and could not be passed from father to son.

They came to *beis din* for a *din Torah*. Rafi claimed that the *gemach* was established as his personal *gemach*. The other managers were appointed by him to help maintain the *gemach*. The *gemach* was named for Rafi's father, not as part of the shul. Lastly, the money he collected from the shul members was given in appreciation of his delivery of the *Daf Yomi shiur*, and was entrusted to him.

The community claimed that although the *gemach* was named for Rafi's father, it was established within the shul. Their support for this claim was the fact that the name and address of the shul appear on the loan application form, as the address of the *gemach*. Although Rafi was the originator and first manager of the *gemach*, he was not meant to be the owner of the *gemach*. He became the manager only because of the respect and appreciation the community had for him. Appreciation, they claimed, is not something that can be passed from father to son.

Who is right?

It would seem that since Rafi solicited the funds for the *gemach*, the *gemach* belongs to him. The Gemara in *Megillah*[140] states that if a shul was donated under the auspices of a great person, that person has the right to sell the shul. The same is true for the money of the *gemach*, as it was donated for Rafi to do with it as his judgment dictated.

However, the *Beur Halachah*[141] explains that this halachah does not apply to just anyone. It has to be someone of great stature, as the Gemara's example was the great Rav Ashi, one of the authors of the Talmud! A regular person who leads a project is not endowed

---

140. 26a.
141. 153 *Sheba'in*.

with the license to do with communal funds as he sees fit.

It would appear that the true test to decide the ownership of the *gemach* would be in the way it was run. Since Rafi had a unique position in the management, as he was never elected, and it was he who appointed the other managers, it is apparent that the *gemach* is his.

The *Terumas HaDeshen*[142] was asked to settle a dispute in a particular city. One *Rav* settled in a city and would process *Gittin* and officiate *Chalitzos*. Later, a different *Rav* came to town, and the first *Rav* refused to let the second *Rav* practice, as he claimed that the position already belonged to him. The *Terumas HaDeshen* answered that as long as the first *Rav* had not been appointed by the community as their Rabbi, he had no claim to prevent anyone else from filling the position.

This is not similar to our case, because a *Rav* needs to be accepted. Without a community, he cannot be a *Rav*. In our case, this was Rafi's personal *gemach*, and he does not have to be appointed by anyone. He may therefore appoint his son in his stead.

<hr />

An Expensive House Call

וְאֵת הָאֶלֶף
And from the one thousand
(38:28)

Dr. Chilon was the closest physician the Cohens could find on Shabbos afternoon. He was certainly not the

---

142. Vol. II, 126.

most personable, but under Mr. Cohen's life-threatening condition, the Cohens had no other choice but to consult him.

Dr. Chilon insisted that he would not administer the life-saving medicine that his patient needed until he was paid in full. The Cohens promised to pay him immediately after Shabbos, but could not move the stonehearted doctor. He refused to take a collateral or even a signed blank check. The Cohens knew that saving a life takes precedence to abstaining from doing "melachah" on Shabbos, and asked the doctor how much he wanted. Chilon named his fee for the weekend house call: 500 shekels.

Mrs. Cohen did not have that much cash on hand. As she reached for her checkbook, it occurred to her that if she wrote the check for 1,000 shekels (אלף ש"ח) as opposed to 500 shekels (חמש מאות ש"ח) she could avoid writing an extra word on Shabbos. Is she obligated to do so? (The doctor would not give her change.)

*A*The *Rema*[143] rules that one who is being forced to violate a prohibition must forfeit all of his money in order not to transgress. As long as one has the option of giving money in lieu of the violation, he is not considered "forced" to transgress. It would seem that the same would apply in our case and she should write the check for 1,000 shekels.

Perhaps we could differentiate between the two scenarios. It is incumbent on someone to give all of his money in order to avoid something prohibited, but in our case, Mrs. Cohen is doing the mitzvah of preserving life. Maybe in such a circumstance there is no obligation to give away all of one's money.

An example of this can be found in the *Rema*,[144] who rules that

---

143. *Yoreh De'ah* 157:1.
144. Ibid. 374:3.

a Kohen who finds a *meis mitzvah* is not required to hire others to bury it; rather, he may do the mitzvah himself! Even though a Kohen would otherwise have to pay so as not to come in contact with a dead body, when he is involved in a mitzvah that Heaven designated for him, he is allowed to do it himself.

In contrast, Responsa *Zayis Ra'anan*[145] writes that the sick person himself must go to any expense in order not to violate a prohibition. Rabbi Shlomo Zalman Auerbach[146] explains the difference. Burying a *"meis mitzvah"* is a mitzvah that overrides the Kohen's obligation not to defile himself. Therefore a Kohen does not have to spend money in order to avoid defiling himself in the process of the mitzvah. Although a sick person has a mitzvah to save his own life, he also bears a financial responsibility to pay for his medical expenses with all of his assets, if necessary. Therefore, no amount of money is too great to heal him if he can avoid having to transgress a prohibition. Anyone else, however, would not have to spend extra money on behalf of the sick person in order to avoid such transgressions, as they bear no such financial obligation.

In our case, the Cohens would have to write the check for 1,000 shekels since the money belonged to the sick person himself. Even if they would write the check with their left hand, which would render the act of writing into a Rabbinic decree for a right-handed person, that would still not permit them to write the extra word. Even a Rabbinic decree would require one to forfeit all of his money rather than to violate the decree.

----■◆■----

145. *Orach Chaim* Vol. I 2:2.
146. *Minchas Shlomo* I, 7.

Going the Extra Mile

וְאֶת הָאֶלֶף וּשְׁבַע הַמֵּאוֹת וַחֲמִשָּׁה וְשִׁבְעִים

And from the one thousand seven hundred seventy-five

(38:28)

 Dr. Friedman, a pediatrician, receives $10 for every vaccination he administers to an infant. He can buy thicker needles, which would cause more pain, for 50 cents, in which case his profit will be $9.50, or very thin needles, that cause less pain, for $1.50, leaving him with a profit of $8.50. Since he administers thousands of injections, the difference is significant. Does he have to buy the thinner needles for his patients?

 One would have to determine what would happen if the doctor would charge $10 for his services and charge for the thin needle separately. What would most parents do? If most parents would pay the extra dollar to have the thinner needle to spare their baby the pain, then the doctor must buy the thinner needles. If most parents would choose the thicker needle in order to save the dollar, then the doctor may do so as well. The majority opinion is considered the norm, and the doctor should act accordingly.

Since most people would certainly spend a dollar to spare their baby pain, the doctor must buy the thinner needles.

Even though we find that we do not decide monetary issues based on a majority,[147] this case is different. In a case where someone bought an ox for plowing, and the ox proved to be fit only for slaughter, the seller can say that he sold it for slaughter, even though the majority of people buy oxen for plowing. The reason for this is because he is making an absolute claim and he is currently

---

147. See *Bava Basra* 92b.

in possession of the money. Thus, removing the money from him requires a greater burden of proof.

In our case, the doctor himself is unsure what to use, and therefore he should follow the majority opinion.

Shul Business

וַיַּעֲרֹךְ עָלָיו עֵרֶךְ לֶחֶם

He prepared on it the setting of bread

(40:23)

 In Yosef's shul the custom was to sell the *aliyos,* to determine who would be called to the Torah. On a particular Shabbos, Yosef bought an *aliyah* for 50 shekels. Binyamin approached Yosef before the Torah reading and told him that he had a personal reason to receive Yosef's *aliyah* because it contained certain *pesukim* that had special significance to Binyamin, and asked if Yosef would sell it to him. Yosef was a shrewd businessman, and realized that he could name his price. He sold the *aliyah* to Binyamin for 500 shekels!

When the shul members heard about the business deal, they were enraged. They felt that Yosef had no right to conduct business with his *aliyah,* and even if Binyamin was willing to pay that much money, he should pay it to the shul and not to Yosef!

Others supported Yosef's position. If he bought the *aliyah,* he could do with it as he pleased, even to resell it. Who is right?

A The *sefer Olas Tamid*[148] writes that one who bought a mitzvah in shul for a year (e.g., to open the *aron hakodesh*) and died in the middle of the year, his heir must take the mitzvah upon himself and either pay the remainder of money due for the mitzvah, or sell it to others. If they sell it for less money than is due, they must make up the difference. If they sold it for more, it would appear that the profit belongs to the community, because one cannot make profit from *tzedakah*. The *Sheyarei Knesses HaGedolah*[149] argues that the profit belongs to the heir.

It seems that the *Olas Tamid's* reasoning was that the mitzvah is available only due to the existence of the congregation, and the congregation is willing to participate only for the sake of the mitzvah, and not to provide people with an opportunity to make a profit.

Rav Elyashiv ruled that, halachically, one should be able to resell an *aliyah*, like the opinion of the *Sheyarei Knesses HaGedolah*. However, he needs to pass on part of the profit to the shul since their participation is crucial to his business venture. By doing so he will also calm those who opposed the sale.

Even so, it seems improper to profit from a mitzvah, as we find that those who made the *lechem hapanim* in the *Beis HaMikdash* are criticized for wanting to increase their salary by doing this mitzvah.[150]

---

148. 144 § 4.
149. *Orach Chaim* 143:3.
150. See *Yoma* 38a.

ספר ויקרא

Sefer Vayikra

פרשת ויקרא
Parashas Vayikra

A Father's Blessing

וַיִּקְרָא אֶל מֹשֶׁה וַיְדַבֵּר ה׳ אֵלָיו מֵאֹהֶל מוֹעֵד לֵאמֹר

And Hashem spoke to him from the Tent of Meeting, saying

(1:1)

A 35-year-old woman contracted a serious illness. She asked her husband and her doctor not to divulge her condition to anyone. Her husband asked if it would be proper for him to inform his wife's father without her knowledge, so her father could *daven* for her.

Revealing a secret is strictly prohibited. The *pasuk* in *Mishlei*[1] compares revealing a secret to *rechilus* (talebearing). The Gemara in *Yoma*[2] learns from our *pasuk* that unless one has permission to give over information he heard from his friend, that information is *"b'val yomar"* (not to be repeated). In early *sefarim* it is brought that one who reveals a

---

1. 20:19.
2. 4b.

secret will be reincarnated as a mute. The Chofetz Chaim[3] explains that one who reveals information that was conveyed in private, causes damage to the original bearer of the secret and provides an opportunity to thwart his plans; it is also a breach of modesty and a violation of the will of the one who originally passed on the information.

Nevertheless, the father should be informed, despite the request of the daughter, because a parent's prayer is readily accepted. The *Sforno*[4] explains that the Torah records Lavan's blessing to his daughters and their children to teach us that a father's *berachah*, since it is given with his entire heart and soul, is certainly more powerful than that of any other person.

The *Tur*[5] explains that honoring one's parents gives one long life, because it causes his parents to pray for him, and that will bring him longevity.

Therefore her father should be told, because we may assume that if she realized the power of her parent's prayers, she would certainly want her husband to tell him.

It is obvious that if the information will have a detrimental effect on the father's health, he should not be told, and all efforts should be made to hide his daughter's condition.

———————◆———————

---

3. *Rechilus, Klal* 8:5.
4. *Bereishis* 32:7.
5. *Parashas Yisro.*

The Privilege of Ownership

אָדָם כִּי יַקְרִיב מִכֶּם

When a man among you brings an offering
(1:2)

 It seemed that the shul's *shofar* had disappeared. The shul owned only one *shofar*, and it was gone! Fortunately, one of the *mispallelim* (congregants) had a *shofar* in his house. However, he requested that he would let the shul use it only if he would be the one to blow for them. Although he was a worthy candidate for the task, the shul already had someone who blew the *shofar* for them every year.

Should they let the owner of the *shofar* blow for them since it is his *shofar*, or should they explain to him that his request is improper because once someone has acquired the mitzvah by doing it year after year, it may not be taken from him.[6]

 The Gemara in *Yoma*[7] explains that lotteries were conducted among the Kohanim to decide who would bring the communal offerings. For personal offerings, however, the owner could choose any Kohen he wanted.[8] Perhaps in our case as well, since the *shofar* belongs to an individual, he has the right to choose who should blow it.

Upon further examination there is a glaring difference. Regarding a personal offering, the mitzvah belongs to the individual. In

---

6. See *Shulchan Aruch, Orach Chaim* 153:22.
7. 26b.
8. As explained by the *Noda BiYehudah* in his glosses.

our case it is an issue of who will be the messenger of the entire community to blow the *shofar* for them, and help the community do their mitzvah. Merely because he owns the *shofar* does not make him the owner of the community's mitzvah.

If, however, the entire community would come to the man's house to hear the *shofar*, then the one who usually blows would have no claim, since his position is only for blowing in shul, and not anywhere else.

The First or the Most

וְשָׁחַט אֹתוֹ

He shall slaughter it

(1:11)

 The *mispallelim* of Congregation Beis Avrohom intend to invite a noted *tzaddik* to be the *chazzan* for *Selichos* in order to inspire and awaken them to the spirit of the upcoming Rosh Hashanah. Since the *tzaddik* can only be with them for one night, they are unsure whether to invite him for the first night of *Selichos* or for Erev Rosh Hashanah. Which is preferable?

 The Gemara in *Yoma*[9] teaches that the Kohanim would make a lottery to decide who would receive the coveted task of slaughtering the morning offering. Slaughtering does not even require a Kohen, and therefore one would think that the Kohanim would not attribute such importance to it. The *Be'er*

---

9. 14b.

Sheva[10] explains that since it was the beginning of the service, it was especially beloved to them, and in the absence of a lottery there might be an argument as to who would get the job.

Similarly, although Erev Rosh Hashanah's *Selichos* may be more important, as they contain the 13 Attributes of Mercy with greater frequency than any other *Selichos*, it is still likely that the first *Selichos* have more of an impact.

Some explain that the reason the first *berachah* of *Shemoneh Esrei* is so crucial,[11] such that concentration is a prerequisite, is because everything is affected by the beginning. In our case as well, they should invite the *tzaddik* to lead the prayers for the first night of *Selichos*.

---

10. At the beginning of the third *perek of Tamid.*
11. See *Shulchan Aruch, Orach Chaim* 101:1.

פרשת צו
Parashas Tzav

One Dizzy Chicken

זֹאת תּוֹרַת הַחַטָּאת

This is the law of the sin-offering

(6:18)

 Yom Kippur was approaching, and Menachem had just finished circling a chicken around his head during the traditional *kapparos* ceremony. Menachem put the chicken down for just a second — or so he thought. The chicken, still traumatized from its recent harrowing experience, jumped into one of the nearby crates of chickens. Now Menachem had a big problem. No one would want to perform the ritual with a chicken that had previously been used for *kapparos*, and as soon as people realized what occurred, the owner of the chickens stood to suffer a great loss. Does Menachem have to pay for all the chickens in the crate in order to prevent that loss?

 Mi'd'Oraisa (based on the Torah), the used chicken would be nullified among all the other chickens. However, the Sages decreed that living beings or important objects cannot become nullified.[12] Perhaps it is acceptable to do *kapparos* on a chicken that the Torah considers *batel* even though *mi'd'Rabbanan* it is not. If this would be the case, Menachem would be absolved from payment as there would be no loss.

In actuality, it seems that people would not want to rely on such an explanation because they would be apprehensive of taking the previously used chicken. Thus it would appear that Menachem is indeed liable for the loss.

Nevertheless, Rav Elyashiv ruled that the *kapparah* does not take effect until the chicken is slaughtered. Therefore, since the chicken escaped before it could be slaughtered, it is not considered a used chicken.

According to this reasoning, it would seem that Menachem could get his money back for his chicken, since he never used it for *kapparos*.

Rav Zilberstein added that the language of the *Shulchan Aruch* is explicitly in accordance with the ruling of Rav Elyashiv, as it describes the custom of *kapparos* as "**slaughtering** a chicken ..."[13]

The *sefer Torah Lishmah*[14] also follows this reasoning in its ruling that even if the chicken is found to be a *tereifah*, one does not have to do *kapparos* again, because the important part is the slaughtering.

Rav Chaim Kanievsky suggested another solution: perhaps one could nullify the *kapparah* the same way one could nullify a *neder*, by approaching three people to nullify it, and by doing so the chicken would revert to its original status.

---------◼▸◆◂◼---------

---

12. See *Yoreh De'ah* 110.
13. *Shulchan Aruch, Orach Chaim* 605.
14. 155.

No Time to Eat

אִם עַל תּוֹדָה יַקְרִיבֶנּוּ

If he shall offer it for a thanksgiving-offering

(7:12)

Ephraim's custom is to do *kapparos* before Yom Kippur with a chicken. He then has it slaughtered and delivered to a poor person.[15] One year it was already Erev Yom Kippur, and Ephraim was unsure if he should act in accordance with his regular custom, or perhaps, since the poor person probably has so many chickens by this time from the many people who performed this ritual, Ephraim's chicken will go to the garbage instead of going to *tzedakah*. Should he do *kapparos* using money rather than risk his chicken going to waste?

The Gemara in *Pesachim*[16] states that that one does not bring a *todah*-offering on Erev Pesach, as it contains *chametz*, and will have to be eaten in a much shorter span of time than when brought on other days. Later commentaries point out that there seems to be a contradiction to this concept in the Gemara in *Shevuos*.[17] There the Gemara says that one may bring a sin-offering on Erev Yom Kippur, even though the usual allotment for it to be eaten extends into the night, which is not possible on Erev Yom Kippur, as one may not eat on the evening of Yom Kippur.

The *Meleches Betzalel*[18] explains that since as long as one has not brought a sin-offering he is in danger of being subject to suffering, there is no greater benefit for the person than to bring this

---

15. See *Rema, Orach Chaim* 605:1.
16. 13b.
17. 8a.
18. On the Gemara in *Shevuos*.

offering. In deference to such a benefit, the fact that the offering may not be eaten later is not a deterrent to bringing it. A thanksgiving-offering does not have this urgency, and it may thus be delayed until after Yom Kippur.

The *Eretz Tzvi*,[19] in his glosses, brings an additional proof from the Gemara in *Kereisos*[20] that records how Bava ben Buta would offer a conditional sin-offering every day, in case he had inadvertently sinned, with the exception of the day following Yom Kippur, as Yom Kippur would have already atoned for him. One may infer that on Erev Yom Kippur, he did bring the offering even though there was a time restriction for eating it. This shows again that an offering that is meant to protect its owner cannot be turned away by the fact that it may not be eaten for its full time.

Ephraim's dilemma can perhaps be resolved with these sources as well. Since Ephraim uses a chicken every year for *kapparos*, and this inspires him to do *teshuvah*,[21] he should maintain his custom. He should not be concerned that the chicken may be wasted, just as there is no concern that the meat of the sin-offering may have to be burnt after it becomes unfit. However, if he only uses a chicken when it is convenient, then he should use money now as well, and distribute it to the poor.

---

19. 6 §35.
20. 25a.
21. See *Ramban, Vayikra* 1:9.

Can You Take It With You?

לְמֹשֶׁה הָיָה לְמָנָה

It was a portion for Moshe

(8:29)

 Abe was a guest at a wedding, and the waiter served him the main course. Abe was not particularly hungry, and asked for aluminum foil so he could take the portion home to his wife. May Abe take his portion home?

 The *Mahari't*[22] raises a question as to whether food served to a guest belongs to the guest, or if it remains in the possession of the host until it is eaten.[23]

Even according to the latter opinion, it would appear that Abe may take home his portion, as the *Tosefta*[24] states, "What may one take home from the *simchah* hall? A piece of meat, a small roll, and a seasoned cracker. Rabban Shimon ben Gamliel says, in a place where the custom is to distribute nuts and toasted grains (ancient candies) he may take his children with him to the *simchah*." The *Tosefta* delineates those foods that a host does not mind his guests taking home. If, however, there are not enough portions for all the guests, Abe would likely not be allowed to take his home as the host's priority is to provide for those in attendance.

---

22. Vol. I, 150, quoted by the *Ba'er Heiteiv, Even HaEzer* 28 § 32.
23. See "Whose Matzah is It?," *Parashas Bo* (p.161).
24. *Beitzah* 4:9.

פרשת שמיני
Parashas Shemini

You Have the Right to Remain Silent

וַיִּדֹּם אַהֲרֹן

And Aaron was silent

(10:3)

 Zevulun had an idea for a lucrative investment. He wanted to begin to import a certain product that required licensing from the local authorities. He proposed to his friend Naftali that if Naftali would be successful in acquiring the license, as well as renting a storefront with a good location and hiring a staff to manage the store, Zevulun would give him 20 percent of all the profits. Zevulun thought that was a fair commission for the several months' work that the job demanded. To his surprise, Naftali, with special assistance from Above, was able to secure everything in less than a month! Zevulun refused to pay that much for so little effort and informed Naftali that either he could accept only 10 percent of the profits, or Zevulun would not proceed to open the business, in which case there would be no profit at all. Nafatali was silent, but in his mind he refused to accept this change in terms. Several months later, when they met to divide the profits, Naftali demanded 20 percent. Zevulun countered that Naftali had agreed to take less, and only under such terms had Zevulun agreed to open the business. Naftali insisted that he never truly accepted Zevulun's "new" terms. How much should Zevulun pay Naftali?

The *Imrei Yosher*[25] deals with a similar case. A *shadchan* (matchmaker) proposed a match between a young man and young woman. They met several times, but before the couple became engaged, one of the sides informed the *shadchan* that they were willing to proceed with the engagement only if the *shadchan* would lower his fee for suggesting a successful match.

The *Imrei Yosher* rules that if the *shadchan* expressed willingness to accept the cut in salary, even though he did so under duress, we cannot force the family to pay, since they maintain that they continued with the match only due to such an understanding, and they have possession of the money in question.

However, if the *shadchan* says that he is not satisfied with their terms, but continued to work on bringing the match to fruition, in spite of his dissatisfaction, then they must pay him his full wage. If they had told the *shadchan* initially that they will only pay less than his normal wage and the *shadchan* did not consent, but nevertheless made the match, they could pay him less. In this case, when the match is close to completion and the services have already been rendered, he deserves his normal fee. Even though he is not entitled to be paid unless the couple get engaged, that is only a condition that needs to be met, but the payment is for services that have already been rendered.

---

25. Vol. 3, 91.

This proves that even if the *shadchan* was silent and did not refuse the reduction in payment, the fact that he continued to work in order to keep the parents from ending the match is not interpreted as accepting the new conditions.

In our case as well, Naftali invested his time, energy, and connections to set up the business, and therefore has already earned his commission. Zevulun cannot retract his original offer, and Naftali's silence proves nothing.

Please Pass the Ketchup

זֹאת הַחַיָּה אֲשֶׁר תֹּאכְלוּ
These are the creatures that you may eat
(11:2)

 A hospital patient has to eat the nonkosher hospital food because of his life-threatening condition. (No kosher food is now available.) May he season his food in order to enjoy it? If he is offered a choice of chicken or meat, and either one is sufficient to preserve his life, may he choose meat because he prefers it over chicken? If a Jew is taken captive and forced to eat nonkosher meat, because his captors want him to violate his religion, may he salt the meat so he can enjoy it?

 In a case of someone who is sick, it is permissible, but in a case of duress it is not. A sick person is allowed to eat nonkosher foods in order to save his life, and therefore he may enjoy them as well. If, however, he is being forced to eat nonkosher, the food does not become permissible; rather, the fact that he is eating under duress exempts him from any punishment. If, however, he expresses a desire to eat the food by making it more tasty, his desire to eat makes his eating a prohibited act. Although there is also duress, there is desire, and no leniency exists for such a circumstance.

The *Mishnah Berurah*[26] makes this distinction in regard to making a *berachah* on nonkosher food. A sick person does make a *berachah*, whereas one who ate under duress would not. For a sick person, his eating is not responsible for his life-threatening circumstance; his sickness is. Thus, his eating is not only permissible, but is a mitzvah, because he is doing so in order to save his life. If, however, the source of his duress is whether he will eat or not, for example if he is being forced by gentiles, we cannot obligate him to make a *berachah* on the benefit he receives from the food since he is only eating under duress and is not considered to be eating for enjoyment.

If he would also have intent to enjoy the food, it would not be considered duress at all.

<hr />

To Eat or Not to Eat

לֹא תֹאכֵלוּ

You shall not eat

(11:4)

 A man was dangerously ill and was instructed to eat on Yom Kippur. He refuses to eat unless his wife will eat with him, even though his wife is healthy enough to fast. May she eat with her husband in order to save his life?

<hr />

26. 204 § 45.

A similar incident took place in Amsterdam several hundred years ago. A man was instructed to drink milk from a donkey in order to save his life, and he refused. His son decided to attempt to fool his father. He brought his father a cup of donkey's milk and informed him that it was goat's milk. The father suspected something was amiss and instructed his son that he would drink it only if the son would drink first! The son asked Hagaon Rabbi Yitzchak Saruk if it would be permissible for him to drink, and he was told that it is forbidden.

A source for this ruling could be found in *Maseches Kesubos.*[27] A man would refuse to eat his own food unless he received money from *tzedakah*. R' Shimon ruled not to give him funds from *tzedakah*, and if he dies, so be it. We are only required to help someone who is not capable of helping himself. If, however, he can support himself, but he refuses to do so, we have no obligation to help him. This would seem to apply in our cases as well, since the people can save themselves.

This is not to be compared to the situation in the time of Rav Yisrael Salanter when a terrible epidemic was rampant, and Rav Yisrael was concerned that people who needed to eat on Yom Kippur would not do so, risking their lives. After *davening* he made *Kiddush* and ate. In that case, Rav Yisrael was concerned that people would not realize the severity of the situation, and if Rav Yisrael did not eat, even though he personally had no need to, they would think that they were also not allowed to eat. Similarly, if the husband was deranged and incapable of rational decisions, his wife would be allowed to eat in order to ensure that her husband eat as well, since under such circumstances he is unable to help himself, and she would actually be saving his life by eating.

---

27. 67b.

Mandatory Attendance? I

לֹא תֹאכְלוּ

You shall not eat

(11:4)

Q Darryl Segal — or as he is now known, Dovid Segal — is a recent *baal teshuvah*. Unfortunately, he is the only one in his family who has earned that title. The entire family is planning to gather in a nonkosher restaurant in honor of his father's 50th birthday, and his father has a strong desire to have all of his children there, whether they eat or not. Dovid wants to do the right thing. Should he attend, solely to honor his father's wishes? And if so, should he dress in the mode he has become accustomed to, and people will recognize that he is religious, or should he dress down in order to prevent a desecration of Hashem's Name by being in a nonkosher restaurant?

A He is forbidden to enter a nonkosher restaurant regardless of whether he is dressed as an observant Jew, and certainly not dressed otherwise. He should maintain his dignity and stay home. How could he possibly attend the affair, in the hope of honoring his father, while simultaneously disregarding the Honor of our Father in Heaven, Who is our King and our Shepherd?!

———◆———

Bac-Os

וְאֶת הַחֲזִיר

And the pig

(11:7)

 There were some immigrants to Israel who had become accustomed to eating pork in their mother countries. These immigrants are in the process of returning to their *Yiddishkeit*, but have difficulty refraining from their familiar foods. Would it be permissible to produce for them kosher food that tastes like pork?

 The *Chida*[28] comments on the Gemara in *Chullin*[29] that relates the story of Yalta, the wife of Rav Nachman, who asked her husband to feed her the permissible equivalent of milk cooked with meat. Rav Nachman instructed his cook to serve her cow udders that had been roasted on a spit. The *Chida* used this as a proof regarding whether the "*mahn*" that nourished *Bnei Yisrael* in the desert could assume the taste of something forbidden. We can learn from Rav Nachman, who acceded to his wife's request, that as long as a person knows that the food he is consuming is permissible, he may eat it, even if its taste is identical to that of something that is forbidden. Moreover, the fact that the "*mahn*" was able to assume the taste of whatever the person wanted was a miracle. If eating the "*mahn*" in such a fashion would be prohibited, it would not have had the desired taste.

Rav Elyashiv said that if not for the words of the *Chida*, it would be better for people to refrain from eating foods that simulate forbidden foods. *Chazal* warn us to stay away from those things that

---

28. *Pesach Einayim.*
29. 109b.

resemble forbidden behavior (*harchek min hakiyur*). Although Hashem created foods that resemble the tastes of forbidden foods, such as the *Shibuta* fish (that tastes like pork) and the udders of a cow (that tastes like milk and meat), those foods are entirely kosher, created by Hashem Himself. But to manufacture imitation foods that taste like pork, which Hashem considers an abomination, we should also be sensitive and refrain from eating those items that attempt to duplicate nonkosher foods.

פרשת תזריע
Parashas Tazria

The Preferred Sandek

וּבַיּוֹם הַשְּׁמִינִי יִמּוֹל

On the eighth day he shall be circumcised

(12:3)

Boruch and his wife had been childless for many years after their wedding. His *Rebbe* told him that if he will be *sandek* at the *bris* of a holy and pure child, he will merit to have a child of his own. Boruch went to his neighbor who was a *talmid chacham* and asked if he would allow him to be *sandek* at his son's *bris*, explaining the reason for his request. The neighbor had wanted his *Rosh Yeshivah* to be *sandek*, as the *Rema*[30] prescribes that one should try to use a *sandek* who is very righteous. Whom should the man choose, his *Rosh Yeshivah* or his desperate neighbor?

It seems that he should allow Boruch to be *sandek*, since the issue of having a righteous *sandek* has no source in the Gemara, whereas doing kindness is a mitzvah from

---

30. *Yoreh De'ah* 264:1, based on *Or Zarua*.

the Torah, as the Gemara in *Bava Kamma*[31] learns from the *pasuk* in *Parashas Yisro*.[32] Because his neighbor is suffering, it is certainly a great kindness to make him *sandek*. This will be a greater merit for the baby than having a righteous *sandek*!

We find a similar ruling in the laws of mourning. Although it is a great mitzvah to *daven* specifically in a shul, we are taught that it is a mitzvah to *daven* in the house of a mourner, because by doing so, he is doing kindness with the living as well as the dead.[33]

Here, where a person is not giving up a mitzvah, only forgoing a recommended practice, it would seem obvious that doing kindness takes priority.

Family First

וּבַיּוֹם הַשְּׁמִינִי יִמּוֹל

On the eighth day he shall be circumcised

(12:3)

 Reuven's wife gave birth to a baby boy, and he is unsure to whom he should give the honor of being "*kvatter*" at the *bris*. (Being *kvatter* is known as a *segulah* — an omen — for having children.) On the one hand, his brother does not have any children yet, and would certainly appreciate the honor. On the other hand, there is a couple who have done abundant kindness with Reuven and his wife, and he feels that perhaps he has

31. 100a.
32. *Shemos* 18:20.
33. *Shulchan Aruch, Orach Chaim* 90:9.

an obligation to give them *kvatter* in appreciation of their benevolence. To whom should he give *kvatter*?

 It seems that Reuven should give the honor to his brother. His brother needs the *segulah*, and from whom else should his brother receive such an honor if not from his own family? It is regarding such an instance that it is said not to forsake one's flesh.[34] His appreciation to his benefactor can be expressed in many other ways, and does not have to come at his brother's expense. If a person had a delicious fruit that could heal someone ill, or it could be given as a token of appreciation, would anyone ask the question, to whom should the fruit be given?

Let us consider, however, if the person to whom he has a debt of gratitude is also waiting to be blessed with children, would the *p'sak* be different?

The Gemara in *Kesubos*[35] tells the story of someone who bequeathed his earthly possessions to Tuvia. Two Tuvias came to claim them. One was a neighbor and one was a relative. The Gemara concludes with *pasuk* in *Mishlei*,[36] "A close neighbor is better than a distant brother." The *Tur* explains that a neighbor does not refer to someone who merely lives next to the person, but rather someone with whom he is friendly and with whom he has regular dealings. Based on this, Baruch should choose his neighbor as *kvatter*.

However, the Gemara is probably only relevant to someone who has already given away his property, and we have to determine what his intention had been. But in a case where he is coming to ask to whom he should give his property, he would be instructed to give it to his relative. A possible proof may be brought from the *Rema* in *Hilchos Tzedakah*.[37] He says that relatives have priority over all others.

---

34. *Yeshayahu* 58:7.
35. 85b.
36. 27:10.
37. *Yoreh De'ah* 251:3.

The *Chacham Tzvi*[38] rules that if a baby's father dies and the *beis din*-appointed guardian wishes to perform the *bris milah*, and the baby's brother also wishes to perform the mitzvah, the brother has priority. The source for the ruling is the aforementioned *Rema*. If for livelihood in this world a relative has priority, certainly for spiritual livelihood a relative comes first.

We see that although the guardian certainly deserves appreciation, the relative has priority.

In addition, if Reuven's father wants Reuven to give it to his brother, he will be showing appreciation to his father by observing *kibbud av*.

Rav Shmuel Rosenberg provided an additional reason to give *kvatter* to the brother. In the mitzvah of *yibum*, Hashem instructed a brother to ensure the perpetuation of his deceased brother's name. Therefore, it makes sense that if a brother could assist his **living** brother in having children, this would certainly be a fulfillment of Hashem's will. Thus, it would be appropriate to give *kvatter* to one's brother, as opposed to anyone else.

Care for Tefillin

וְהִסְגִּיר הַכֹּהֵן
Then the Kohen shall quarantine
(13:4)

 A man was diagnosed with a highly contagious disease, and he must be hospitalized and quarantined. The hospital's rule is that after the patient's demise, all of his

38. Responsa 70-71.

possessions must be incinerated. May the *Yid* bring his *tefillin* with him to the hospital, when he knows that should he die they will be burned?

A The Responsa *Dovev Meisharim*[39] writes about a similar case that it is prohibited to bring the *tefillin*. This is based on the *Rashba* in *Maseches Shabbos*,[40] who writes that wherever it is clear that one's actions will cause Hashem's Name to be erased, one may not proceed. In our case as well, although the *tefillin* will be burned by gentiles, and the Jew is only causing it to happen, it is prohibited since the eventuality is obvious.

Similarly, the *Igros Moshe*[41] forbids bringing *tefillin* into such a situation, as he compares it to the obligation to save the holy Scripture from a house that has caught fire. Even though not saving the holy writings is even less involvement than actually causing them to burn, nevertheless one may not leave them in such a situation. Rav Moshe elaborates that bringing *tefillin* into such conditions is actually commensurate to actively burning them (see the *teshuvah* for further explanation).

In contrast, Rav Elyashiv rules that one may bring *tefillin* to such a hospital patient, since at the present time he has a mitzvah to wear the *tefillin*, and one does not have to be concerned what will happen in the future. The prohibition of causing something to happen is only when one is causing the *tefillin* to burn at the time that he is doing the mitzvah. If at the time of the action there is only a mitzvah taking place, and the threat of the *tefillin* being burned is merely looming in the future, that does not exempt the patient from his obligation to wear *tefillin* today.

39, Vol. I 99.
40, 120b
41. *Orach Chaim* Vol. I, 4.

פרשת מצורע
Parashas Metzora

Classified Information

זֹאת תִּהְיֶה תּוֹרַת הַמְּצֹרָע

This shall be the law of the metzora

(14:2)

It is the practice of certain hospitals to accept young doctors for a one-year trial period, after which their performance is evaluated, and their future in the hospital is determined by their superiors. The department head dictates his reports, to be typed by his secretary, and he signs them.

Even if the department head has to report the shortcomings of the young doctors, and there is no problem of *lashon hara* because it is for a constructive purpose *(to'eles),*[42] is there any reason to permit relating the information to the secretary who has no need to know?

It seems that the department head should dictate the report without identifying the name of the doctor he is reviewing. Afterward, he could insert the name of its

---

42. See *Chofetz Chaim, Rechilus* 9:8.

subject into each report. That way the secretary will not know who is the subject of each report, and there is no problem of *lashon hara*.

Rav Elyashiv agreed to this requirement, and added that in a case where this would not be possible, because the identity of the doctor would be apparent anyway, the department head would even have to take vacation days if need be, to write the report himself! Avoiding *lashon hara* is at least as important as other things for which he takes his "personal days."

Responsa *Tzitz Eliezer*[43] writes that since it is known that it is the accepted practice for doctors to dictate reports to their secretaries, the young doctors accepted their posts with that premise in mind, and have thereby granted permission for it to be done. The secretaries also enable the report to be written more efficiently, by removing room for errors that could otherwise occur, e.g., mislabeling a report. That is why secretaries are allowed to be privy to patient's medical information, even for children who cannot forgo their right to privacy.

Rav Elyashiv did not agree with this reasoning. He maintained that *"mechilah"* — forgoing one's right not to have others speak about him — does not always work,[44] especially since the young doctor agreed to the condition only because he thought he would receive a favorable report. Had he known he would get a negative report, he would not have agreed. Therefore, the department head may not tell his secretary to type it.

There seems to be a precedent that one can allow others to report about him negatively. The Chofetz Chaim writes[45] that if a girl's father brings a prospective son-in-law to be tested by scholars to determine the boy's proficiency, the scholars must tell the truth, since both sides agreed to this proviso.

Nevertheless, in that case only interested parties will discover the results. The secretary, however, does not have to know about each doctor's performance.

---

43. Vol. XX, 52.
44. See *Kiddushin* 19b.
45. *Rechilus* 9, *tziur* 6.

Another example might be that one who reveals personal information in front of three people has thereby granted permission to pass on the information to others.[46] If so, we see that *mechilah* on *lashon hara* is effective. However, in such a case the person gave over the information himself, and it is not considered *lashon hara*. In our case the doctor does not want negative information about himself to become known, so the department head must avoid having anyone on his staff know the identity of the doctor being negatively reviewed.

Service Call

זֹאת תִּהְיֶה תּוֹרַת הַמְּצֹרָע
This shall be the law of the metzora
(14:2)

 As she ascended the steps of her apartment building, Rochel was shocked to overhear her neighbor Sarah's tirade against Yocheved, who also lived in their building. When Rochel reached the landing, she saw a repairman standing in front of Yocheved's door.

"Do not take her washing machine," Sarah told the repairman. "She never pays for repairs! You will have only heartache from her! She will complain that the work was not satisfactory, and you will never see your money," she concluded.

The repairman was convinced that Sarah's words were sincere, and decided not to take the washing machine.

After he left, Rochel approached Sarah and ques-

---

46. *Hilchos Lashon Hara* 2:13.

tioned her about her behavior. They had both known Yocheved for years as a fine and honest person. Rochel could not understand how Sarah could speak so harshly against Yocheved.

Sarah explained to Rochel that Yocheved had arranged for the repairman to take her washing machine into his shop for repairs. When the man came, Yocheved had to leave for a doctor's appointment, so she left the man alone in her apartment to detach the machine and cart it off. A few minutes later, Yocheved called Sarah and told her that she had just remembered that her husband had hidden a large sum of money in the washing machine. She asked Sarah to make up any excuse to stop the repairman from taking the machine.

Rochel chastised her on two accounts. First, she asserted that the repairman deserved to be paid for his service call to Yocheved's house to pick up the machine, and now she had caused him a loss. Secondly, she caused him to believe her *lashon hara* about Yocheved.

Is Rochel right?

 It would seem that there is no obligation to pay the repairman for his visit, since he has only himself to blame for believing *lashon hara* about his client. He should have suspected that maybe Sarah had had a conflict with her neighbor Yocheved that caused her to speak so unkindly.

In addition, the first repairman was contracted to do a job and since Yocheved will have to pay the full fee to a different repairman to fix the machine, she should not have to pay the first man anything.

However, since he did not leave the job of his own will, but was tricked into doing so, they must pay him his wages. As far as the fact that he accepted *lashon hara*, the Gemara in *Niddah*[47] states, in the name of *Rava*, that although one may not believe *lashon hara*,

---

47. 61a.

he must be suspect that what he is being told may be true.[48] in order to protect himself. So the repairman did nothing wrong by heeding Sarah's words.

Regarding whether Sarah had the right to speak *lashon hara* about Yocheved since by doing so she may have caused the repairman to sin by believing her, it seems that since Yocheved gave her permission to say what she said, there is no prohibition for the repairman to believe it.

The Chofetz Chaim[49] writes that one who is asking for information, before entering a partnership or the like, must reveal his motivation for asking about his proposed partner, in order that the one he is asking will have a constructive intent in revealing the character of the one about whom he is being asked. If one did not do so, he has caused the one giving the information to speak *lashon hara*, even though the one gathering the information is permitted to do so. In our case, even if Sarah did not state that she was telling him for a constructive purpose, it would still be permitted since Yocheved had given her permission to say what she said.

<hr />

Trojan Couch

וּבָא אֲשֶׁר לוֹ הַבַּיִת

The one to whom the house belongs
(14:35)

 Michoel informed his neighbor Shimmy that he would be leaving town for a week, and would like to leave a key with him. He warned him not to give the key to anyone.

---

48. See *Chofetz Chaim, Klal* 6:2.
49. *Klal 4 (Hilchos Lashon Hara):*11.

Two days later a delivery man knocked on Shimmy's door. "Michoel ordered a couch and I came to deliver it. Do you have a key to the house?" he asked. "Michoel told me not to give the key to anyone," came the reply. The man answered Shimmy, "You are right. Do not give me the key. Just open the door for me, and watch me the whole time. You'll see, I won't touch a thing." Shimmy agreed. The workers put the couch inside and left.

That night, the delivery man returned. "There has been a mistake," he apologized as he waved the invoice in front of Shimmy. "Michoel ordered a brown couch, and today we delivered a maroon couch. Would you mind letting us switch it?" Shimmy agreed, and watched the workmen trade the couches, not letting them out of his sight.

At the end of the week Michoel returned and came to get his key from Shimmy. He returned a few minutes later to Shimmy's house, frantic. His safe, which had contained several hundred thousand dollars, was found empty. Shimmy claimed his innocence. "I did not give the key to anybody!" Michoel asked him, "Who brought the couch inside the house?" Shimmy told him, "That's the couch you ordered." Michoel retorted, "You fool, I never ordered a couch!" It seems that the original couch had a thief hiding inside of it. He emptied the safe, and when they traded couches at night, they removed the man inside with his loot. Can Shimmy still claim innocence for being fooled by a Trojan couch?

 If Shimmy would have taken responsibility to watch Michoel's house we could decide if he was negligent in his job by letting the workers go in or not. Since he only accepted responsibility to watch the key, he had no responsibility to watch the house.[50] The issue at hand is only if he is liable for the action of letting them in, as if he himself was an accessory to the robbery.

The *Maharashdam*[51] writes of one who had bolts of fabric in his friend's store. He asked the store owner for the key in order to retrieve the fabric. The store owner gave the key on condition that the store be opened in the presence of the store owner's brother. The owner of the fabric did not wait for the brother, and the store owner claimed that an expensive silk robe was stolen from his store. The *Maharashdam* ruled that the owner of the fabric does not need to pay for the robbery because his actions were only a *gerama*.

The *Shevet HaLevi*,[52] in explaining the opinion of the *Rema*,[53] writes that if one was warned specifically, he would have to pay if he violated the warning even in a case of *gerama*.

In our case, although Michoel warned Shimmy not to give the key to anyone, by letting the men in, Shimmy did not violate Michoel's instructions since he did not give over the key; rather, he watched the men the entire time, and did not have to suspect that someone was hiding in the couch. It would seem that he is absolved of any obligation as he only facilitated the robbery unknowingly. וצ״ע.

---

50. See *Avodah Zarah* 70b.
51. *Choshen Mishpat* 365.
52. Vol. IV, 201.
53. *Tur, Choshen Mishpat* 157.

Color Coordination

כְּנֶגַע נִרְאָה לִי בַּבָּיִת

Something like an affliction
has appeared to me in the house

(14:35)

 Eli was warned by *beis din* to fix his water pipe. Eli was negligent, and caused water damage to the neighbor's wall. To repair the damage, Eli painted the neighbor's entire wall. However, the neighbor was not satisfied. Since the other three walls had been painted many years earlier, the room looked strange with only one freshly painted wall. The neighbor demanded that Eli paint the other walls as well, since he was responsible for making the paint job neccesary.

Is the neighbor entitled to this?

 The *poskim* discuss one who borrowed a pair of earrings. The set costs $100, but if one is lost, the remaining is only worth $30, since it does not have a match. How much would the borrower need to pay if he lost one earring? The *Zera Yaakov*[54] maintains that the borrower must pay $50, because that is the value of each earring in the set. The *Kol Eliyahu*[55] claims that the borrower must pay $70, as that is the loss incurred by the lender. The *Divrei Geonim*[56] agrees with the latter opinion. Even though the additional $20 is only a *gerama* (i.e., the depreciation of the earring is only circumstantial, because it was part of a set), since the borrower was responsible to return the item intact, he is responsible for losses that are incurred even indirectly.

---

54. 67.
55. 14.
56. *Klal* 96:58.

According to this reasoning, one who did not borrow earrings, rather he just damaged one earring, would have to pay only $50 since he never accepted responsibility for the set of earrings.

In our case, Eli did not borrow his friend's apartment; rather he caused damage to just one wall, so it should be sufficient to paint just one wall. The other walls that are now mismatched are not Eli's responsibility.

However, we could differentiate between these two cases. Eli's neighbor does not want a painted wall. He wants all the walls to look uniform. If Eli cannot accomplish this by painting one wall, then he should paint all the walls. In other words, painting the wall is not called repairing the wall. A repaired state would translate into painting the wall the same color that it was (five years old), not to repair the wall so that it looks like it was painted recently. In addition, painting one wall without treating the other walls, as well, is in itself making the wall ugly. Just as we understand that Eli could not just paint the stains on the wall and leave the rest of the wall unpainted, because that would not look nice, so too Eli is required to paint all the walls.

Regarding earrings, each one is a separate entity. But all the walls of the room stand together and should be viewed as one unit. וצ״ע.

Even if Eli must paint all the walls, if his neighbor considers the freshly painted walls a benefit, he will have to pay Eli the small amount that the benefit is worth.[57]

---

57. See Shulchan Aruch, Choshem Mishpat 375:1.

Wet Paint

וְטָח אֶת הַבָּיִת

And plaster the house

(14:42)

Shmuel and Chaim are neighbors in a two-family home. The front of their house was sorely in need of a paint job. Shmuel decided to have the house painted in Chaim's absence, and since he could not paint only his side, as the house would look terrible if it was done only halfway, he had Chaim's side painted as well. When Chaim returned, Shmuel presented him with a bill for half the price of the painting. Chaim refused to pay. A short while later Shmuel noticed Chaim painting a small corner on his side that had remained unpainted. Shmuel took the opportunity to ask Chaim why he refused to pay for the painting of the house. Chaim replied that he did not have the money to pay for such an expense that he considered unnecessary. The small corner that he finished cost very little to paint, and that much he could afford. Does Chaim have to split the cost of painting the entire house?

The *Shulchan Aruch*[58] rules that although neighbors who share a courtyard may force each other to share certain expenses that pertain to their shared property, painting is not one of them. If, however, one of them painted on his own, and his neighbor expressed his consent to the painting, then the neighbor must share in the expense. According to this, Chaim, who expressed his pleasure in having the house painted, needs to pay Shmuel for the job.

---

58. *Choshen Mishpat* 161:1.

Had Chaim not painted his corner, he could have claimed his lack of interest in painting the house. Had he claimed that he painted his corner only because the house looked worse than before, since there was an unfinished patch, he also could be excused from paying, as painting his corner would not be an expression of consent that he is happy with the paint. He only painted the corner to remove the eyesore of a partially painted house. But now that he admitted that he is happy that the house is painted, even though he would not have gone through the expense, he is required to pay, like someone whose field needed to be planted, and someone else came and planted it for him. In such a case the halachah would be that the owner of the field must pay the planter whatever is less; the appreciation of the field because it is planted or the planter's expense. In our case Chaim must pay Shmuel either the increase of the value of Chaim's house now that it is painted or the expense that Shmuel incurred by painting Chaim's part of the house.[59]

59. See *Chazon Ish, Bava Basra* 2 § 3-6.

פרשת אחרי

Parashas Acharei Mos

It's Only Water

וְרָחַץ בַּמַּיִם אֶת בְּשָׂרוֹ וּלְבֵשָׁם

He shall immerse himself in water and then don them

(16:4)

Aharon washed his hands before performing the mitzvah of taking the *lulav*, and his hands were still wet when he held the *lulav*. Is the water a *chatzitzah* (a barrier) between his hands and the *lulav*, which would invalidate the mitzvah?[60]

The Mishnah in *Yoma*[61] states that on Yom Kippur the Kohen Gadol immersed himself and dried himself before he put on a new set of garments.

The *Tiferes Yisrael* explains that it was necessary for the Kohen Gadol to dry himself in order for the garments to remain dry and clean. The *Mishneh LaMelech* offers a different explanation, that the Kohen Gadol had to dry himself lest the water interfere

---

60. See *Shulchan Aruch, Orach Chaim* 651:7, *Mishnah Berurah* § 32.
61. 31b.

between his body and the garment. According to this opinion, it would have to be determined if water would interfere with the mitzvah to hold the *lulav*.

With regard to donning *tefillin,* the *Birkei Yosef* writes[62] that those who follow the opinion of the *Shela"h,* and wash the area where the *tefillin* rest, must dry the area well before putting on their *tefillin,* to preserve the honor of the *tefillin* and in order that the *tefillin* should rest directly on the body, similar to the Kohen's garments.

The *Amudei Or*[63] discusses this question, and records that someone tried to prove from the Gemara in *Succah*[64] that the *esrog* gets wet from the *lulav*, which implies that the *lulav* is wet when taken for the mitzvah. If so, the water is obviously not an interference. The *Amudei Or* rejects this proof, because maybe the area where it was held was dried prior to the performance of the mitzvah.

It would seem that this proof is not valid for another reason. Since the water was intended to preserve the *lulav,*[65] the water is considered as part of the *lulav* it is servicing. This would not be true about water used to wash one's hands.

The *Amudei Or* concludes that water is not a *chatzitzah*, based on the Gemara in *Zevachim*[66] that states that during the service in the *Beis HaMikdash*, the Kohen's foot must have direct contact with the floor, and yet the Gemara subsequently records[67] that blood on the floor was not considered a barrier since it was wet. Thus, water would likewise not be an interference between one's hand and the *lulav*.

------•◆•------

62. *Orach Chaim* 27:1.
63. 37.
64. 35b.
65. *Succah* 42a.
66. 24b.
67. 35a.

Special Delivery

וְשִׁלַּח אֶת הַשָּׂעִיר בַּמִּדְבָּר

And he should send the he-goat to the desert

(16:22)

 Bernie would love to send *Mishloach Manos* to his friend Moish who lives across town, but has no time to battle the traffic. His wife suggests that he call a messenger service that zips around town on mopeds. Bernie thought it was a great idea, and phoned the service. When the messenger arrived, it occurred to Bernie that it might be problematic to send *Mishloach Manos* with a messenger who is not Jewish. Does Bernie have to hire a Jewish messenger if he wants this *Mishloach Manos* to count for the mitzvah?

 Rabbi Akiva Eiger[68] asked this same question, if one could fulfill the mitzvah with a gentile messenger. The *Chasam Sofer* answered that had the mitzvah been to deliver the *Manos* personally, one would need a Jewish messenger in order to fulfill the mitzvah by proxy. However, since the mitzvah is to send the *Manos*, even a gentile messenger is sufficient.[69]

According to this, Responsa *D'var Avraham*[70] questions if the Yom Kippur scapegoat that was sent to Azazel to be thrown off a cliff could be sent via a child or a gentile, since the mitzvah requires simply that the goat be sent off.

Even without the *Chasan Sofer's* response, in our case, Bernie could send the *Mishloach Manos* with the gentile; since the

---

68. Quoted in *Sefer Likkutei Chaver,* notes on Responsa *Yehudah Ya'aleh (Orach Chaim* 204).
69. See also *Chasam Sofer, Gittin* 22b *"V'ha Lav."*
70. Vol. II, 8, § 1.

messenger is being paid for the service, he is not merely a messenger, but an employee. The *Nesivos*[71] writes that even though
ordinarily a gentile cannot be a proxy, it is permitted when he is
acting in his capacity as the Jew's employee.

The Yolk Is on Whom?

לֹא יֹאכַל דָּם

You may not consume blood

(17:12)

 Blimi borrowed an egg from her neighbor to make an
omelet. When she cracked it in a glass to check for a
blood spot she was dismayed to find that there was indeed
blood in the egg. Does she need to return an egg to her
neighbor, or since she was unable to use it, maybe she did
not borrow anything of value that needs to be returned?

 The *Shulchan Aruch* writes:[72] "One who sells eggs to
his friend, and they were found to be inedible (because
chicks started developing in them), the sale is null and
void, and the money should be returned to the buyer. However,
that is not the prevailing *minhag*, and the *minhag* supersedes the
law!" The *custom* is that the sale is in force, and the buyer has lost
his money. According to this, Blimi should have to pay her neighbor back for the "wasted" egg.

However, Rav Elyashiv ruled that the *"minhag"* the *Shulchan
Aruch* speaks about is relevant only to an egg salesman whose

---

71. 188 § 8.
72. *Choshen Mishpat* 232:19.

eggs are merchandise. Had he not sold it to a specific person, he would have sold it to someone else. Therefore he could claim that the fact that the buyer could not use the eggs is not a reason that the salesman should not receive payment for the eggs. This is not so regarding a neighbor whose eggs are meant for private use. Even if Blimi had not borrowed the egg, her neighbor would have had to take the loss on the egg anyway when the neighbor would have found the blood spot. In such an instance there is no prevailing *minhag* to require the one who found the blood spot to absorb the loss, and therefore Blimi does not need to return the egg.[73]

To Call or Not to Call I

וָחַי בָּהֶם

And by which he shall live
(18:5)

 A *Hatzalah* member received a call on Shabbos to respond to an emergency. He does not know if someone else has already answered the call. Should he call the base to find out before he sets out on his mission in order to prevent his driving on Shabbos? Similarly, if a *Hatzalah* member gets a call on Shabbos and he is on the other side of the city, should he call the base first to verify if an ambulance is already on the way?

---

73. Editors Note: Why can't the neighbor claim that she might have boiled the egg, and would never have found the blood? I asked the question to Rav Zilberstein. The *Rav* answered that if in reality the egg contained blood and may not be eaten, the spiritual damage caused by eating it far exceeds the value of one egg. Therefore she didn't suffer any loss.

A The Gemara in *Menachos*[74] states that if 10 people ran to pick figs on Shabbos in order to save a life, then even if in the end one fig was sufficient, they are all innocent of desecrating the Shabbos.

Rav Elyashiv, explaining the words of the *Ramban,*[75] says that the Gemara means that even though before one of them went to pick a fig, he could have verified if it was still necessary for him to go, he is still innocent from any sin as his actions were for the sake of saving a life. So too in our case, when the *Hatzalah* members do not call the base, and immediately answer the calls, they are innocent of any sin; to the contrary, they have done a great mitzvah.

Moreover, it appears that it is forbidden to call the base to find out if someone else took the call, since the verification is not for the sake of saving a life, only for the member to save himself from responding to the call for nothing. The *Parashas Derachim*[76] writes that one may not violate a less serious prohibition when his sole purpose is to prevent doing a more serious prohibition that would be allowed because it is related to saving a life. One may only violate a prohibition to save a life, not to save from worse violations.[77]

———◆◆◆———

---

74. 64b.

75. *Milchamos, Yoma* 4b.

76. *Derush* 19.

77. There are numerous reasons that many *Poskim* give to allow members to communicate with the base and respond only if they are closest. *Hatzalah* members should follow the protocols set by their local *Poskim*.

To Call or Not to Call II

וָחַי בָּהֶם

And by which he shall live

(18:5)

 A child came down with a high fever on Shabbos. The father could drive the child straight to the hospital, since a high fever could be life threatening. Should the father do so, or should he phone the doctor first and ask him if he should try to bring down the fever at home, thereby possibly avoiding taking his child to the hospital on Shabbos?

 Rav Elyashiv answered that if it would be normal procedure on a weekday to call the doctor first, one should do so on Shabbos as well.

Rav Zilberstein explained that apparently it is not similar to our previous discussion, the case of the *Hatzalah* member calling his base, where the call is made in order to protect violating the Shabbos unnecessarily. In the case of the child, if it is not necessary to take him to the hospital, it is better for the child's well-being to be at home. The hospital will not admit the child without reason, out of fear that he could catch something worse in the hospital. Therefore, calling the doctor is a lifesaving medical need, as much as taking him to the hospital, and is allowed on Shabbos.

פרשת קדושים
Parashas Kedoshim

A Business Expense

וְלִפְנֵי עִוֵּר לֹא תִתֵּן מִכְשֹׁל

And you shall not place a stumbling block before the blind
(19:14)

 Joseph Fine is the owner of a large corporation that is involved in multimillion-dollar business transactions in many different countries. One day he discovered that one of his vice presidents was embezzling money from the company. Joseph confronted him on several occasions, but the vice president denied taking any money. Joseph does not want to fire this particular employee because the corporation needs his skills. The amount of money he steals does not come close to the amount of profit he engenders. The only question is: Is Joseph allowed to retain him (and essenially give him license — without telling him — to continue his embezzling), or must he fire him so that he will not be an in violation of *"lifnei iver"* (literally, putting a stumbling block in front of someone, i.e., providing an opportunity to commit a crime)?

The Gemara in *Kiddushin*[78] relates that Rav Huna ripped a fine silk in front of his son Rabbah. He wanted to see if his son's reaction would be respectful or not. The Gemara questions Rav Huna's actions: Perhaps this would cause his son to get angry at him, thereby causing the son to sin? The Gemara answers that Rav Huna forgave his son in advance for any disrespect that would be shown. *Tosafos* adds that Rav Huna must have informed his son that he forgave him, for otherwise his son would be unaware that his father had negated the son's obligation to honor him, and the son would still be responsible for perpetrating an act that, according to his knowledge, would be a violation of his father's honor.

One may infer from *Tosafos* that it is wrong to allow someone to commit an act that he thinks is improper, even if in reality he is doing nothing wrong, since the deed was forgiven in advance. According to this, Joseph would be required to fire the vice president.

Our case, however, is different, since no action is being done to enable someone to sin. It is not similar to the case of Rav Huna who actively baited his son. Therefore it would not be necessary to remove the vice president from the position that gives him an opportunity to steal since in reality, he is not stealing, as his employer is willing to write the loss off as a necessary business expense.

Another reason to allow keeping the status quo would be based on a ruling of the *Maharil Diskin,*[79] that a person is not obligated to lose money in order not to violate *lifnei iver*. Since the vice president is responsible for significant income to the corporation, Mr. Fine would not have to let him go and forgo these earnings.

Rav Zilberstein ruled[80] that Joseph must fire the employee. Because he knows the man will continue to steal and Joseph gives him the opportunity to do so, it is tantamount to baiting him.

As for the *Maharil Diskin,* unlike the case where someone is being compelled to allow someone to sin, where he need not

---

78. 32a.
79. *Kuntrus Acharon* 145.
80. As reported by a close disciple.

take a loss, here Joseph is voluntarily keeping the man, which is prohibited.

━━━━━◆◆◆━━━━━

Driver's Test

off

וְלִפְנֵי עִוֵּר לֹא תִתֵּן מִכְשֹׁל

And you shall not place a stumbling block before the blind
(19:14)

 A wealthy American tourist landed in the airport in Lod. He hailed a taxi to Yerushalayim. In the middle of the trip the tourist looked through his pockets for his money, to no avail. Since it was night, and the cab was dark, he asked the driver for a flashlight so he could find his money. The driver claimed he did not have one. When he reached his destination, the passenger asked the driver to wait for him to bring a flashlight from his relative's house. As soon as the man entered his house, the driver drove away. It seemed the driver was hoping to find the money and keep it for himself.

The passenger went to a *Rav* and confessed that he had not really lost any money in the cab. He had just wanted to test the honesty of the driver! If the driver would drive away, hoping to find the lost money, he would never collect his fare for the trip from the airport! If the driver would prove his honesty by waiting, he would receive the payment he deserved. Did he have a right to teach the driver a lesson in integrity? If not, must he track down the driver to pay him the fare from the airport?

The passenger is guilty of two misdeeds: *lifnei iver*, for allowing the driver the opportunity to attempt to steal, and of telling a lie in order to avoid paying, in the event that the driver would drive away. *Bedi'avad*, he need not seek out the driver to pay the fare, since the driver knowingly gave up his fare, hoping to gain more by finding the lost money.

This is so only if the driver charged a fair price for the trip. If the passenger understood that the driver was taking advantage of his wealthy client, he would be allowed to fool the driver in order to save himself from overpaying.[81]

A Choice of Mitzvos

לֹא תַעֲמֹד עַל דַּם רֵעֶךָ
You shall not stand aside while your fellow's blood is shed
(19:16)

 Dr. Gross is on call, and has only one hour free on Purim night. He cleared this hour from his very busy schedule to allow himself to hear the *Megillah*. As he was leaving to shul, he received a phone call from a patient who was suffering great pain, and asked Dr. Gross to come administer drugs to relieve the pain. Which mitzvah should Dr. Gross choose to do this Purim night: *Megillah* reading or treating a patient in great, though not at all life-threatening, pain? (He will be able to do only one of them.)

It would seem that if the patient is in great pain, even though there is no danger to his life, the doctor should attend to him, even at the expense of missing *Megillah*

---

81. See *Yerushalmi Sotah* 3:3.

reading. Treating this patient is a *mitzvah min haTorah.*[82] The Gemara in *Kiddushin*[83] states that if a woman is being chased by a dog, every person is commanded by the Torah to save her. The *Meiri* explains that this obligation stems from the prohibition of *"Lo sa'amod al dam rei'echa,"* not to stand by idly when your friend's blood is being spilled. In addition, there is a positive command of returning your friend's lost property, which *Chazal* explain to include returning his body to its health.

The fact is that being bitten by a dog is not a threat to one's life, as is explained in *Bava Kamma,*[84] unless the dog is rabid. Evidently saving her from pain of being bitten is also a *mitzvah min haTorah.* If so, Dr. Gross also has a Torah command to attend to his patient. According to the *Rema,*[85] no Torah command is to be set aside in order to read the *Megillah.* Even according to the opinions that *Megillah* reading has priority over positive Torah commands, in our case there is a **prohibition** to stand by while your friend's blood is being spilled, and that has priority even over *Megillah* reading.

If the pain is at the level that had the doctor himself had the pain he would still have to hear the *Megillah*, he would not have to spare his friend from the same pain at the expense of hearing the *Megillah.* The mitzvah to heal a patient is learned from the mitzvah to return a lost item.[86] If one needs to return lost property, certainly one has to heal his friend, if he can. Anything of his own, that one would not trouble himself to recover, does not have to be returned to his friend, either. Similarly, one would not have to tend to his friend's pain, if had the doctor had such pain, he would also not treat it. If, however, the patient is forced to go into bed because of the pain, certainly such a condition would exempt someone from the obligation to hear the *Megillah*, and then Dr. Gross would have to treat him.

---

82. Of Biblical origin.
83. 8b.
84. 83a.
85. *Orach Chaim* 687:2.
86. See *Sanhedrin* 73a.

Mandatory Attendance? II

לֹא תִקֹּם

You shall not take revenge

(19:18)

Chananya received an invitation to Eli's son's bar mitzvah. He did not feel it necessary to attend, since Eli had not come to his son's bar mitzvah His wife suggested the possibility that maybe this would be considered taking revenge and therefore would be forbidden by the Torah. Is that prohibition applicable in this case?

The Gemara[87] states that the prohibition of taking revenge is limited to cases of money matters, e.g., if someone did not lend me his tools, and I wish to repay his unkindness. However, the *Rambam*[88] and the *Chinuch*[89] omit this limitation when they explain the prohibition of revenge, so apparently they rule that revenge is prohibited regardless of the misdeed, be it monetary or otherwise.[90]

In practice we do not consider revenge over non-monetary matters to be a Torah prohibition, but it is certainly not a practice of the pious. The Chofetz Chaim in his opening to his *sefer* says that since there is a difference of opinion as to whether non-

---

87. *Yoma* 23a.
88. Chapter 7, *Hilchos Dei'os*.
89. Mitzvah 241.
90. See *Minchas Chinuch* and *Chofetz Chaim* for an explanation of why the *Rambam* and the *Chinuch* do not contradict the Gemara.

monetary revenge is a Torah prohibition, one must be stringent in this matter.

If so, it would seem that he must attend the bar mitzvah.

However, if he is truly very busy, and attending the bar mitzvah would be very taxing, and he would only have made a special effort to reciprocate had Eli come to his son's bar mitzvah, then his lack of attendance is not an expression of any ill feeling toward Eli. He just does not feel obligated to overextend himself to attend. That would not be considered revenge.

Sincere soul-searching is necessary to discern the root of his desire not to attend. If he does have any ill will toward Eli, he would have to attend the bar mitzvah.

✦

Keeping Your Co-workers

וְאָהַבְתָּ לְרֵעֲךָ כָּמוֹךָ

You shall love your fellow as yourself

(19:18)

 Dr. Stern works in a hospital in Eretz Yisrael. One day he opened a letter he found in his in-box, and realized that the letter was actually intended for his co-worker, Dr. Fried. Dr. Fried is an expert at the top of his field, and this letter was offering him a prominent position in a foreign country at a salary much higher than he was currently earning. Dr. Stern knows that losing Dr. Fried would be a great loss for all of Eretz Yisrael, and he also knows that if he would inform the administration of the hospital of the pending offer, they would be able to offer competitive terms to ensure that Dr. Fried will remain. May Dr. Stern reveal to the hospital administration what he accidentally learned by opening his friend's letter?

 The *Kol Bo*[91] writes that there is a *"cherem"* of Rabbeinu Gershom against one who reads his friend's letters without permission. The Responsa *Chikekei Lev*[92] brings two possible reasons for the *"cherem."*

1) *V'ahavta l'rei'acha kamocha*, one certainly would not want someone else to open mail intended for him.

2) It is *geneivas da'as* (deceit).

The Responsa *Toras Chaim*[93] adds an additional reason, that it is considered stealing as he is using his friend's property without permission.

Even if one viewed the contents of his friend's letter by mistake, Responsa *Beis Dovid*[94] writes that the uninvited reader needs atonement. It is likely that Dr. Stern would be completely innocent, as he was an *"oneis"* (he had no reason to believe that someone else's letter had been placed in his box).

Dr. Stern is not doing his friend any harm by telling the hospital about the letter; on the contrary, he is obtaining for Dr. Fried a generous offer from the hospital. In addition, there is no deceit involved since he opened the letter unintentionally. Therefore Dr. Stern may inform the hospital that Dr. Fried might be leaving.

---

91. 116.
92. *Yoreh De'ah* 49.
93. Vol. III, 47.
94. *Yoreh De'ah* 158.

Uh! Uh! Nu!

וְאָהַבְתָּ לְרֵעֲךָ כָּמוֹךָ

You shall love your fellow as yourself

(19:18)

 The *Poskim* write that on Seder night one should not talk about anything that is not connected to the meal from after *Rachtzah* until after he has eaten the *korech*, in order that the *berachah* that he made on the matzah, as well as the *berachah* that he made on the *maror*, should count for the *korech* as well.[95] What would be the halachah in a case where a small child fell down and is crying right before the eating of the *korech*? Should one talk to the child to calm him down, and forfeit the preferred way of doing the mitzvah?

 To calm down a crying child is a fulfillment of the positive commandment of *V'ahavta l'rei'acha kamocha*, and takes precedence over this preferred way of doing the mitzvah of *korech*.

It is also possible that talking to the child would not be considered an interruption between *korech* and the *berachos*, since doing so is also related to the meal. How could one possibly concentrate and enjoy the mitzvah when a child is crying? The *Maharil*[96] expresses that anything that is related to the *seudah* is not an interruption.

---

95. See *Shulchan Aruch* 475:1.
96. *Minhagim Seder Haggadah.*

פרשת אמור
Parashas Emor

Kiddush Hashem

וְנִקְדַּשְׁתִּי בְּתוֹךְ בְּנֵי יִשְׂרָאֵל
Rather I should be sanctified among the Children of Israel
(22:32)

 A Holocaust survivor brought bloodstained fragments of a *Sefer Torah* into the *beis midrash*, and told the people learning there that her husband had given his life to save the *Sefer Torah* from the savage Nazis who had thrown it to the ground and trampled it. Is it permissible for a Jew to put his life in danger to preserve the honor of a *Sefer Torah*?

 The Gemara[97] relates that Nikanor traveled to Alexandria to purchase beautiful copper doors for the *Beis HaMikdash*. A storm broke out on his way home, and they needed to lighten the weight of the ship in order to save their lives, so they threw one of the doors overboard. When they wanted to throw over the second door, Nikanor embraced it

---

97. *Yoma* 38a.

and challenged them to throw him overboard together with the remaining door. Immediately the storm abated.

Rav Elyashiv asked: How could Nikanor forfeit his life for the sake of the door? There was no sin involved that justified giving up a life, and yet Nikanor's dedication was rewarded with a miracle. Why?

Rav Elyashiv answered that if Nikanor's door would have been thrown over it would have been a *chillul Hashem*. Nikanor had traveled all the way to Alexandria, and spent a considerable sum of money. If the doors would have been lost at sea, and all of his efforts would have been in vain, then people would conclude that beautifying the *Beis HaMikdash* is not that important after all. Saving the door was a *kiddush Hashem* and since Nikanor's intentions were pure, he was rewarded with a miracle.

In our case as well, the man made a *kiddush Hashem* in front of the beastly murderers by showing them that the Torah is so important that he would give his life for its honor, and that is permitted.

The *Ein Yaakov* differs in explaining Nikanor's motives. He maintains that Nikanor relied on the fact that those enroute to a mitzvah shall suffer no harm.[98] According to this view, during the Holocaust, when Jewish blood was spilled with such frequency and disregard, one would not be able to rely on the mitzvah to protect him.[99] Where harm is apparent, one may not be saved and therefore it would not be proper to risk one's life.

---

98. *Pesachim* 8b.
99. Ibid.

Priorities

וְעִנִּיתֶם אֶת נַפְשֹׁתֵיכֶם
And you shall afflict yourselves
(23:27)

 A cardiac patient required an angiogram to determine how to proceed with his treatment. The procedure was scheduled for the day before Yom Kippur. The patient asked his doctor if the procedure could be postponed until after Yom Kippur, and the doctor answered that it could. The difference between waiting or not, would amount to whether the patient could suffice with an intravenous tube on Yom Kippur, or if he would have to eat. Should the patient postpone the procedure so he can fast on Yom Kippur, or since there is a minimal danger in waiting, he should have it done as soon as possible?

 The *Shulchan Aruch* rules[100] that if one has an internal wound on Shabbos, we should do anything that we would do during the week in order to heal it. If, however, we know that there is no danger in waiting, no desecration of Shabbos is necessary. One should therefore wait to treat it, so as not to desecrate the Shabbos.

In our case, where the danger is unlikely and the doctor says that it could be postponed, it would seem that one should not undergo the procedure and negate the mitzvah to fast on Yom Kippur.

In truth, there is a difference between our case and that of the *Shulchan Aruch*. The *Shulchan Aruch* is discussing a case where one would be desecrating the Shabbos. In our case, he is having

---

100. *Orach Chaim* 328:4.

the procedure done in advance of Yom Kippur. As a result he will have to eat on Yom Kippur, but there is no desecration of Yom Kippur now. Later, when Yom Kippur comes, he will have to eat because of his health. To cause himself to have to eat on Yom Kippur is only a violation of a *Rabbinic* decree, and under these circumstances, where there is even a small chance of danger, the Rabbis never made their decree. Even if his intention in having the procedure right now is because he wants to eat on Yom Kippur, it would still be permitted because his health dictates that it is correct to undergo the procedure, whether his intentions are pure or not.

Which Mitzvah to Choose

וּלְקַחְתֶּם לָכֶם בַּיּוֹם הָרִאשׁוֹן

You shall take for yourselves on the first day

(23:40)

 A man bought two beautiful *esrogim*: one for himself and one for his father. Should he keep the nicer of the two for himself since in regard to mitzvos one's own life has priority, or should he give the nicer one to his father because of the mitzvah of *kibbud av*?

 The Gemara in *Succah*[101] relates that Rabban Gamliel, R' Yehoshua, R' Elazar ben Azaryah, and R' Akiva were on a ship, and only Rabban Gamliel had a *lulav*, for which

---

101. 41b.

he had paid 1,000 *zuz*. The Gemara explains that the mention of the price is to teach us how beloved the mitzvah was to "them."

The *Ben Yehoyada* asks how the Gemara teaches us that the mitzvah was precious to "them," if only Rabban Gamliel incurred the expense of buying the *lulav*. He explains that if Rabban Gamliel could pay such an amount, it must be that there was only one *lulav* available. That explains why only Rabban Gamliel had one. Since there was only one, it was only fitting to allow the *Nasi*, Rabban Gamliel, to buy it.

The *Ben Yehoyada* implies that even with regard to mitzvos it is proper to honor those greater than ourselves, and not to say that our own lives have priority.

However, the *Sha'arei Teshuvah*[102] records how one wealthy man sought to purchase a *lulav* for the *Rav*, Rav Dovid Cohen, and the father of the author of *Sheyarei Knesses HaGedolah* outbid him and bought the *lulav* for himself. He was rebuked for his disrespect to Harav Cohen, but he replied that although the *Rav* deserves tremendous honor, in regard to Hashem's mitzvos we do not give honor to others over ourselves, because a person has a greater obligation to himself to do Hashem's command than to any other person. He was praised for his answer.

In truth, there is no contradiction between the two episodes. In the case of the *Sha'arei Teshuvah*, only the person who bought the *lulav* would have the opportunity to do the mitzvah, as they did not live in the same area. In the Gemara in *Succah*, everyone was going to do the mitzvah, and there was only a question as to who would be allowed to buy the *lulav* in order to enable all of them to do the mitzvah. If it is a question of doing the mitzvah or not, one cannot afford to honor others, as one's own life has priority. On the other hand, if everyone will get to do the mitzvah, it would be proper to honor those greater than ourselves.

In our case, since both *esrogim* are beautiful, one should buy the nicer one for his father, as there is no issue of putting one's

---

102. 658 §12.

own life first. By giving his father the nicer one, he has a mitzvah of *kibbud av*, as well as the mitzvah of owning a beautiful *esrog*.

<hr />

The Chofetz Chaim's Preference

וּלְקַחְתֶּם לָכֶם בַּיּוֹם הָרִאשׁוֹן
You shall take for yourselves on the first day
(23:40)

 The story is told that one year there was an *esrog* shortage. In the entire town there was only one set of the *Arba'ah Minim* to be shared by all. Everyone took a turn holding the precious *lulav* and *esrog*. When it came to *Hallel*, the community wanted to honor the Chofetz Chaim with holding the *lulav* and *esrog* to shake during *Hallel*, but he refused. He explained that there were other *talmidei chachamim* present, and he did not want to be chosen over them. Why is that a reason to forgo something as important as shaking the *lulav* and *esrog*, which the Gemara[103] says has the power to protect from tragedy?

 The Gemara[104] says that when they would divide the *lechem hapanim* among the Kohanim, each Kohen would get the size of a bean. The humble ones would

---

103. *Succah* 37b.
104. *Yoma* 39a.

abstain totally, while the ravenous ones would take and eat.[105]

We see that there is a certain refinement that prevented them from taking a bean-sized piece of *lechem hapanim*, even though it was certainly a mitzvah to eat it. Since there was not enough for everyone, and by taking, it would cause someone else not to get, they abstained in order to leave it for someone else.

So, too, the modest Kohen, the Chofetz Chaim, understood that under such circumstances of having only one *lulav* for the whole city, certainly there would be others who would want to hold the *lulav*. So the Chofetz Chaim abstained in order to leave the honor to someone else.

The *Maharatz Chayes*[106] cites the question of the *Shevus Yaakov*, whether one who has only less than a *kezayis* of matzah, has a mitzvah to eat it at all, since it is less than the minimum amount required to fulfill the mitzvah.

He tries to prove from the fact that the modest Kohanim abstained, that there must be no mitzvah at all to eat less than a *kezayis*, for if there were a mitzvah, they would not have abstained. The *Chasam Sofer* dismisses this proof by saying that although there was a mitzvah, the obligation to eat the *lechem hapanim* is not on any specific Kohen; there is only a general obligation that it be eaten. The humble Kohanim abstained because as long as someone would eat it, the mitzvah would be accomplished.

According to this, there is no parallel to the *lulav*, where each person has an individual obligation and maybe one would be obligated to take it even though by doing so, others will have to be without.

It would seem that if there would be only one *kezayis* of matzah on Seder night, the Chofetz Chaim would not have refused the offer on the basis of sparing someone's feelings, since he had an

---

105. See also *Chullin* 133a.
106. On the *Gemara* in *Yoma* 39a.

actual obligation.[107] As the *Sha'arei Teshuvah* writes, when it comes to doing Hashem's mitzvos one does not refrain in order to honor his *Rav*. The reason why the Chofetz Chaim refused to take the *lulav* for *Hallel* is because shaking the *lulav* is only an addition onto the mitzvah. It shows one's love for the mitzvah and is not obligatory. The Chofetz Chaim would rather show love for the mitzvah of loving another Jew, as well as not causing pain to another Jew.

━━━━━ ◆ ━━━━━

Cramped Quarters

כִּי בַסֻּכּוֹת הוֹשַׁבְתִּי אֶת בְּנֵי יִשְׂרָאֵל

That I caused the Children of Israel to dwell in booths

(23:43)

 Nosson did not have a lot of space in which to build a *succah*. It was not really such a problem until his oldest son became bar mitzvah. Now the question arose as to how their small *succah* could accommodate two people for sleeping. There seemed to be two choices. Either father and son could sleep curled up next to each other, which would not be very comfortable, or they could take turns, the father sleeping in the *succah* one night, and the son on the next. What should they do?

 The *Rema*[108] rules in the name of the *Terumas HaDeshen* that one who cannot sleep in the *succah* because he does not have the room to stretch out his arms and legs

---

107. *Siman* 658.
108. 640:4.

must nevertheless sleep in the *succah* and does not have an exemption of *mitzta'er*. (One who does not enjoy living in the *succah* is exempt with the exception of eating a *kezayis* on the first night, because the Torah commanded to live in the *succah* only as one would live in his home. If one would leave his home because the standards are not livable, one may leave his *succah* under similar conditions.) The *Terumas HaDeshen* proves this from the fact that the minimum size of a kosher *succah* is 7 x 7 *tefachim*,[109] approximately 28 x 28 inches (70 x 70 cm.). The only way one could sleep in such a small *succah* is if he curls up. It must be that sometimes people sleep that way, and therefore that is not called *mitzta'er*.

Although the *Chacham Tzvi*[110] argues on the *Terumas HaDeshen*, the *Avnei Nezer*[111] brings a proof for the *Terumas HaDeshen* from *Rashi*. Therefore, if there is room for them both to sleep, albeit in a crowded position, they should do so.

The *Sha'arei Teshuvah*[112] quotes from Rav Hai Gaon that brothers or partners who share a small *succah* should take turns sleeping there on alternate nights. If they could share each night, they will certainly be blessed for their efforts.

In our case, however, where they are father and son, if there is only room for one of them, the father should sleep there all seven nights. Since the son is not a partner in the *succah*, the father's obligation takes precedence. If the father will give his son a turn to sleep in the *succah*, it will appear that the father does not have the proper respect for the mitzvah as he is willing to give it away.

———◆———

109. *Succah* 3a, *Shulchan Aruch, Orach Chaim* 634.
110. 94.
111. *Orach Chaim* 479.
112. 639:1.

The Best Way to Live

כִּי בַסֻּכּוֹת הוֹשַׁבְתִּי אֶת בְּנֵי יִשְׂרָאֵל

That I caused the Children of Israel to dwell in booths

(23:43)

 The Gemara brings a dispute as to the minimum size of a *succah*. According to everyone, 7 x 7 *tefachim* is sufficient, which is the minimum amount required for one's head, most of his body, and a small table (one handbreadth), and such is the halachah. One who has such a *succah*, but could invest in a *succah* that could contain his entire body, would that be preferable, or is it enough *le'chatchilah* to be mostly in the *succah*, as he has still fulfilled all the opinions with a *succah* that size?

 It would seem that the Gemara would not give a measurement with which one could not fulfill the mitzvah to its fullest.

However, Rav Chaim Kanievsky said that we find a similar situation at the Pesach Seder, where it is sufficient to drink most of the cup to fulfill the mitzvah of the "four cups" of wine, yet *le'chatchilah* (initially) one should drink the whole cup. So too, it is better to be fully inside the *succah*.

Without Rav Chaim Kanievsky's observation, we would have thought that since one must "live" in the *succah* the way one normally lives during the year, and since sometimes one sleeps with his feet sticking into a different room, therefore it would be sufficient to do the mitzvah of *succah* in that way as well, even *le'chatchilah*.

Rav Elyashiv proved that one does not need to be fully in the *succah*, from the fact that one could put his feet under the table. Sitting under a bed or table that is ten *tefachim* high is equivalent to sitting outside the *succah*, and yet no one is careful to sit with their feet sticking out from under the table. It must be that it is sufficient that one is mostly in the *succah*.[113]

(See also *Tosafos* in *Rosh Hashanah*,[114] where he explains that there is no violation of *bal tosif* by making a four-walled *succah*, even though it is sufficient to have just three, since four walls are better since they are more livable. Having a *succah* that can contain the entire person would also seem to be more livable, and thus a better way to fulfill the mitzvah, albeit not the mandatory way to do the mitzvah.)

Oops ! Sorry

וּמַכֵּה בְהֵמָה יְשַׁלְּמֶנָּה

One who strikes an animal shall make restitution
(24:21)

 Daniel placed his glasses on the bench next to him in shul. His friend Yosef came to sit next to him, and cracked the glasses in half. Does Yosef have to reimburse Daniel for the damage that was done?

 It would seem that Yosef needs to pay, because people are liable for their actions, even if those actions are unintentional.[115] Rav Elyashiv ruled that we cannot obligate

---

113. Editor's Note: In the olden days, when they would eat in a reclining position it seems that they did not put their legs under the table, especially if the whole table was only one *tefach* wide. Nowadays, our tables are about 30 inches (76.2 cm.) high, which is less then 10 *tefachim*, and therefore there would be no reason not to put one's legs under the table. Rav Elyashiv's proof would seem to be from the fact that there is no mention of a restriction not to put one's legs even under a higher table.
114. 28b.
115. *Bava Kamma* 3b.

him in *beis din* to pay, because everyone has a right to use the shul. Yosef sat where he was allowed to sit. It is as if Daniel had put his glasses on Yosef's living-room chair. Daniel should have been careful not to put his glasses on Yosef's seat!

It is also similar to a shared yard that is designated for leaving cattle and not for leaving fruits. If one partner's cow ate a different partner's fruits, there would be no obligation to pay. Here, as well, the seats are provided for sitting, and not for leaving fragile eyewear.

Nevertheless, it would seem that Yosef has an obligation *b'dinei Shamayim* to pay for Daniel's glasses, even though the earthly courts cannot force him to pay.

פרשת בהר
Parashas Behar

Conflicting Interests

וְחֵי אָחִיךָ עִמָּךְ

And let your brother live with you

(25:36)

A man was injured in a car accident and lost sight in one of his eyes. The hospital determined that he was 35 percent handicapped. When he submitted his claim to the insurance company to collect damages, the company sent him to their doctor for evaluation. Upon examination the doctor revealed that the other eye had also suffered damage, which placed the patient in the category of 60 percent handicapped. The doctor came to ask if he is required to tell the patient about the additional handicap. This would entitle the claimant to a larger settlement, but since the insurance company will view his diagnosis as "traitorism" against them, they will stop sending him patients for evaluation. Is he obligated to lose their patronage?

*A*Rav Elyashiv answered that the insurance company is obligated to pay the victim retribution because of the payments they received from the assailant. If they will not pay the victim his full due they will be guilty of stealing from the victim. Therefore the doctor should reveal the patient's true level of handicap so that the patient can receive full payment. It is as if he bears testimony that could benefit his friend. He is obligated to come testify on his behalf.[116]

However, if the doctor will lose business from the insurance company, it makes sense that he would not have to tell, since his own loss has priority over the loss of his friend. Even so, the *Shulchan Aruch*[117] says that one should go beyond one's obligation and not be so exacting to put his own interests first, unless he will certainly sustain the loss. Even under such circumstances, if the doctor could let the patient know "off the record" that he is entitled to more, he should do so.

Too Cheap to Be True

אַל תּוֹנוּ אִישׁ אֶת אָחִיו

Do not aggrieve one another

(25:14)

Yoel was passing a wine store the day before Purim and noticed a display of a familiar wine. He asked the salesman for the price.

The salesman responded that it was 18 shekels.

---

116. See *Shulchan Aruch, Choshen Mishpat* 28:1.
117. *Choshen Mishpat* 264:1.

Yoel thought that at such a price, he could buy a large quantity of the wine and distribute them for *Mishloach Manos*. He loaded up the trunk of his car, and paid for the wine.

After Purim Yoel wanted to buy some more of the same wine for himself. He brought a few bottles to the counter and asked how much it cost. It was a different salesman who informed Yoel that the wine cost 50 shekels per bottle.

Yoel asked how there could be such a discrepancy in the price now than from before Purim. The salesman answered that before Purim he had been very busy and had asked his father to sit at the counter. His father had made a mistake when he quoted a price of 18 shekels, and had sold tens of bottles at a loss! The salesman requested that Yoel pay the difference on each bottle that he had bought! Is he required to do this, as it was not his fault?

 When a bottle of wine costs 50 shekels and is mistakenly sold for 18 shekels, since the discrepancy is more than a sixth of its price, this constitutes a *"bitul mekach,"* a retroactive nullification of the sale.[118] Therefore, the customer must return the bottles or pay the difference in price.

In Yoel's case, he had already distributed the bottles to his friends on Purim. Had it not been for the inexpensive price, he never would have been so generous. He would have given his friends a less expensive wine instead. In addition, Yoel had been misled, albeit accidentally, by the salesman's father, who had been left in charge of the store. It would therefore seem sufficient for Yoel to pay the amount of his benefit.

The Gemara in *Kesubos*[119] states a halachah concerning chil-

---

118. *Shulchan Aruch, Choshen Mishpat* 227:1.
119. 34b.

dren whose father died, and had left a cow in the yard. The children mistakenly thought that it was their father's cow, so they slaughtered it and ate it. Afterward, they discovered that the cow had actually been borrowed from someone else. The halachah is that they must pay two-thirds of the price of the meat. The *Rashbam*[120] explains that this halachah is relevant to anyone who ate something for which he did not have reason to believe that he would have to pay. Had Yoel known he would have to pay 50 shekels, he would not have bought the wine. Therefore, if he cannot return the wine, he can claim that he only has to pay two-thirds, which is the value of his benefit.

However, one *Rav* claimed that the scenarios are not comparable. In the Gemara in *Kesubos*, the children had no idea that the cow may not belong to their father, and are really not to be blamed.[121] In Yoel's case, he should have known that 18 shekels was a very cheap price, and he should have verified that there was no mistake being made. Therefore we cannot allow him to pay only two-thirds. However, since he was not totally at fault either, we should make a compromise and have him pay the cost price, which is approximately 40 shekels.

In a similar incident, a man once bought an old *sefer* from a store owner for an inexpensive price. The next day, the seller claimed that he had made a mistake and asked for additional money. The customer went to ask the Chazon Ish, who answered that there was no obligation to add money, since an old *sefer* does not have a set price, and it was bought from the owner himself. It would only be *middas chassidus* to do so. In Yoel's case, the wine had a set price, and the discrepancy was clear. This is in addition to the fact that the customer was minimally at fault.

------- ◆ -------

120. *Bava Basra* 146b, s.v. *Shamin.*
121. See *Tosafos, Bava Kamma* 27b s.v. *Shmuel.*

A Misinformed Seller

וְאִישׁ כִּי יִמְכֹּר בֵּית מוֹשַׁב

If a man shall sell a residence

(25:29)

 Itzik contacted a broker to locate a buyer for his house. The broker sent Mr. Silver, who was willing to pay a certain amount for the house. Itzik agreed to the price, and they signed a contract. The next day Itzik met his old friend Motti, and told him that he had just sold his house. Motti asked Itzik why he had not wanted to sell the house to him. It seems that Motti had already offered the broker an even higher price than Itzik agreed to with Mr. Silver. Itzik was surprised; he had not known about Motti's offer. Certainly if the broker had informed him of this, he would have sold the house to his friend. Upon further investigation, it seemed that Mr. Silver had agreed to pay the broker a higher fee for his services, and therefore the broker had only told Itzik about Mr. Silver's offer, and not Motti's. May Itzik claim that the sale was a mistake, and sell the house to his friend Motti?

 There was no mistake in the sale. Itzik agreed to sell the house for the amount that was offered. His mistake was in something external to the sale.

The Gemara in *Kiddushin*[122] states that if one secured an agent to marry a woman on his behalf, and instead of the agent acting on behalf of the one who sent him, he married the woman himself, the marriage is valid despite the fact that the agent has

---

122. 58b.

acted dishonestly. The *Ran* asks: Why would one have thought that the marriage should not be valid? He explains that one might have thought that had the woman known that the one who sent the agent was interested in marrying her, she never would have accepted the agent's offer to marry her, and therefore the marriage is a mistake. That is why the Gemara needed to tell us that the marriage is valid nevertheless, as the mistake was not about the marriage itself, rather in an external detail.

Rav Meir Arik[123] used this as the basis for his ruling that even if a man had sold a *Sefer Torah* because he was unaware that it is prohibited to do so, the sale is nevertheless valid.

In our case, even though the sale is valid, the *beis din* should fine the broker the excess amount that he was paid as an agent's fee for acting dishonestly with Itzik. The broker was unfaithful, and did his job without loyalty to his client. He certainly does not deserve to be paid extra for a job done improperly.

Seller Beware

וְאִישׁ כִּי יִמְכֹּר בֵּית מוֹשָׁב

If a man shall sell a residence

(25:29)

 Shalom needed a kidney transplant and was desperate for cash. He approached a broker in order to sell his house to the highest bidder.

After two days, the broker returned, saying that the only buyer he has is willing to pay $150,000. Shalom had no choice, so he accepted the offer. Afterward,

---

123. *Sefer Minchas Pittim.*

Shalom discovered that the buyer was actually the broker himself. It was true that he had not found another buyer, so he had bought it for himself. A few months later the broker sold the house for $250,000.

Shalom summoned the broker to a *din Torah*. Shalom claimed that his house was actually worth $250,000, and that the broker had not exerted himself to sell it, because he wanted to buy it for himself cheaply, in order to make a large profit. The broker claimed that there really was no buyer interested in Shalom's house, and since he knew that Shalom needed the money desperately, he decided to do Shalom a favor by buying his house. The broker reasoned that he would be able to sell the house without pressure for a higher price, and so he did. Who is entitled to the extra $100,000?

 The Gemara in *Kesubos*[124] declares that a widow who appraised the estate of her late husband for the purpose of acquiring it herself in fulfillment of the *kesubah* has not accomplished anything. She must have the estate appraised by *beis din* and sold to a third party. The reason for this is because when she takes the property for herself, she did not buy it from a second party, i.e., the *beis din* or the heirs, and the property remains as it was. Had she had sold the property to someone else, she would have the power to make the sale and take the proceeds for her *kesubah*.

The *Tur*[125] quotes the *Rashba*, who infers from this Gemara that an agent to sell a property cannot acquire the property for himself, even if he pays the price that was set by the owner. The agent is empowered to sell the property to a buyer, but not to himself. A transfer of ownership is required, and a person cannot transfer something from himself to himself. Since the agent is in place of the owner, no transfer can occur without another party's involvement.

---

124. 98a.
125. *Choshen Mishpat* 185.

The *Tur* writes elsewhere[126] that when one appoints an agent to sell a field, the agent may not buy the field for himself, even if he shares a common border with the field for sale, because he is not trusted to make the deal honestly since he has a vested interest. This is the same as a trustee, who must sell to others and may not sell to himself.

The *S'ma* asks why the *Tur* designated the reason of an agent to be that he lacks the ability to transfer ownership, and about one who shares a border that he is not trusted.

The *S'ma* explains that in the case of the agent, the seller wanted to retract, while in the case of the one who shares a border, the seller did not object. The *S'ma* gives an additional answer: It depends if the seller had set the price. If the price is set, there is no suspicion upon the agent, whereas if the price was left open, there is room for suspicion that the agent will not offer a fair price.

According to this, had Shalom empowered the broker to sell the house, and his intention was for the broker to represent him in the sale, there would be three reasons why the broker could not buy the house for himself.

1) There is no one to sell it to him, as he is acting as both the seller and the buyer.

2) He is putting himself under suspicion that he has his own interests at heart and not that of the owners, which according to the *S'ma* would invalidate the sale if the seller wished to retract.

3) The seller did not set a price and therefore the agent cannot buy it for himself.

In contrast, Shalom's broker was only given the job of finding a buyer and not of selling the house. Therefore the first reason does not apply. The reason of suspicion itself however is sufficient to invalidate the sale.

Rav Chaim Kanievsky added that since the Gemara makes it clear that a custodian cannot sell a property to himself, and this ruling is reflected in *Shulchan Aruch*, when someone gives a

---

126. *Choshen Mishpat* 175.

property to an agent for sale it is as if the seller has specified that he wants to sell it to someone other than the agent. Accordingly, the broker cannot buy the property for himself and the profit the broker made should go to the original owner. וצ״ע.

Your Life Has Priority

וְחֵי אָחִיךָ עִמָּךְ
And let your brother live with you
(25:36)

 An American tourist visited Russia during the days of religious persecution. Before he returned home, the people begged him to leave them his *tefillin*, as all of their *tefillin* were *pasul* and they could not get others because of the Iron Curtain. If he would leave them his *tefillin*, tens of Jews would be able to wear *tefillin* every day. The tourist would be happy to give them his *tefillin*, except for the fact that if he would do so, he would miss one day of wearing *tefillin*, since he would not arrive in the United States until one day had gone by. What should he do?

 It would appear that he should take his *tefillin* with him, because his mitzvah take precedence over theirs. In addition, they are prevented from wearing *tefillin* due to duress, whereas he would be willfully ignoring his obligation to wear his *tefillin* every day, even though it is for a good cause.

One may infer this from the *Mishnah Berurah*:[127] "A man who has a special *esrog*, and in a different city there is no *esrog*, it is better for him to send them his *esrog*, and he will use the *esrog* that belongs to his community. The *Machatzis HaShekel* writes that in our times it often happens that after a few days of Succos have passed, the community's *esrog* becomes ruined from being handled by so many people, so perhaps one would not have to send away his own *esrog* for the benefit of his friend."

We see from the *Mishnah Berurah* that although one could provide another city with hundreds of mitzvos, one's own mitzvah has priority.

The *Sha'arei Teshuvah*[128] also seems to concur in a case where two Jews are in jail, or in a desert, and have only one *kezayis* of matzah. He rules that the one who has it should eat it himself. For if in life-and-death situations one must save his own life first, when it comes to spiritual matters, certainly one's own spiritual life comes first! This is how the *Igros Shmuel* explains why Boaz stressed to the redeemer that Rus was a Moabite, in order to dissuade him from marrying her, so that *Boaz* could marry her. For Boaz had seen with *ruach hakodesh* that Rus would bear the Davidic dynasty, and every person is commanded to enrich his soul and gather mitzvos.

Moreover, Rav Elyashiv said that if two people had only a half a *kezayis* of matzah each, according to the *poskim* who rule that there is a mitzvah to eat a half a *kezayis* (even though one has not completely fulfilled the mitzvah by doing so) neither person must give up his portion so that at least one of them should have a complete mitzvah.

The Gemara in *Berachos* tells how R' Eliezer freed his *eved Cena'ani* (Canaanite slave) in order to enable him to be the 10th man in a *minyan*. The Gemara questions how he could do so, since there is a mitzvah not to free an *eved Cena'ani*. The Gemara

---

127. 658 § 42.
128. 482.

answers that it was for the sake of allowing many to do a mitzvah. This would seem to contradict everything we have said until now!

However, the answer is that there is a distinction between violating a prohibition and accomplishing a mitzvah. Even though a negative command is more stringent as it carries a penalty of *malkos* (flogging), whereas failing to fulfill a positive command has no penalty, on the other hand, *teshuvah* wipes away a transgression of a negative command, but cannot replace the lost opportunity of doing a positive mitzvah.[129]

In our case as well, although one may violate the prohibition of freeing an *eved Cena'ani* in order to allow the public to do a mitzvah, this is because the *Rabbanan* understood that such a need is ample justification to do so, yet to give up one's chance to put on *tefillin* for a day, which is an irreplaceable loss, one should not do. To send out an *eved Cena'ani* in such a case is not considered a transgression, since the benefit justifies the act of setting him free, whereas giving away one's *tefillin* cannot be considered as if he put them on. Therefore, one's own spirituality comes first, and one should not forgo his own mitzvah in order to give opportunity to those who are otherwise not obligated, since it is beyond their capability.

---

129. See *Avnei Nezer* II, 455 § 3.

פרשת בחקתי
Parashas Bechukosai

The Right to Remain Silent

וּשְׁכַבְתֶּם וְאֵין מַחֲרִיד

And you will lie down with none to frighten you
(26:6)

There is a quiet neighborhood on the outskirts of the city. Certain residents want public transportation to service the neighborhood. Other residents vehemently oppose this plan, as the traffic will increase the noise level in the neighborhood. Upon further investigation it was discovered that all the people who object to bringing in buses have their own cars, and do not use buses. May they still object?

The Mishnah in *Pe'ah*[130] states that *pe'ah* is given while it is still attached to the ground. Even if 99 poor people request that the *pe'ah* be divided among the poor and

---

130. 4:1-2.

not left attached, and one man wants that the *pe'ah* be left to the first taker, we listen to the single individual, since his words are in accordance with the halachah. The *Tosafos Yom Tov* adds that even if that one person is stronger than all the others, and therefore has the best chance of grabbing it, we still listen to him, since his words are according to the halachah.

Therefore, if the neighbors who object to the buses have the law on their side, it is irrelevant whether they own cars or not.

The Gemara in *Bava Basra*[131] states that one may prevent his neighbor from opening a store in their shared courtyard by claiming that he will be disturbed by customers coming and going. Therefore, we would have to decide the status of this neighborhood, by determining: a) if it was originally built on the outskirts of the city so that it would be a quiet neighborhood, and b) who stands to lose more, the neighbors who need the public transportation or the neighbors who want quiet streets. If public transportation is available within a short distance, and the noise is really disturbing, the objection would be justified even if the neighborhood was not meant to be especially quiet. We will not punish the objectors, and subject them to undue noise, just because Hashem gave them cars.

The Chazon Ish writes[132] that there is a difference between one who disturbs his neighbor by doing something that is essential for living as opposed to something that most people do not do. For example, a neighbor has no right to complain about crying babies who disturb his sleep, since that is a normal use of a home.

According to this, we could say that buses are not an essential part of a neighborhood, while peace and quiet are crucial to the character of a peaceful neighborhood. Therefore the ones who do not want the buses have a legitimate claim. The ones who need the bus will have to walk to catch one, provided the closest bus stop is within reasonable distance.

131. 20b.
132. *Bava Basra* 13.

Measure for Measure II

אַף אֲנִי אֶעֱשֶׂה זֹּאת לָכֶם

Then I will do the same to you

(26:16)

 Boruch was on his way to buy a lottery ticket when he spotted his friend, Dovid. Boruch suggested to Dovid, that since according the Gemara,[133] "The fortune of two is better than that of one," they should each have in mind to buy a lottery ticket for the both of them, and they will be partners in the tickets, as well as the prize. Dovid agreed, and each went on their way.

The next time they met, it was after the drawing, and again Boruch had an offer for Dovid. "I do not know the numbers on your ticket, and you do not know the numbers on mine. Let's decide that each of us will keep the tickets that we are holding." Boruch's motive for doing so was that he had already checked the results of the drawing, and his ticket had won 50,000 shekels.

Surprisingly, Dovid agreed that Boruch could be the sole owner of the ticket he was holding, and Dovid would be the sole owner of the ticket that he was holding.

It was not until later that Boruch discovered that while his ticket had won 50,000 shekels, Dovid's ticket had won 200,000 shekels. Dovid had known this already, which explains why he agreed to Boruch's offer

---

133. *Bava Metzia* 105a.

to dissolve their partnership. Can Boruch invalidate his offer?

The *Maharsham*[134] was asked about someone who sold a lottery ticket after the drawing had already taken place, and the seller had been unaware that he was selling the winning ticket. The question was if the sale was binding or if it could be invalidated, as the seller would never have sold it had he known that his ticket had won.

The *Maharsham* quoted the Gemara in *Kesubos*[135] that tells of a drought that affected the city of Nehardea, and there was no food for its citizens. People sold their houses, preparing to relocate to a place where they would have sustenance. Shortly afterward, a large shipment of grain arrived, and there was plenty of food for everyone. Rav Nachman ruled that all the sales of houses were invalid because they were sold based on a false premise. The sellers did not realize that the shipment was on its way. Had they known, they never would have sold their houses. In the case of the lottery ticket as well, perhaps the sale is invalid because the seller did not know the true value of his ticket.

On the other hand, if the seller could have verified whether his ticket had won, and he did not do so, he cannot claim that he sold the ticket by mistake. The *Maharsham* concludes that since the seller knew that the drawing had already taken place, the sale was with the understanding that any possible gain should belong to the buyer. Certainly if the possibility existed to check the results of the lottery at the time of the sale, it would be obvious that no claim exists to invalidate the sale, as the seller knowingly sold the ticket without concern if it had won. Only if the seller had not known that the drawing had already taken place could he have claimed that the sale was invalid, as in that case he was unaware of the ticket's real value.

---

134. Vol. II, 34.
135. 97a.

In our case as well, the final agreement was not a mistake. Since Boruch could have found out what Dovid's numbers were, by not doing so, he is responsible for his own loss. Boruch fulfilled that which is said "as he has done, so will be done to him."[136]

———◆———

Absolute Value

וְהֶעֱרִיךְ הַכֹּהֵן אֹתָהּ

The Kohen shall evaluate it

(27:12)

 A man walked into the grocery store to do some shopping. As he was strolling down the aisle, his hand brushed one of the bottles of wine, and it fell to the floor with a great impact. Wine splattered and glass shattered. Obviously, the man has to pay for the bottle of wine. Even though it was an accident, a person is always responsible for his actions.[137] The question remains: How much does he need to pay? The owner of the store bought the bottle at wholesale price, but he sells it at the retail price. Does the customer only have to replace the store owner's cost, or, since the bottle has a value of its retail price because that is how much it is sold for in the store, the customer should have to pay that price?

 The *Shulchan Aruch*[138] rules that a delivery man who breaks a barrel of wine has to pay the store owner. If on market day the barrel is sold for $4.00, and on

---

136. *Vayikra* 24:19.
137. *Bava Kamma* 3b, *Adam mu'ad l'olam*.
138. *Choshen Mishpat* 304:5.

a regular day only $3.00, then if the damage happened on market day, the delivery man needs to pay $4.00. This proves that the damage is estimated according to the sale price.

One could argue that on market day one cannot buy wine for less than $4.00. Certainly if a store owner bought the wine for $10.00, and because of inflation the price went up to 20, the customer could not pay just $10.00. In such a case it is obvious that the value of the wine is more than his cost, and the damage is estimated by the value of the object. Similarly, on market day, the wine has greater value. In our case however, there are two prices for the wine, concurrently — the wholesale price and the retail price. It is not similar to market day, where there is only one value for a barrel of wine.

It would seem that the customer could request that the next time the storekeeper buys from his wholesaler, he should buy an extra bottle to replace the broken one, at the customer's expense. That way the customer will have to pay only the wholesale price. For the store owner to refuse would be *middas S'dom* as he stands to lose nothing.[139]

One scholar wanted to argue that the reason the retail price is higher is because of the store's overhead, i.e. rent, utilities, etc. Therefore, the customer should have to add the additional expenses that are included in the price of the wine. In truth, it seems that the expenses are incurred only for the sake of people who come to buy, and not for someone who damaged the merchandise. One who buys the wine pays for the service of being able to buy the wine. One who has to pay for damaging merchandise is not enjoying the convenience of buying wine in the store, and therefore does not have to pay for the store owner's expenses.

---

139. Editor's Note: It is not similar to the bottles in the hotel (see "It's the Ambiance," *Parashas Shemos*, p. 144), which are meant for sale, and the hotel is opposed to having the bottles replaced. In this case the bottle is broken, and cannot be sold. At this point, the store owner has nothing to lose. Certainly if the customer owned a bottle of the same wine he could replace the broken bottle. Therefore, he can ask the store owner to buy him one. This would not be the case in the incident with the hotel's bottles.

If the store owner has an agreement with his suppliers that he can be credited for broken items by producing the broken bottle, no payment is necessary.

ספר במדבר

Sefer Bamidbar

פרשת במדבר
Parashas Bamidbar

Going Down?

שְׂאוּ אֶת רֹאשׁ וכו'

Take a census

(1:2)

The sign on the elevator said clearly, "OCCUPANCY: 4 Adults." None of the five people who entered the elevator bothered to read the sign, until the elevator jolted to a halt in between floors. The elevator had broken from the exertion of pulling the additional weight.

Who needs to pay for the repair? All of them, the last one who entered the elevator, or the one who pushed the button for their destination?

The *Shulchan Aruch*[1] rules, "If five men sat on a bench together, resulting in a broken bench, the halachah is as follows: If they all sat down at the same time, they all need to pay. If the fifth man sat down last, then it depends. If the

---

1. *Choshen Mishpat* 381:1.

bench would have broken even without his weight, he is exempt. But if it was due to his weight that the bench broke, he alone must pay for the bench's repair."

This is applicable if the fifth person entered the elevator and subsequently someone on a different floor summoned the elevator. In such a case the fifth person must pay since he is responsible for the damage. He should have known that someone might call for the elevator without knowing that there was additional weight in the elevator. (The fact that the fifth passenger did not know the weight limit is not an excuse, as a person is responsible for any damage he does, even accidentally.)[2] However, if it was one of the five passengers who pressed the button to a destination, then the one who pressed is responsible to pay for the repair because he made the elevator move with five people on board. Even if it was the first person who pressed it after the fifth person boarded, he is liable because he had no right to press the button with so many people in the elevator.

———◆◆◆———

Hashem Knows

וְהוֹרִדוּ אֶת פָּרֹכֶת הַמָּסָךְ

And take down the Partition-curtain

(4:5)

 The custom of Congregation Magen David was to sell the *Pesichah* (opening of the *aron hakodesh*) for Neilah on Yom Kippur for a significant sum. One year, no sooner had the purchaser climbed the platform to draw

---

2. *Bava Kamma* 3b.

the *Paroches*, when a young child drew the curtain and opened the *aron hakodesh*. The *gabbaim* were aghast. What should they do? Should they close the *aron hakodesh* again to allow the man to open it, or should the man be absolved from paying since someone else did the mitzvah?

It would seem that the man still has to pay. The man "purchased" the honor and it was now his. Just because someone else stole his mitzvah, why should he not have to pay for what he bought?

Rav Elyashiv did not see it that way. It is clear from the words of the *Ran*[3] that the mitzvah is not actually sold. Rather, a person obligates himself to give money in return for having done the mitzvah. According to this, if he never did the mitzvah, he has no reason to pay.

On the other hand, the *Chasam Sofer* writes[4] in the name of the *Shav Yaakov* that one who recited a *Kaddish* that was supposed to be said by his friend, has not only gained nothing for himself, but he has also not taken anything away from his friend. The *Kaddish* is attributed to the one for whom it was originally intended to be said. This is supported by the Gemara in *Bava Kamma* that states that one who stole his friend's offering and sacrificed it for himself does not need to pay his friend. Since Hashem knows whose offering it was, it is attributed to its true owner, and therefore it is considered as if it had been returned to its rightful owner.

According to this, perhaps the merit of opening the *aron hakodesh* still belongs to the man who was supposed to have done it. Therefore, he must pay for the mitzvah.[5] וצ״ע.

3. *Shabbos* 64a, in the pages of the *Rif*.
4. *Yoreh De'ah* 345.
5. See "The Most for Your Money," *Parashas VeZos HaBerachah*, p. 476)

פרשת נשא
Parashas Nasso

An Outstanding Loan Payment

וְנָתַן לַאֲשֶׁר אָשַׁם לוֹ
And give it to the one to whom he is indebted
(5:7)

 Dov borrowed $100,000 from his friend Meir. When the loan came due, Meir asked Dov to repay the loan promptly as Meir owed $100,000 to the bank and would face severe penalties if he would not repay his loan on time. Dov visited Meir's bank without Meir's knowledge, and informed them that Meir did not have the money to repay his loan. Dov made the following proposal to the bank's manager. Dov would pay the bank $60,000 today, if they would erase Meir's loan totally. Otherwise, Dov would pay them nothing, and the bank would have to struggle to get their money from Meir, and they would risk never being paid. The bank manager researched the options, and decided to accept Dov's offer. When

Meir heard what had happened he asked Dov to pay him the remaining $40,000, since he had only given the bank $60,000. Is he justified?

A The *Shulchan Aruch* rules:[6] One who sent an agent to collect a loan from an idolater who, by mistake, overpaid the loan, the profit belongs to the messenger. If however, the messenger was sent to repay a loan and the lender denies having loaned the money, the messenger must return the money to the one who sent him. The *S'ma* explains that any new income belongs to the messenger, whereas any money that belonged until now to the one who sent him, remains in the owner's possession. According to this, since the bank's agreement to forgive $40,000 is not new income, it would seem that Dov would still have to give Meir his money.

However, the *Shulchan Aruch*[7] rules that a widow who wishes to forgive a debt owed to her late husband has no right to do so, since it is not hers to forgive, and it must be repaid to the man's heirs. The *Taz* explains that this is specifically when the heirs have other funds to pay the widow her *kesubah*. But if she can collect her *kesubah* only from the repayment of this loan, she is considered the owner of the loan and may forgive it.

In our case, since Meir owes the bank, and Dov owes Meir, it is as if Dov owes the bank.[8] And if the bank manager forgave "Dov's" loan, he would not have to pay the difference to Meir.

However, since in actuality the bank, in accordance with its protocol, would never try to collect from Meir's debtor, there would be no real obligation from Dov to the bank. Therefore, it would seem that the bank cannot forgive the debtor's loan either. On the other hand, if the bank would come to a Jewish court, they could collect the money from Dov, and therefore maybe they could indeed forgive Dov's loan. וצ"ע.

---

6. *Choshen Mishpat* 183:7-9.
7. *Even HaEzer* 96:6.
8. This is known as *Shibuda D'Rebbi Nassan;* see *Kiddushin* 15a.

It should be noted that the bank does not actually erase the discrepancy between the original loan and the amount that was repaid; rather they pay it to themselves as a bank expense. Therefore it could be that Dov paid the loan in full, between his money and the bank's money. וצ"ע.

———◆◆◆———

Would You Care for Another Cheese Blintz?

וּמָחָה אֶל מֵי הַמָּרִים

And erase it into the bitter waters

(5:23)

 Nachman stopped at a local restaurant on his way home from work. He wanted a snack after a hard day in the office. When he arrived home, his wife greeted him with a special *milchige* meal that she had prepared in his honor. He was very surprised, as they usually ate *fleishig*, and his recent snack had been *fleishig*. Nachman knew that if he would tell his wife he had already eaten she would be very upset. He was not able to withstand the test that was put in front of him, and ate the meal that was prepared for him. Does he need to atone for his actions?

 Nachman did not do the right thing by not admitting to his wife that he was *fleishig*. Although eating milk *after* meat is only a Rabbinic prohibition, it should not have been violated for the sake of *shalom bayis*. Telling his wife would not have created such a rift, and is therefore not similar to the case of a *sotah*,[9] where one is instructed to even erase the Name of Hashem for the sake of restoring *shalom bayis*. If he was afraid of his wife's reaction, he could have told her that when he was passing by the restaurant, he was stopped and invited for a *seudas mitzvah*, and could not refuse. One may alter the facts to maintain peace.[10]

In our case, where he already transgressed the prohibition, he should establish a fixed time to learn the laws of milk and meat, as well as a chapter of *Sha'arei Teshuvah* on the detrimental effects of eating forbidden foods.

━━━◆◆◆━━━

Shalom Bayis — At What Cost?

וּמָחָה אֶל מֵי הַמָּרִים

And erase it into the bitter waters

(5:23)

 Mr. Kahn lent his car to his son. His son was caught by a police camera traveling 20 miles per hour over the speed limit. Since the car was registered in Mr. Kahn's name, he received a summons to appear in court. Mr. Kahn pleaded guilty, and since he had a clean record, he was given just a fine, and sent home. Had he told the court that the driver had been his son, his son's license

---

9. See *Nedarim* 66b. A wife suspected of unfaithfulness was, in certain circumstances, given a drink into which verses from the Torah, including the Name of Hashem, had been erased.

10. *Yeramos* 65b.

would have been revoked for two years, as his son is a repeat offender. Mr. Kahn lied to protect his son's marriage, which was troubled, and losing his license would add to the strife and put the marriage in jeopardy. Was Mr. Kahn justified?

 Driving a car is a great responsibility. For this reason, the law requires one to have a license. If the son deserves to have his license revoked, he does not have the right to drive. Even if we could justify Mr. Kahn's dishonesty in order to save his son's marriage, what right does the son have to drive for the next two years? The son is a possible menace to society, and a potential murderer, since he does not respect traffic regulations. Therefore, despite his precarious marital state, there is great doubt as to whether his father was allowed to lie.

Since Mr. Kahn already did his damage, he should approach a *beis din* to request that they sternly warn the son never to violate the traffic regulations. They should require the son to place a very large sum of money to be held in escrow as insurance for his being careful. In addition, they should warn him that he will be ostracized from the community and punished to the extent that he will learn his lesson well if he continues to violate traffic safety laws. Only then will Mr. Kahn have atoned for not allowing his son to face the consequences of his reckless actions, and enabling him to continue driving.

פרשת בהעלותך
Parashas Beha'aloscha

Age Before Beauty

בְּהַעֲלֹתְךָ אֶת הַנֵּרֹת

When you kindle the lamps

(8:1)

Yudi had two options when buying a Chanukah *menorah*. Either he could buy a beautiful silver *menorah*, or he could buy an antique *menorah* that had been lit for many generations. Which *menorah* makes the mitzvah more beautiful?

It depends on the individual. To some people, an antique *menorah* is very precious, and they would be willing to spend a lot of money to have one.

The Gemara[11] relates that worn-out Scrolls of Scripture were appraised at a high price. Rav Elyashiv noted that this shows that antiques are considered valuable. To others, antiques have little value, and they see them simply as something old. For them, it would be preferable to light a new silver *menorah*.

In other words, beauty is in the eye of the beholder.

---

11. *Gittin* 31a.

Steak Out

מֵאַיִן לִי בָּשָׂר
Where shall I get meat
(11:13)

Yoni moved into his new second-story apartment one Thursday night, and he could not sleep. After tossing and turning restlessly for some time, he arose from his bed well after midnight and went to the window for some fresh air. He noticed a truck across the street unloading merchandise. He thought it was a strange time for the butcher store to accept a delivery, so he went downstairs to take a closer look. He was horrified to discover workers unloading nonkosher meat to be sold the next day as kosher! The truck completed its delivery and drove away.

Yoni was in shock. What should he do? He had two options: He could expose the dishonest butcher immediately, and save many Jews from eating *tereifeh,* or he could wait for the next delivery, and follow the truck along its route. With Hashem's help he could expose the entire ring that was involved in this terrible fraud, as well as all the other stores participating in this crime. If he exposes the store immediately he will lose the opportunity to save all the other people who are buying *tereifeh* meat from other stores. In the meantime, the customers of this store will continue to buy *tereifeh* meat. What should Yoni do?

The Gemara in *Mo'ed Katan*[12] states that the borders of graves are marked so that Kohanim should be able to avoid walking on them. However, the Gemara stipulates that we do not mark off an area where a partial corpse, the size of a *kezayis,* is buried.[13] Rav Pappa explains that the *kezayis* will eventually shrink, rendering it too small to cause ritual impurity. While keeping the area unmarked may result in people comtaminating *terumah* (and having to burn it) for a short period of time until it shrinks, marking the site will result in people unnecessarily burning *terumah* that passes over there forever.

Perhaps we could infer from this Gemara that it is better to allow a short-term problem to continue, in order to save a long-term problematic situation in the future.

However, Rav Elyashiv ruled that the derelict store should be exposed without delay. We may not "do business" involving transgressions and allow individuals to eat *tereifah*, in order to save many more people in the future. We have to deal with the situation at hand without considerations of "profiting" elsewhere. Rav Elyashiv explained that the Gemara in *Mo'ed Katan* is discussing a case which may only possibly cause a problem, but is not certain to, for there is no *terumah* in the vicinty of the *tumah*, and it is therefore only a potential hazard. On the other hand, people will *certainly* buy the *tereifah* meat and transgress by eating it.

In addition, marking off the grave is an action that may cause problems in the future, so *beis din* may choose not to do anything. In our case, exposing this store will not actively cause people to eat *tereifah*; rather, it will fix the current situation, at least in this store. Therefore, Yoni should do what he has to, now.

---

12. 15a.
13. Only an olive-size piece of the flesh of a corpse can render a Kohen or *terumah* impure.

Sensitivity

עַד אֲשֶׁר יֵצֵא מֵאַפְּכֶם

Until it comes out of your nose

(11:20)

 Rav Adler delivered a wonderful *shiur* to his congregants each night before the 8:30 *minyan* for *Ma'ariv*. One night, there was a new participant who was especially malodorous. It was the local butcher on his way home from work. He had not had time to shower before the *shiur*. Rav Adler was barely able to make it through the *shiur* due to the pungent odor, and cannot conceive tolerating such conditions on a nightly basis. What should the *Rav* do? Should he request that the butcher attend only after he has showered? Or should he cancel the *shiur* in order not to offend the butcher?

 The Gemara in *Sanhedrin*[14] relates that Rebbi was once delivering a *shiur*, when he smelled garlic from the mouth of one of his students. Rebbi requested that whoever had eaten garlic should please leave. R' Chiya, one of the most prominent students, arose and exited the room. The entire class followed him, and left the room as well.

The next morning, R' Shimon, the son of Rebbi, asked R' Chiya, "Are you the one who caused my father such aggravation?"

R' Chiya, answered, "May such a thing never happen in Jewish history!"

Rashi explains that R' Shimon questioned R' Chiya as to how he could have eaten garlic before the *shiur*, causing Rebbi such discomfort. R' Chiya responded that Heaven forfend such a thing;

---

14. 11a.

he had only left the room so that the real culprit should not be embarrassed to leave the room.

The *Maharsha* questions *Rashi's* explanation. Since everyone left the room afterward, it was clear that R' Chiya had not been the true culprit, and R' Shimon would not have asked such a question. Rather, R' Shimon asked R' Chiya, "How could you have disturbed the entire *shiur* by causing everyone to follow you out of the room?" R' Chiya answered that although terminating the *shiur* is a very serious responsibility to bear, Heaven forfend to embarrass a Jew, and such a sin should never happen in Jewish history!

It would seem that Rav Adler's next step is dependent on the difference of opinion between Rebbi and R' Chiya. Rebbi felt it was preferable to ask the guilty *talmid* to leave, and not to disrupt the *shiur*. R' Chiya held that it was better to preserve the *talmid's* dignity, even if it meant disturbing the *shiur*.

However, it is likely that in our case, both Rebbi and R' Chiya would agree that the *Rav* should approach the butcher. In the Gemara's case, the *talmid* would have been embarrassed in front of the whole class. The butcher could be told in private. Also, the Gemara's case was the cancellation of a single *shiur*, whereas our case requires the cancellation of many *shiurim*.

On the other hand, the student who ate the garlic should have known that he would offend people, and therefore Rebbi thought that the *talmid* was responsible for his own shame. In our case, the butcher's smell is because that is his livelihood, and the result of providing a community service. Maybe even Rebbi would agree that the butcher should not be shamed. וצ"ע.

פרשת שלח

Parashas Shelach

The Situation Is Not So Grave

וַיָּבֹא עַד חֶבְרוֹן

And he arrived at Hebron

(13:22)

A tour group traveled to Morocco to *daven* at the gravesites of *tzaddikim* (righteous people). They left their hotel in the morning, intending to travel to a different part of the country. After about half an hour, one of the tourists cried out in dismay that he had left an expensive electronic device in the hotel, and requested that the bus turn around and allow him to recover his lost object.

(It is impossible for him to find his own means of transportation to return to the hotel and rejoin the group later.)

A different member of the group protested that this would cost the entire group a full hour, to travel back to the hotel and then return to where they were, and since they were on a tight schedule, that would mean skipping some of the holy sites on their itinerary. The protestor refused to miss out on the opportunity to make the most of his trip, for which he had paid no small fee. Even though he was aware that there is a mitzvah to return a lost item, his determination was not swayed.

To whom should the group defer? The one who had lost the expensive object, or the one who does not want to miss out on the purpose of his trip?

If the obstinate tourist would suffer a financial loss by participating in returning the lost object, he would certainly have to be compensated by the owner of the lost item.[15] However, in our case, we are dealing with a spiritual loss, of not being able to pray at the holy gravesites. It would seem more important to return the lost object than to visit the righteous deceased, since the very people buried in those places would tell the would-be supplicant that performing the mitzvah of returning the lost item takes precedence over praying at their gravesites. In the merit of fulfilling the commandment to return the lost object, the *tzaddikim* will pray for him, as one should not ignore a mitzvah in which he is obligated, in favor of visiting holy gravesites, which is not an obligation.

———————•◆•———————

---

15. See *Bava Metzia* 31b.

Too Easy

וַיָּבֹא עַד חֶבְרוֹן

And he arrived at Hebron

(13:22)

 A man and his wife had hoped for many years to have children, but to no avail. The husband's rabbi advised him to visit the graves of *tzaddikim* to *daven* there, as it is propitious for prayers to be accepted at the resting place of *tzaddikim*.[16] Perhaps in the *tzaddikim*'s merit Hashem would grant them children. The man vowed that he would travel to the graves of the righteous as his rabbi advised.

Subsequently he noticed an advertisement soliciting people to travel to the gravesites of righteous people to pray on behalf of others, with the offer of monetary compensation. The man decided to apply for the job. Then he remembered his vow. Does he need to donate the cost of the trip to *tzedakah* since he promised to spend the money to that end, or is he exempt?

 The *Shulchan Aruch*[17] rules that one who vowed to travel to the graves of the righteous, and was subsequently hired to do so, can fulfill both obligations at the same time. The *Mishnah Berurah* explains that the vow was to go, and he did go. If, however, he had vowed to spend money on travel expenses, and was subsequently hired to go, then he cannot count his trip as a fulfillment of his vow. The *Sha'ar HaTziyun* writes that if he will give the money to *tzedakah* perhaps that would suffice.

16. *Mishnah Berurah* 581 § 27.
17. *Orach Chaim* 568:10.

A related incident occurred in the time of Rav Azaria Figo (author of the *Gidulei Terumah*). A young man fell deathly ill, and swore that if he would recover, he would marry an orphan and take care of all her needs. Hashem heard his prayers, and he had a full recovery. He approached matchmakers to fulfill his pledge, and was told of a very wealthy young lady who happened to be an orphan. This orphan had many choices of a marriage partner, and the young man was unsure if marrying this girl would be a fulfillment of his promise. On the one hand, she was certainly an orphan. On the other hand, one who is in trouble and vows to marry an orphan intends to do kindness with an underprivileged girl who has no one to look after her, not a girl who has her choice of a match due to her wealth. This question was sent to the *D'var Shmuel*.[18] He answered that this case is different from the case of one who swore to visit holy gravesites, because in that case the main objective was to pray there. The trip was only a means to an end. This is not so when one vows to take an orphan for a wife, where the intention is to do charity, and since the orphan in question does not need his assistance, it would not be considered a fulfillment of his vow.

In our case, if the *Rav* had intended that the trouble involved in the trip itself should also be a merit for him, perhaps this goal would not be realized if he was hired to make the trip. וצ"ע.

---

18. *Siman* 27.

To Give Him Another Chance

וְכִי תִשְׁגּוּ וְלֹא תַעֲשׂוּ

If you err and do not perform

(15:22)

 A guest was called upon to recite one of the *berachos* under the *chupah*. Unfortunately, he made the wrong *berachah*. Even more unfortunate was the fact that the mistake was not discovered until after the *chassan* and *kallah* were danced into the *Yichud* room. Luckily the assembled people were able to ask Rav Elyashiv what to do. He ruled that the young couple must be brought from the *Yichud* room so that the proper *berachah* could be recited in the presence of 10 men. (The order of the *berachos* is not mandatory.)[19]

Now the debate began: Does the guest who was originally called upon to make the *berachah* still have the right to make it, since it was "his" *berachah*, or did he lose the right to make the *berachah*, due to his mistake, and the honor may be given to someone else?

 Once someone has been given the honor to perform a mitzvah, it should not be given to someone else, as is brought in *Shulchan Aruch* in reference to one who asked a *mohel* to perform a *bris* on a baby where one may not then ask another *mohel* to do the circumcision.[20] In our case, the honoree had already made the *berachah*, but did so improperly.

---

19. *Shulchan Aruch, Even HaEzar* 5:1.
20. *Yoreh De'ah* 264:1.

Has he already gotten what he was promised, or, since he has not properly fulfilled the task that he was given, is he still ready and waiting to accomplish that which he intended to do?

If the *chassan* or the *kallah* do not want the same person to make the *berachah* because they are fearful that it is a bad omen, they could certainly give the *berachah* to someone else. This is similar to the right one has to choose a different *mohel* if he has a good reason to do so, as is explained in the aforementioned *Shulchan Aruch*. Our question is when the *chassan* and *kallah* do not mind.

It would seem that someone else could make the *berachah*, unless it would cause embarrassment to the person who made the mistake. Since the first person already received his honor, there is no problem to now honor someone else.

פרשת קרח
Parashas Korach

Know Your Place

וּמַדּוּעַ תִּתְנַשְּׂאוּ

Why do you exalt yourselves

(16:3)

 Shimon and his wife had a baby boy and decided to give the honor of *sandek* to the head of his *Kollel*. At the *bris*, to everyone's surprise, one of the *gedolei hador* entered the hall. Should the *Rosh Kollel* defer being *sandek* in order to give the honor to the *Gadol*?

 The *Radva"z* writes:[21] "If one's *Rebbi* was called to the Torah for *shlishi*, the *talmid* may not be called for *mashlim*,[22] in a place where that is considered to be a greater honor. Even if the *talmid* was called for *mashlim*, he should not accept the *aliyah*, lest he cause shame to his *Rebbi*. Even though it is a terrible thing not to accept an *aliyah* when one is called to

---

21. *Pischei Teshuvah* 242 § 1.
22. The final *aliyah*.

the Torah,[23] since he is abstaining only to protect his *Rebbi's* honor, it is not considered disrespectful to the Torah.

This being the case, the *Rosh Kollel* should give the honor to the *Gadol*, because it is not respectful to the Torah to accept an honor in the presence of a *gadol hador*.

We Want to Pay!

לֹא חֲמוֹר אֶחָד מֵהֶם נָשָׂאתִי

I have not taken even a single donkey of theirs

(16:15)

 Harav Fried is a *Rosh Yeshivah* who gives his *talmidim* 110 percent of himself. He is totally involved in the needs of the yeshivah, as well as its maintenance. Would it be *middas chassidus* (an act of piety) for the *Rosh Yeshivah* to refrain from taking money from the yeshivah for his livelihood?

 One who is constantly involved in the needs of the community should certainly take a salary for his efforts, as needed. The proof to this is from Moshe Rabbeinu.

Moshe Rabbeinu told Hashem, "I did not take from the Jews even one donkey!"[24] The *Netziv* asks why Moshe did not say even more than that, that even the bread he ate in Mitzrayim did not come from the community. The answer is, because it did! This proves that one who is totally dedicated to the community should not refrain from taking a salary for his work. The reason for this is because if he

---

23. *Berachos* 55a.
24. *Bamidbar* 16:15.

does not take money from the community, he will be forced to interrupt his communal work in order to provide a livelihood for himself. Since it is essential to the community to have someone who is solely dedicated to serving their needs, even at their expense, there is no virtue in not taking a salary. That is why even Moshe Rabbeinu ate at the community's expense. However, when he went to Midyan, and was in need of a donkey to return to Mitzrayim, it was his personal decision to bring his wife and children with him, as is mentioned in the *Mechilta*. His wife wanted to see the glory of *Yetzias Mitzrayim*. Such an expense was not mandatory, and therefore Moshe's piety would not allow him to let the community pay for it.

Rabbi Fried should therefore take a salary to cover his family's needs.

A Picture Is Worth ...

וַתִּפְתַּח הָאָרֶץ אֶת פִּיהָ
The earth opened its mouth
(16:32)

 Due to flaws in the structure of the wedding hall, the floor caved in, in the middle of a wedding. It was a terrible tragedy, as many of the guests fell through the hole into the gaping pit below. The photographer, who was hired to take pictures of the wedding, continued taking pictures of the disaster, and hurried to sell his pictures to the media for a large sum of money.

Sometime later, the parents of the *chassan,* who had hired him to take pictures of the wedding, claimed that since they had engaged his services for the entire evening, any pictures taken during that time belonged to them. The photographer claimed that he was hired to cover the wedding, not the collapse of the hall, and therefore the rights to the pictures were his. To whom do the pictures belong?

A The Gemara in *Bava Metzia*[25] states that a worker who finds something during his working hours is allowed to keep it. The Gemara stipulates that this is true only if he was hired for a specific job, which does not include finding things. If, however, he was hired for general work, anything the worker finds belongs to the one who hired him. *Rashi* explains that picking up lost items is also included in general work, and since he is hired for such labor, any benefits belong to his employer.

The *Shulchan Aruch*[26] rules according to an alternate explanation of the Gemara that only if he was hired to specifically find lost items would the items belong to the employer.

Perhaps in our case it is similar to someone who was hired to find things, as the photographer's job is to take pictures of anything interesting that happens that evening.

In truth, taking pictures of a collapsing building requires special effort, including putting one's self in danger. When everyone else is running for their lives, the photographer must muster his courage and remain calm. Such efforts are certainly not included in the job description of a wedding photographer, and therefore any pictures of the catastrophe belong exclusively to him.

Additionally, the photographer was hired to take pictures of the wedding. This includes the guests, the dancing, and all that pertains to the *chassan* and *kallah*. The collapse of the building is not the domain of the people who made the wedding, but rather the one who owns the building, or the police. If an airplane would have crashed into the hall, would that also be included in the work

---

25. 10a.
26. *Choshen Mishpat* 270:3.

of the photographer? Obviously that is not part of his job, and neither is the collapse of the building.

* * *

Taking a Risk to Do Mitzvos

מִבֶּן חֹדֶשׁ תִּפְדֶּה

From one month shall you redeem

(18:16)

 Mrs. Klein was in the delivery room, about to give birth to a firstborn son. There was a sudden complication in the labor, and the doctors decided to deliver by Caesarean section. Mrs. Klein vehemently refused because she wanted her husband to have the once-in-a-lifetime mitzvah of *Pidyon Haben* which is applicable only for children born naturally, and the danger involved in letting the birth progress naturally was minimal.[27] Should we let her deliver naturally, even though there is a small danger involved, or should her wishes be disregarded, and the operation performed immediately?

 The *Noda BiYehudah*[28] was asked if hunting is permissible. He answered that if it is for amusement, it is prohibited since there is danger involved (in addition to other prohibitions). However, if it is for the sake of earning a living

---

27. The danger was only to the mother, and not to the child.
28. *Yoreh De'ah, Tinyana* 10.

it would be permitted, just like it is permissible to travel in ships to earn a living, even though doing so is dangerous [at that time].

This shows that it is permissible for a person to put himself at a certain amount of risk in order to obtain a real benefit. However, the guidelines of how much risk and for what purposes are unclear.

Perhaps it would be permissible to allow the risk for the sake of *kiddush Hashem*, as we find by Nikanor, who risked his life to save the door he brought for the *Beis HaMikdash* from being tossed into the sea.[29]

If this woman wants to sanctify Hashem's Name, and show that Hashem answers those who call out to Him in times of need, perhaps she could take the risk in order to allow her husband to do a *Pidyon Haben*. This is in addition to the fact that she is involved in the mitzvah of giving birth, and those en route to a mitzvah shall suffer no harm.[30] Although this is not a ruling for everyone, one who wishes to take a *small* risk may do so.[31] If, however, the risk is not so small, it seems that doing so would be prohibited and would be considered an *aveirah*.

If the woman would ask if it is worth taking the risk, we would not recommend entering even a small danger for which she is not commanded.

The *Leket Yosher* writes that in the house of a gentile one should light only one candle and one *shamash* (for Chanukah). Even if the gentile does not mind if the Jew lights more candles, there is a small chance that a fire may break out, thus bringing shame to the mitzvah, and this must be avoided even at the cost of the enhanced fulfillment of the mitzvah. A proof may be brought from the lettuce that we eat all year round, yet on Pesach we eat it (for the mitzvah of *maror*) dipped in *charoses*. The reason for this is because there is a small possibility that there may be a poison in the lettuce, and the *charoses* serves to neutralize it. This shows that when it comes to a mitzvah we do not

---

29. The story of Nikanor is discussed in "Kiddush Hashem," *Parashas Emor* (p. 291).
30. *Pesachim* 8b.
31. A "small risk" is up to 16.6 percent.

take even a small risk, lest the person be harmed and bring shame upon the mitzvah.

In our case as well, Mrs. Klein should be more wary of exposing herself to even a small danger and possibly bringing shame to the mitzvah than the fact that they may not be able to become obligated in the mitzvah of *Pidyon Haben*.

פָּרָשַׁת חֻקַּת
Parashas Chukas

Seize the Moment

פָּרָה אֲדֻמָּה תְּמִימָה

A completely red cow

(19:2)

 Yeshivas Beis Yitzchok desperately needed a building for their growing student body. Unfortunately, their building fund was not growing at the same rate. Finally, they located a donor who was willing to give a substantial donation to erect the much-needed building. It was an older gentleman who lived many hours' travel from Eretz Yisrael, but he had plans to travel to Eretz Yisrael in a week's time. The *Rosh Yeshivah* found himself in a quandry: should he wait for the donor to come to Eretz Yisrael, or maybe it would be more prudent for the *Rosh Yeshivah* to subject himself to the difficulty and expense of traveling that day to the potential donor to collect the donation? On the one hand, even though at the moment, the donor was ready and willing to fund a building, it is possible that by the following week the circumstances would change. On the other hand, maybe the *Rosh Yeshivah* should wait the week and continue to *daven* to Hashem that the donor would remain willing to give the yeshivah the grant.

 The Gemara in *Yoma*[32] says that the Kohen who prepared the *parah adumah* was sequestered for seven days prior to the preparation, in order to insure that he be ritually pure. Rav Elyashiv explains why precautions were taken to guarantee his status, as opposed to delaying the preparation of the *parah adumah* in the event that the Kohen became impure. There is concern that the cow could become unfit, either by growing black hairs, becoming blemished, or being worked. The first Mishnah in *Maseches Parah* brings Rebbi Meir's opinion that in reality, even a five-year-old red cow is valid, but the cow is not permitted to age lest it grow black hairs.

This shows that it is a valid concern that as time goes on, circumstances may change. Therefore there is good reason to solicit the grant as soon as possible, so that the donor should not lose his will, energy, or ability to perform the mitzvah. The *Rosh Yeshivah* should make arrangements to travel as soon as possible.

---

32. 3b.

In the Absence of a G.P.S.

וְכָל אֲשֶׁר בָּאֹהֶל יִטְמָא

And anything that is in the tent shall be contaminated

(19:14)

Gershon Katz took a trip to the Rockefeller Museum to view ancient relics, in order to help him understand the properties of different utensils that are discussed in the *Mishnayos* of *Maseches Keilim*. Suddenly, he caught sight of a human skull on display, and he panicked. A human skull!? Gershon is a Kohen, and is not allowed to be under the same roof as a human skeleton. He started to run for the nearest exit, except in his haste, instead of running out of the museum, he ran into an inner courtyard. The only way out would be to go back into the museum building and from there, out to the street.[33] Gershon waited in the courtyard, not knowing what to do. Eventually it was time for the museum to close, and Gershon was asked to leave. He tried to explain that he was a Kohen, and needed to consult with a rabbi as to his next course of action, but the security guard had very little sympathy for anyone who dallied in leaving the museum after closing time. The security guard radioed his friend to join him and make the museum Gershon-free. They threatened that if Gershon did not leave peacefully, they would drag him out amid beatings and other unpleasantries. At that point,

---

33. It seems a helicopter to lift him over the museum's roof was not a viable option. What an idea for a *gemach*!

may Gershon enter the museum building willfully, or should he wait until he is dragged inside?

 Rav Elyashiv answered that once there are guards who are prepared to drag him against his will, he may enter the building willingly.

A basis for this ruling is the dispute in the Gemara in *Pesachim*[34] whether, under certain circumstances, one may actively contaminate *terumah* that is about to become contaminated anyway. Here too, since Gershon will be compelled to enter the building anyway, he does not have to wait to be the victim of violence.

"Has Anyone Seen My Contacts?"

וְלֹא הָיָה מַיִם

There was no water

(20:2)

 A yeshivah *bachur* came back to his dormitory room late at night, and he was very thirsty. He picked up a glass from the table and poured himself some water. Although the water tasted bitter, he did not attribute any significance to that fact, until the next morning. His roommate asked him if he had seen the contact lenses that had been left soaking in a glass on the table. Does the boy who drank the lenses have to pay for them, or was he not required to suspect that maybe the glass contained lenses?

---

34. 20b, as explained by *Rashi* to 15a.

Rav Chaim Kanievsky instructed the boy to pay, since a person is liable for damages even when done accidentally.[35] In addition, he should have realized from the bitter taste of the water that something was amiss.

Rav Elyashiv differed, and said the boy is not liable for three reasons.

1) His behavior is not classified as damage since the damage was done by an act that is normally benign (i.e., drinking). 2) There was no reason to suspect that a drinking glass had lenses in it! Therefore he is considered to have done the damage as a complete *oneis* (against one's will).[36] 3) The owner was negligent in leaving expensive lenses in a public place, in a glass! Therefore, even though one needs to pay for damage done even by accident, if the victim caused himself to be damaged, no payment is necessary.

You Get What You Pay For

לֹא נִטֶּה יָמִין וּשְׂמֹאול
We shall not veer right or left
(20:17)

The local grocer has a kosher newspaper stand at the front of his store. His goal is to sell the newspapers, and he explicitly forbids passersby to read the news, even without handling them! Does he have a right to prohibit people from looking at his newspapers, or, since a

---

35. As explained in *Shulchan Aruch, Choshen Mishpat* 421:3.
36. See *Shulchan Aruch, Choshen Mishpat* 378:1-2, and *Shach* § 1.

person who does not, in any case, intend to buy the paper due to lack of money, this would be a case of "*Zeh neheneh v'zeh lo chaser,*" a person benefiting from someone else without causing him any harm or loss?

 In the *Halachos Ketanos*[37] the author indeed gives license to prohibit someone from reading one's book. The *Ya'avetz*[38] concurs, and quotes the *Shulchan Aruch*[39] in an identical ruling. The only exception would be regarding a holy book, since its use is a mitzvah, and mitzvos are not done for the sake of pleasure. Reading newspapers, however, is not a mitzvah, and clearly one could insist that others not read them unless they will purchase them.

In addition, although many customers claim that they would not buy the paper anyway, the grocer maintains that some of them actually would, if they could not read it otherwise, and therefore the grocer is considered to be incurring a loss by their reading and may insist that passersby not read his papers without payment.

———————◆———————

37. Vol. I, 6.
38. I, 61.
39. *Yoreh De'ah* 221.

Caution in Repaying a Loan

וַיִּשְׁבְּ מִמֶּנּוּ שֶׁבִי

And took a captive from it

(21:1)

Shimon was a wealthy businessman. One day he received a visit from his friend Rafael, a diamond dealer who was about to declare bankruptcy. Rafael told Shimon about his desperate situation and asked for a loan of $10,000 so he could stay in business. Shimon gave him a check on condition that the loan be repaid in two month's time. After two months, Shimon came to Rafael to collect, but Rafael could not pay. He asked Shimon for an extension, which was granted begrudgingly.

Sometime later Shimon went overseas on business and was taken captive. When the community tried to ransom him, his captors refused. The captors were willing to free Shimon only on condition that a certain member of their community who owned a beautiful diamond ring would be willing to trade it for Shimon. The owner of the ring was Rafael.

The leaders of the community approached Rafael and begged him to save Shimon's life. Rafael agreed to part with his expensive ring in order to secure Shimon's release. That night Shimon returned home and came to visit Rafael. Shimon brought with him a huge bouquet of flowers and thanked Rafael from the bottom of his heart. Before he left, Shimon turned to Rafael and reminded him that he still owed him $10,000.

Rafael was aghast. He emphatically informed Shimon that he had just parted with a diamond ring that was worth twice as much, in order to secure his release. He noted Shimon's audacity in asking him to repay the loan.

Shimon did not see a connection between the two matters. He felt that Rafael had given his ring to perform the mitzvah of *pidyon shevuyim*, and the loan was a completely separate matter! Who is right?

 This question is discussed in the *sefer Torah Lishmah*.[40] He proves the halachah from the Gemara in *Kesubos*.[41] There was a man who had an outstanding loan of 100 *zuz*. He died, and left to his children a piece of land valued at 50 *zuz*. His creditor collected the piece of land to repay the debt, and the children paid him 50 *zuz* to release the land. The creditor came to collect the land again, as 50 *zuz* of the loan was still outstanding. The case came before Abaye, who ruled that since there is a mitzvah for the heirs to repay the loan of their inheritors, the original 50 *zuz* was given for the purpose of doing a mitzvah, and the creditor had the right to collect the second half of his loan. If, however, at the time the children had given the 50 *zuz*, they would have expressed that the money is in place of the land, the land could not be collected again.

In our case as well, since Rafael did not say anything at the time he gave the ring, Shimon can claim that the ring was given in order to do the mitzvah of *pidyon shevuyim*. Had Rafael expressed that by giving the ring, he is repaying the loan, he would have been released from his obligation. As he did not do so, he actually proved that his intention was for the mitzvah.

It would seem that we could ask a question on the decision of the *Torah Lishmah* from the ruling of the *Rema*.[42] The *Rema* states that if one redeemed his friend from captivity, the one who was redeemed

---

40. *Siman* 347.
41. 91b.
42. *Yoreh De'ah* 252:12.

must repay his redeemer immediately, if he has the means. The *Rema* concludes that without such an understanding, people would be unwilling to redeem captives. It is clear that Shimon cannot claim that Rafael does not deserve payment for doing this mitzvah, and therefore the loan should indeed be canceled.

Perhaps the *Torah Lishmah* was only relevant to his case, where it was clear that the redeemer gave the money for the sake of the mitzvah, whereas in any other situation, the redeemer could certainly demand payment, or, as the case may be, the cancellation of the debt.

<hr/>

Theft Deterrent

וְהָיָה כָּל הַנָּשׁוּךְ
And it will be that anyone that was bitten
(21:8)

 Fishel was concerned about robbers, so he wanted to hang a sign in his yard, "BEWARE OF DOG IN YARD." He did not own a dog, but he thought it would scare away unwanted "guests." Is that permissible, or would it be considered lying or *geneivas da'as*?

 We can prove from the Gemara[43] that there is no prohibition of lying in such a case. The Gemara says that one who is selling a field and is asked by the purchaser to write the deed in another's name is not then required to write another document containing the name of the actual buyer. The Gemara says that the buyer cannot claim, "You knew I was buying

---

43. *Bava Kamma* 103a.

it for myself, and I only had you write the other person's name in order to ward off those who would make trouble for me."

We see that one could write such a contract to ward off troublemakers. So too, he could write "Vicious Dog in Yard," and it would not be considered a lie.

It is not called tricking people either, since the prohibition to trick someone is only if you seek a benefit by tricking them, and not if you are just trying to save yourself.

Of course, he could just write "vicious dog" and avoid the whole problem.

Accidental Insurance

בֹּאוּ חֶשְׁבּוֹן
Come to Heshbon
(21:27)

 Sara would never have gone over her bank statement if her last check hadn't bounced. She did not have time for such things. As long as she deposited her paycheck every week, she would leave the balancing to the bank. Somehow her account got into the red, and she needed to find out why. Her eye caught an automatic debit on her statement. A phone call to the bank revealed that this payment was made to an insurance company. Sara was confused; she did not own any insurance! She placed a quick call to the company and the fax they sent her shed light on the mystery. It seems that the insurance agent had forged her signature on a contract, and had supplied her bank account number for the automatic payment. She had been paying monthly. for medical insurance, for four and a half years, and she had never even noticed!

Her indignation was soon replaced with a wonderful thought. She had undergone several medical procedures in the past four years for which she had paid from her own funds. Could it be that she could claim reimbursement from the company and make the entire investment *very* profitable?

It would seem that even if the insurance company is amenable to paying, Sara cannot make a claim because she never bought insurance. The Gemara in *Bava Metzia*[44] teaches that if Yehudah bought a field from a swindler, even if the swindler subsequently bought the field from its rightful owner, Yehudah is not entitled to the field by right of the original sale. The reason for this is because at the time of the sale the swindler had no ability to sell it. Even though the Gemara concludes that the field does belong to Yehudah, it is only his from the moment that the swindler bought it from the original owner and not before such time.

Certainly if the insurance company refuses to pay, Sara cannot make a claim. The insurance company is not interested in insuring people against their will, and their agent was not working on their behalf when he signed Sara's name. Obviously they have to reimburse her premium for four and a half years, but they do not owe her anything more than that. That being said, if the insurance company wishes to pay her, she may take the money as a gift. וצ"ע.

---

44. 16a.

פרשת בלק
Parashas Balak

Be Kind to Animals

וַיִּפְתַּח ה' אֶת פִּי הָאָתוֹן
Hashem opened the mouth of the she-donkey
(22:28)

 A stray cat got caught on a wire fence and is wailing in pain. Yoni could free it, but he is hurrying to an important appointment and he does not want to be late. Does he have a mitzvah to free the feline because of *tza'ar baalei chaim*, or since he did not cause the animal's pain, he has no obligation to rescue it?

 The Gemara in *Bava Metzia* explores whether *tza'ar baalei chaim* is a Torah obligation, or one that was Rabbinically instituted. The Gemara brings a proof that it is a Torah obligation from the mitzvah of *"perikah,"* the obligation to unload a donkey that has collapsed under its burden. Obviously the Gemara understands that this is the mitzvah even though the one who is required to unload it did not cause the animal's pain.

An additional proof can be brought from the *Shulchan Aruch*,[45] that allows instructing a non-Jew to milk a Jew's cow on Shabbos to relieve it of its milk because of *tza'ar baalei chaim*.[46] This reason exists even though the Jew did not cause the cow's pain.

The *Ya'avetz*[47] explains that the prohibition against eating before one's animals is because of the animals' pain, even though their hunger is not the fault of the owner.

Rav Yaakov Kamenetsky[48] observes that the *Rambam*[49] states that causing pain to animals is a Rabbinic decree.

Yet in the *Moreh Nevuchim*[50] the *Rambam* says that we learn not to cause pain to animals from Bilaam who, after hitting his donkey three times, was chastised for doing so. That would imply that the prohibition is a Biblical one. Rav Yaakov answers that causing an animal pain is indeed a Biblical prohibition, while saving an animal from pain that one did not cause is a Rabbinic decree.

Certainly Yoni should help the poor feline, but he has no obligation to do so if it will cause him pain or loss.

---

45. *Orach Chaim* 305:20.
46. As explained by the *Mishnah Berurah* § 71.
47. Vol. I, 17.
48. *Emes LeYaakov, Bava Metzia* 32b.
49. Ch. 13, from *Hilchos Rotze'ach*.
50. *Ma'amar* 3, Chapter 17.

Using the Law for Your Own Purposes

מַה טֹּבוּ אֹהָלֶיךָ יַעֲקֹב

How goodly are your tents, O Yaakov

(24:5)

 Yanky and Chaim are neighbors whose yards are adjacent to each other. Yanky wants to build a wall to separate the two yards, and asked Chaim to share the cost. According to *Shulchan Aruch*,[51] Chaim must agree, since the wall is a protection from *hezek re'iyah* (others looking into the private property). The truth is that Yanky is not really concerned with *hezek re'iyah,* he just wants the wall built so he can use it as a wall for his *succah.* Can Yanky take advantage of his right to force Chaim to help him build a wall for a purpose other than that for which the halachah intended?

 The *sefer Mishpatim Yesharim*[52] rules that one has no right to use a claim for his own purposes. He proves this from *Shulchan Aruch.*[53] A woman may demand a divorce from her husband if they were not blessed with children and she wishes to marry someone else in the hope of bearing children. However, if at the same time she requests to be paid for her *kesubah, beis din* will not force her husband to divorce her. The reason for this is that her claim is accepted only when her purpose is to bear children, and not when she has financially influenced

---

51. *Choshen Mishpat* 157:1.
52. Vol. I, 7.
53. *Even HaEzer* 154:6.

ulterior motives. The *Mishpatim Yesharim* concludes that the matter still needs resolution.

Rav Zilberstein suggests that the reason the *Mishpatim Yesharim* was not convinced of his proof is because there is a difference between the two cases. In the case of the wall, we find that the Torah favors the modesty and privacy created when neighbors do not have access to viewing their neighbor's property. *"Mah tovu ohalecha Yaakov."*[54] *Rashi* explains that the Jews were praised that their doorways did not face each other so that they should be prevented from looking into their neighbor's homes. Divorce, on the other hand, is not something that the Torah encourages, and is an acceptable solution only under specific circumstances. Therefore, unless the woman has pure motives we will not force the husband to grant her a divorce.

Even so, the *Mishpatim Yesharim* is inclined to say that Yanky cannot force Chaim to build the wall if his intentions are not for the reasons for which the halachah intended the wall to be built.

---

54. *Bamidbar* 24:5.

פרשת פינחס
Parashas Pinchas

Shul Policy

אַךְ בְּגוֹרָל יֵחָלֵק

Only by lot shall the land be divided

(26:55)

 In Congregation Ohev Shalom they made a rule that anyone who wishes to reserve a particular *aliyah* to be called to the Torah must do so six months in advance; in the case of a conflict, the decision is made by a lottery. Menashe responsibly notified the *gabbai* that his son's bar mitzvah would be in six months' time, and he would like his son to receive *Maftir*.

Six months later, on Friday afternoon, Ephraim, who was also a congregant of Ohev Shalom, called the *gabbai* on his cellphone. "Hi!" said Ephraim. "I just wanted you to know that this week is my son's bar mitzvah, and my son prepared the *Maftir*!"

The *gabbai* checked his calendar and saw that Menashe had already reserved that Shabbos six months ago. Does Ephraim's son lose out because his request failed to comply with the rule?

Rav Elyashiv answered that Ephraim's son does not lose his chance to have the *Maftir*. It is not the son's fault that his father did not adhere to the shul's rules. Being under bar mitzvah exempts the son from knowing shul policy, and he should not be penalized. He is a congregant as much as Menashe's son, and deserves to be called to the Torah. Therefore they should decide by lottery which boy should get the *Maftir*.

Jackpot!

אַךְ בְּגוֹרָל יֵחָלֵק
Only by lot shall the land be divided
(26:55)

Yehoshua gave *Matanos La'evyonim* to a poor man on Purim afternoon. Later that afternoon Yehoshua discovered that the poor man with whom he had done the special mitzvah of *tzedakah* on Purim had won the lottery that morning, and neither Yehoshua nor the poor man had been aware of that fact at the time. Has Yehoshua fulfilled his obligation, or must the no-longer-poor man return Yehoshua's money and Yehoshua will need to do the mitzvah with a truly needy individual?

It would seem that Yehoshua has indeed fulfilled his obligation and the money does not have to be returned.

The *Shulchan Aruch* rules,[55] if a businessman is traveling from place to place and has run out of funds until the

---

55. *Yoreh De'ah* 253:3.

point where he has nothing to eat, he may take *tzedakah*, and when he returns home he need not pay it back. Although he may have a lot of money at home, when he runs out of money on the road, he and the poor man are exactly the same. When he returns home to his money he is similar to a poor man who became wealthy, who does not have to repay all the *tzedakah* he received in the past.

In Yehoshua's case as well, the poor man who had yet to discover, and certainly to collect, his money, is temporarily poor and is allowed to take money from *tzedakah,* and Yehoshua has fulfilled the mitzvah.

Priority to Be Chazzan

יִפְקֹד ה' אֱלֹקֵי הָרוּחֹת
May Hashem, G-d of the spirits of all flesh, appoint
(27:16)

 Yossi stood outside the shul late at night asking passersby to come and join a *minyan* for *Ma'ariv*. It was his grandfather's *yahrtzeit*, and his grandfather had left behind four daughters and no sons. Yossi had taken upon himself to be the *chazzan* as a merit for his grandfather's *neshamah*, but he was unable to attend an earlier *minyan*.

Yossi painstakingly gathered a *minyan* one by one, and when the tenth man arrived, the man announced that he is a mourner, and has an obligation to be *chazzan*. Does Yossi have to step aside?

A Rashi in *Parashas Pinchas*[56] tells that Moshe Rabbeinu wanted his children to inherit his position as leader of the Jews. Hashem told him that it is befitting that his faithful student, Yehoshua, should reap the reward of his constant and dedicated service, as Shlomo HaMelech said in *Mishlei:*[57] "One who guards the fig tree will eat its fruits."

Based on this, the *Aderes,* in his *sefer Oveir Orach,*[58] rules that one who gathered the 10 men needed for a *minyan,* and without him the *minyan* would not have gathered, is more deserving to be the *chazzan* than one who has *yahrtzeit* or the like.

Similarly, the *Elef HaMagen*[59] writes that one who volunteers his house for a *minyan* has precedence to be the *chazzan,* more than other mourners. The same is true concerning one who gave a *shiur* or who read from the Torah. He deserves priority to say the *Kaddish* that follows, in spite of the fact that other mourners are present.

Even if Yossi could find another *minyan,* and the mourner will not be able to find another *minyan,* Yossi still has the right to be the *chazzan,* and does not have to give it away.

---

56. *Bamidbar* 27:16.
57. 27:18.
58. On the *sefer Orchos Chaim* 132.
59. On the *Mateh Ephraim, Kaddish Yasom* 1 § 3.

פרשת מטות
Parashas Mattos

False Alarm?

לֹא יַחֵל דְּבָרוֹ

He shall not desecrate his word

(30:3)

Reuven was diagnosed with a disease that was believed to be fatal. He fervently *davened* to Hashem for a complete recovery, and vowed that if he would recover, he would donate a large sum of money to the poor. Subsequently, Reuven underwent additional testing, and to his immense relief, the results showed that the disease he actually had was never really fatal at all. Does Reuven still have to honor his pledge, or was the whole thing just a mistake?

The *Shulchan Aruch*[60] rules that if an individual started to fast as a merit to avert a tragedy, and subsequently discovered that the tragedy had been averted even

---

60. *Orach Chaim* 569:2.

before he had accepted upon himself to fast, he does not have to complete his fast.

In our case, though, there is ample reason for Reuven to fulfill his vow. It is completely possible that Reuven did have a fatal disease, and only after his *tefillah* was accepted, and his vow tipped the scale, his condition changed. It is a known fact that before a tragedy has become known, one can avert it more easily through *tefillah*.

Once there was a terrible decree issued against the Jews of a certain city. The Jews sent a letter to a *tzaddik*, who was known to work miracles, to *daven* for their salvation. The *tzaddik* requested that the Jews of the city send him money to distribute to widows and orphans. A short time after they sent their money, a letter arrived that the decree was rescinded. The letter was dated prior to the sending of the money. There were some scoffers who demanded to have the money returned, since it seemed apparent to them that they had sent it by mistake! The question was brought to the *Maharsham*, who ruled that the money does not have to be returned.

The *Maharsham* proved his ruling from the Gemara in *Berachos*[61] that relates that the house of Oved Edom HaGiti was blessed because he swept and dusted in front of the *Aron HaKodesh* of the Mishkan while it was kept in his house. The blessing came in the form of his wife and eight daughters-in-law each giving birth to six babies at a time! The *Aron HaKodesh* only spent three months in his house. How could they give birth to the babies so quickly? It must be that since Hashem knew that the *Aron HaKodesh* would be there and receive such honorable care, Hashem sent the *berachah* in advance, so that the manifestation of the *berachah* would coincide with the presence of the *Aron HaKodesh*. In the case of the *Maharsham* as well, Hashem had repealed the decree with the knowledge that the Jews would send the money for *tzedakah*.

---

61. 63b.

The difficulty that remains is how to explain the *Shulchan Aruch* that exempts the person from completing his fast. Why would we not have to be suspect that Hashem had removed the tragedy based on His prior knowledge that the person would eventually fast?

Perhaps the *Maharsham's* ruling is applicable only when we can attribute the willingness to do the meritorious act, to the period that preceded the salvation. Oved Edom HaGiti always held the *Aron HaKodesh* in great esteem, and was just waiting for the opportunity to show it honor. As such, Hashem rewarded him in advance because of his desire to do the mitzvah. The Jews who engaged the services of the *tzaddik* were already prepared to give *tzedakah* at the *tzaddik's* behest. The *Maharsham* ruled that this readiness (with the understanding that their intentions would be carried out), which preceded the actual giving of the *tzedakah*, caused them to be deserving that the decree be revoked. In the case of the fast however, the tragedy had been averted even before the person had accepted upon himself to fast. Thus, the salvation had nothing at all to do with the person's decision to fast.

Every case must be decided according to its individual circumstances, and in our case, it is appropriate to suspect that Reuven's vow was the reason for his tragedy to be averted before it became known. Therefore Reuven should indeed give the money to *tzedakah*, and keep his promise.

———◆———

Expensive Garbage

אֶצְעָדָה וְצָמִיד טַבַּעַת עָגִיל

Anklet and bracelet, ring, earring

(31:50)

Simcha happily ran down the steps of his apartment building on the way to his *kollel*. As he was passing his neighbor's doorway, he noticed that Meir had left a full garbage bag in the hallway, waiting to be taken downstairs to the receptacle. Simcha decided to do Meir the favor of relieving him of the duty of bringing the bag downstairs, certain that his neighbor would be happy not to have another chore.

A few hours later, Meir's wife noticed that her engagement ring and wedding band were not on her finger. She tried to recall where she had left them, and remembered taking them off before washing her hands for lunch. She had left her rings on the disposable tablecloth, which Meir had promptly rolled up after the meal and disposed of in a garbage bag.

When Meir and his wife opened the door to retrieve the rings they were horrified to discover that the bag was no longer there. As a matter of fact, the city's garbage truck had just emptied the receptacle, and the rings were, by now, very far away. Somehow, Simcha's "good deed" came to light, and Meir is now demanding that Simcha pay him for the expensive rings. Simcha believes that the rings were in the bag, but he claims that he could not possibly have known the contents of the garbage bag and is therefore not at fault. Who is right?

At first glance it would seem that Simcha has to pay, as a person is responsible for any damage he causes whether he intended to do so, or not.[62] In truth, however, it seems that he is innocent for the following reasons:

1) There is a difference of opinion if one is liable for damages he causes when he is an *oneis gammur*. Whereas the *Shulchan Aruch*[63] rules that he is responsible, the *Rema* says that he is not. Since this ruling is not universally agreed upon, Meir cannot force Simcha to pay. וצ״ע.

2) The *Shulchan Aruch* rules[64] that one does not have to believe the one who was damaged as to the contents of an opaque container, if it is unusual that it should contain such an object. The *Rema* adds that there is an opinion that even if there were witnesses as to the contents, there is no obligation to pay, as it was negligent to put such an item into such a container.

Again, since the final ruling is the subject of debate, Meir cannot force Simcha to pay.

3) An argument can be made that Simcha did not actually do the damage. He merely placed the bag in the receptacle, and the city workers took it away. Although he may have caused the damage to take place, this is a lower level of responsibility. There are opinions that one is responsible in such a case only if he had intended to do damage, as the liability to pay is actually a penalty *mi'd'Rabbanan* and is only in force when there was intent. Certainly, in our case, there was no intent to cause any harm, only good.

4) Since a neighbor does not have a right to leave his garbage in the hallway, Meir could not fault any of his neighbors for removing the garbage from their common property (unless this was the accepted practice in their building). What Simcha did was completely within his rights, and he is not considered as having done damage.

---

62. *Bava Kamma* 3b; *Choshen Mishpat* 421:3.
63. *Choshen Mishpat* 378:1,2; *Shach* § 1.
64. *Choshen Mishpat* 388:1.

5) Since the bag was intended to be placed in the receptacle anyway, one cannot consider one who brought it to its destination as having done damage.

———◆———

And You Shall Be Clean

וִהְיִיתֶם נְקִיִּם

Then you shall be vindicated

(32:22)

 Chaim is the head adminstrator at Beis Refuah Hospital. Chaim's father contracted a horrible disease and requires very expensive medication. May Chaim purchase the medicine at his hospital and have it sent to his father, if by doing so people will suspect that Chaim took the medicine from the hospital without paying? The alternative would be for Chaim's father to travel to be admitted to Beis Refuah, and have the medicine administered there.

 The Torah relates that Yosef requested that his father Yaakov travel down to Mitzrayim. He promised to sustain his father and family in Mitzrayim for the duration of the famine in order to save them from total poverty and deprivation. The *Ramban* explains that Yosef was unable to send his father sustenance in the land of Cana'an, since sending food out of Mitzrayim would bring suspicion upon Yosef that he was exporting food for sale to amass riches for himself. Only if Yaakov and his family would come to Mitzrayim would it be obvious that Yosef was providing for them. If such a suspicion is sufficient reason for Yaakov to uproot his family from Eretz Yisrael, it would seem ample reason for Chaim's father to come to Beis Refuah for treatment. וצ״ע.

פרשת מסעי
Parashas Mas'ei

Metered Parking I

וַיִּסְעוּ ... וַיַּחֲנוּ
They journeyed ... and encamped
(33:5)

Yossi and Mendy arrived at the shul at the same time. Each parked his car in a metered parking space on the street in front of the shul. Mendy noticed that Yossi was heading for the shul without putting a quarter in his meter.

"Aren't you afraid of a ticket?" he asked Yossi.

"Nah! They never check this early in the morning!" Yossi assured him.

Nevertheless, Mendy put a quarter in the meter and followed his friend into shul.

Sure enough, when they exited the shul they found a ticket on one of the cars, but it was Mendy's! It seems that in his rush to make the *minyan*, he put a quarter in Yossi's meter instead of his own, and spared Yossi the ticket.

Now Mendy is claiming that Yossi should pay the ticket, since if he would have paid for his parking space, Mendy's ticket could have been avoided. Does Yossi have to pay?

 It seems that Mendy is responsible to pay the ticket, as the parking authorities are demanding payment from him. His claim against Yossi is baseless as Yossi did not do any damage aside from being a very indirect contributor to the consequences of Mendy's mistake. However, Yossi does have to pay Mendy the quarter he put into his meter, since that quarter saved him a ticket. It is like a man who planted his friend's field, who is entitled to compensation for his expenditures.[65]

This is in contrast to one who chased a lion away from his friend's flock of sheep. He would not have to be paid,[66] because he chased the lion away willingly and did not suffer any loss. This was not the case with Mendy.

Even if Mendy had managed to spare Yossi from a parking ticket without paying his meter, Yossi would still have to pay the amount of his benefit to Mendy, as is explained by the *Shach*:[67] If one sent merchandise with an agent to a place that requires a tax to be paid, and the agent was able to avoid the tax, the agent is entitled to payment, since the tax was otherwise a certain expense.

If the ticket had not been a certainty, Yossi would not have to pay. However, since the policeman had indeed come to check the meters, Mendy deserves to be compensated for the quarter expended to save Yossi from a loss.

---

65. See *Bava Metzia* 101a.
66. See *Bava Kamma* 58a.
67. *Choshen Mishpat* 183 § 15.

Metered Parking II

 The next day, Mendy and Yossi drove up to shul at the same time again. Mendy was careful this time to put the quarter in the correct meter. Yossi felt that the previous day's ticket had been an unusual occurrence, and persisted in parking his car without putting any money in his meter.

Sure enough, when they came out of shul there was a ticket on one of the cars, and again it was Mendy's! Mendy checked the meters in disbelief. His meter still had time on it, and Yossi's had none. The policeman had clearly made a mistake and ticketed the wrong car. Mendy knew that the police would never believe him, and he did not have time to call them to the scene.

For the second day in a row, Mendy is claiming that Yossi should pay the ticket since it was his car that caused the policeman to write the ticket. Yossi claims that it was obviously Hashem's will that the policeman make the mistake, and He decided that Mendy should get a ticket. Who pays for this one?

 Tickets have to be paid by people who park without paying and have no one else paying for them either willingly or by mistake — not by people who paid for their parking space and just happen to have their license plate erroneously written on the ticket! The policeman who made the mistake is not licensed to decide who should pay, and who should not. This ticket was meant for Yossi.

The Gemara in *Bava Basra*[68] states that "*Andiski* is Divine Providence." The *Rashbam* explains that the tax collectors would come to a city and collect taxes door to door until the city reached its quota. If they happened to skip someone, and collected enough from everyone else, that person does not have to pay his share to the other citizens. He has been exempted by Heavenly Intervention.

This principle is not applicable to this case, since the obligation to pay the ticket is entirely Yossi's. It was only a mistake that the ticket was placed on Mendy's car.

◆

Defensive Driving

וְאִם בְּפֶתַע בְּלֹא אֵיבָה

But if with suddenness, without enmity

(35:22)

 Avi was driving down a side street when a man jumped into the street. In order to avoid killing the man, Avi swerved and hit a parked car. He had no choice but to choose wrecking the car over ending a life. Now, the owner of the totaled car, Avi, and the man who jumped into the street came to *beis din*. The car owner wants Avi to pay for the damages, Avi wants damages from the man who jumped into the street and caused the accident, and the careless pedestrian says he did not do any damage. Who is right?

---

68. 55a.

Since Avi was obligated by Torah law to smash the parked car because only by doing so could he save a life, he had permission to do what he did, and should not have to pay.[69]

Another reason Avi should not have to pay is based on a ruling from the Chazon Ish.[70] If one sees a missile heading for a group of people, and he could divert the missile but by doing so a different person will die, it would seem that he should nevertheless divert the missile. The *Yerushalmi* tells us[71] that if a warring nation demands from a city to give over one person to be killed, or they will kill out the entire city, they may not give over one Jew, even for the purpose of saving the whole city. This is because handing a person over to murderers is tantamout to an act of murder. Conversely, diverting the missile is essentially an act of saving lives, even though under the circumstances one person will be killed.

According to the reasoning of the Chazon Ish, perhaps Avi's collision into the parked car cannot be viewed as an act of doing damage. Avi performed his act for the purpose of saving a life and therefore may not be guilty of damaging. וצ״ע.

As for the careless pedestrian, it would seem that he should pay. Since he was negligent and caused Avi to barrel into the parked car without any recourse, it is likely that he will be obligated to pay.[72]

<hr />

---

69. See *Bava Kamma* 32b: One who damages with permission does not need to pay.
70. *Yoreh De'ah* 69.
71. *Terumos* 8:4.
72. By the law of *"garmi"* (an act that directly caused damage).

With a Broken Heart

וַתִּהְיֶינָה ... לִבְנֵי דֹדֵיהֶן לְנָשִׁים

And they became ... wives to sons of their uncles

(36:11)

 A young woman had given birth to two handicapped children. A few years later, the woman died, leaving her husband to care for their two children. The woman's family considered the idea that the woman's younger sister would marry the widower, as no one would be able to raise the children with as much love and devotion as their own aunt. There was one problem, however, as the younger sister was presently engaged to another young man. The young woman would like to do what is right. Should she break the engagement, which would certainly cause great pain to her prospective *chassan*, in order to do a tremendous kindness with the poor, unfortunate orphans?

 This question was posed to Rav Elyashiv, who ruled that it would be improper to break the engagement, based on the ruling of the *Beis Meir*. If a man promised a woman that he would marry her in return for her doing him a favor the *Beis Meir* leans toward saying that the man is obligated to fulfill his agreement. It is comparable to a case where one proposed to his friend that he will watch his friend's field today, in return for his friend watching his field the following day, that the proposal is binding to the extent that he is obligated to watch his friend's field as if he were a paid watchman.[73] According to this, Rav Elyashiv determined that the young woman's engagement constitutes a

---

73. See *Shulchan Aruch, Choshen Mishpat* 315.

debt to her fiancé. Even if she wishes to marry another man for the noblest of reasons, she would be stealing the rights of her *chassan*, and she should not do so, even to do kindness with her late sister's children.

It seems, however, that this is only if she is interested to do that which is correct. If, however, she wants to marry her brother-in-law, the *chassan* could not stop her, as she is breaking the engagement in order to give these children the best lives possible.

ספר דברים

Sefer Devarim

פרשת דברים
Parashas Devarim

Picking Your Mitzvos

כַּקָּטֹן כַּגָּדֹל תִּשְׁמָעוּן
Small and great alike shall you hear
(1:17)

 Binny was walking in the street and found two bags whose owners had apparently lost them. He can carry only one of them. Should he attempt to return to its owner the larger (more expensive) of the two, or since it is the same mitzvah of *hashavas aveidah* either way, it makes no difference?

 The Gemara in *Sanhedrin*[1] quotes Reish Lakish's explanation of the *pasuk* that *beis din* should judge equally all cases large or small, to mean that the case determining the owner of a penny should be as beloved as the case regarding $1 million. The Gemara explains that the judges cannot decide to adjudicate the million-dollar case before the case of a penny.

---

1. 8a.

The *Erech Shai*[2] asks: If the case of the penny came in front of the judges first, how could I possibly think that they could have passed it over for the million-dollar case? Reish Lakish himself teaches us[3] that one may not pass over a mitzvah. It seems obvious that *beis din* has to attend to the case that came to them first!

The *Erech Shai* answers, based on the words of the *Chacham Tzvi*, that one may not pass over a mitzvah to engage in a different mitzvah, e.g., *tefillin* versus *tzitzis*. If, however, the two mitzvos are the same, one could indeed prefer the one that seems more pressing, even if the less-pressing mitzvah came to him first! Therefore, it might seem that the million-dollar case is more significant, and the judges could choose to put aside the less-significant case of the penny. That is the point of the *pasuk*, that the cases are equally significant. However, that is true only if the smaller case came before them first. If they came at the same time, *beis din* should hear the larger and therefore more-significant case first, unless the smaller case is for a poor person, since the penny of a poor man is equivalent to a large sum of a wealthy person.

In our case, when Binny cannot return both bags, if one of them belongs to a poor person, he should return it to him, as it is as valuable to its owner as a much more expensive item is to a wealthy person. If the two bags belong to individuals of equal financial standing, he should return the larger of the two, as it is a greater mitzvah to save someone from a greater loss than a less-significant one.

---

2. *Choshen Mishpat* 15.
3. *Yoma* 33a.

One in the Hand . . .

כְּקָטֹן כַּגָּדֹל תִּשְׁמָעוּן

Small and great alike shall you hear

(1:17)

Dovid found a bag of pillows and blankets in the street, and picked them up with the intention of returning them to their owner. After walking a few yards, he found a small case containing diamonds worth thousands more than the pillows and blankets. But Dovid cannot carry both of his finds. Should he put down the pillows and blankets and set out in search of the owner of the diamonds?

The *Erech Shai*[4] writes that if *beis din* started to hear a case concerning a small sum of money and subsequently a million-dollar case came to them, and they will not be able to hear both cases (for example, the witnesses for both cases are about to depart on an extended journey), then if all the litigants are wealthy, it is a mitzvah to adjudicate the greater sum, in order to prevent a greater loss. The mitzvah to judge the smaller case that came to them first is relevant only when they will be able to judge both cases. If they cannot judge both, then since the mitzvah involved in judging both cases is the same, *beis din* may halt the mitzvah in which they are currently engaged, in order to do the mitzvah that involves a greater loss.

Conversely, in the case of returning a lost item it would seem that one should *not* put down the item he is already involved with, in order to return an item of greater value. The *Shulchan Aruch*[5]

---

4. *Choshen Mishpat* 15.
5. Ibid. 12:1.

rules that as long as the judge does not know in whose favor the case is leaning, he may refuse to judge it. Similarly, a judge can opt to arbitrate a different case first. In the case of a lost item, where someone is already involved in returning one item, he cannot decide to return a different item, since one who is involved in a mitzvah is exempt from performing a different mitzvah.

Nevertheless, it seems that Dovid should put down the blankets and pillows in favor of the diamonds. The justification for doing so is because he can estimate the value of the blankets and pillows, and the owner of the diamonds will be obligated to pay the value of the bedding to their respective owner! This is based on the *Shulchan Aruch's*[6] ruling that one who is carrying a barrel of wine must pour out his wine in order to save his friend's honey from spilling on the ground, as the honey is more expensive. The *S'ma* explains that even if the owner of the wine is not present, the owner of the honey may empty the wine barrel to save the honey, on condition that he pays for the wine.

In our case as well, Dovid may set aside the pillows and blankets in order to return the diamonds, on condition that the owner of the pillows and blankets will be compensated for his loss by the owner of the diamonds. If, however, he knows that the owner of the pillows and blankets will not be compensated (e.g., he is leaving imminently and cannot wait to be paid), then Dovid would have to return the lost item that came into his hands first.

———◆◆◆———

6. *Choshen Mishpat* 264:5.

First Come ...

כַּקָּטֹן כַּגָּדֹל תִּשְׁמָעוּן

Small and great alike shall you hear

(1:17)

Ariel walked into an electronics store to buy an extension cord. Before the store owner went to get the cord, a wealthy businessman entered the store and approached the counter. The owner asked him what he needed, and the businessman replied that he needed the most expensive sound system in the store — pronto! The businessman was obviously impatient, and was also willing to spend a lot of money. May the store owner take the more profitable customer before Ariel, even though Ariel was there first, or is that improper?

As noted,[7] the Gemara in *Sanhedrin*[8] notes that if a smaller case came to *beis din* before a larger one, they must judge the smaller case first. The *Maharsha* wonders why one would have thought otherwise. Certainly the smaller case deserves to be tried first, as it is as important to the litigants as the larger case is to its parties. The *Maharsha* suggests that the judges are entitled to collect payment to compensate for their losses due to time spent on the case, time which could have been used to earn money elsewhere. However, compensation can be collected only if the judgment exceeds the compensation plus the minimum amount that would justify a hearing. If the amount of the sum awarded by *beis din* that remains after the judges have been compensated will be less than the minimum amount for a

---

7. See the previous 2 questions.
8. 8a.

court case, then the judges may not collect the money. Therefore, it might seem that the judges can choose to take the valuable case first, in order to allow them to be compensated for their time. That is why Reish Lakish had to teach us that they may not do so.

The *Erech Shai*[9] questions the conclusion of the *Maharsha*. Just as one does not have to spend his own money in order to return someone else's lost item, why would the judges have to forgo the more valuable case that would allow them to be compensated for their time?

It would seem that the *Maharsha's* opinion is that since judging in *beis din* is a mitzvah *bein adam la'Makom*, not *bein adam la'chaveiro* like *hashavas aveidah*, a judge would have to judge the inexpensive case first, even though he will lose money as a result. When the obligation is to one's fellow man, one's own loss takes precedence to the loss of one's friend. A mitzvah in which one is obligated to Hashem, such as judging a court case, requires one to expend money as well.

In our case, everyone would agree that the store owner may help the more profitable client first, since there is no mitzvah to sell electrical equipment, and the store owner's livelihood takes precedence to serving the customer who entered the store first!

———◆◆———

---

9. *Choshen Mishpat* 10.

Preferential Treatment

כְּקָטֹן כַּגָּדֹל תִּשְׁמָעוּן

Small and great alike shall you hear

(1:17)

A. Dr. Greenberg has a drop-in clinic in his house to treat patients at night. He accepts patients in order of arrival. One night, a patient entered the waiting room and asked the other patients if he could be seen before them. Although it would not be dangerous for him to wait his turn, he was nevertheless very weak, and obviously more sick than anyone else waiting. The other patients were upset by the request. They admitted that he was in worse condition than they were, but they were also not in good health. Why should they have to wait extra time because of him? Who is right?

B. The *Shulchan Aruch*[10] rules that a judge must adjudicate cases that come to him in the order in which they came. However, there are several exceptions to this rule, in the following order of precedence: 1) an orphan, 2) a widow, 3) a *talmid chacham,* 4) a woman.

Would this hierarchy apply to a doctor's waiting room as well; or perhaps this schedule is relevant only to a judge and cannot be applied elsewhere?

The *Aderes* is quoted[11] as having doubt as to whether a widow would precede a *talmid chacham* in a doctor's waiting room (even if she came first!). He was in doubt as well, if a less-healthy patient would precede his friend who

---

10. *Choshen Mishpat* 15:1,2.
11. *Hizaharu BeMamon Chaveireichem,* page 340.

was better off than he was, or if everything is determined by who arrived first.

The *Meiri* in *Sanhedrin*[12] deals with both of these issues.

The *Meiri* writes that there are some issues that are not within the realm of strict law; rather, the more fitting course of action is to be taken, and one party has to acquiesce to do even that which is beyond his duty (*lifnim mishuras hadin*), along the route of compromise and outstanding behavior. For example, two ships are crossing a narrowing river simultaneously. If both pass together, they will both capsize. If they pass one after the other, they will both pass without harm. Who should pass first? The Gemara says that if one ship is loaded and the other one is empty, the empty ship should allow the loaded one to pass first. If one ship is close to home and the other is far away from its city, let the ship that is closer allow the ship from far away to pass first. Similarly, any time we see that one party can sustain the delay more than the other, the first party should concede to the latter. For example, a healthy person should allow a sick person to precede him. Even in regard to court cases that came before a judge, an orphan is to be judged before a widow, a widow before a *talmid chacham*, a *talmid chacham* before an ignoramus, and a woman before a man. But if all parties are equal, i.e., they don't fall into one of these categories, then whoever came first should go first!

The *Meiri* is clear that the aforementioned hierarchy is relevant to all cases of waiting, *even* court cases, but not limited to them. That being the case, a healthier patient should allow the much-less-healthy patient to go before him. Although that patient arrived later, nevertheless it would still seem that that would be just and proper behavior.

<hr />

---

12. 32b.

Talent Versus Experience

וְהַדָּבָר אֲשֶׁר יִקְשֶׁה מִכֶּם וכו'

Any matter that is too difficult for you, etc.

(1:17)

 Two brilliant, world-famous doctors differed regarding a diagnosis. Who could possibly decide between them? Each doctor had his strong point. Dr. Green was older and more experienced, with thousands of case histories to his credit. Dr. Fine, although younger and less experienced, was incredibly keen and insightful, an ability that had earned him the respect and even awe of the medical elite. And now, each, when invited to offer an opinion on this difficult case, was adamant that his diagnosis was the correct one, and each had a different opinion. Whose advice should the patient follow?

 This question came before the Gerrer Rebbe,[13] the *Chidushei HaRim*, who decided the issue based on the Gemara in *Berachos*.[14] The Gemara asks: Who should be chosen as *Rosh Yeshivah*, one who has tremendous breadth of knowledge (*Sinai*) or one who is incredibly insightful, capable of explaining the most difficult of questions (*Okeir Harim*)? The Gemara concludes that the one with vast Torah knowledge should be chosen. If so, in our case as well, one should heed the doctor with much more experience.

Rav Elyashiv ruled differently on this matter. He points out that the Gemara dealt with who would be a better educator, in order

---

13. See *Meir Einei HaGolah,* Addition 14.

14. 64a.

to choose a leader for a yeshivah. In such a case, the Gemara said that the one with storehouses of information would better serve to enlighten the students in all areas of Torah about which they would inquire.

For diagnosis of a specific case, a sharp and discerning mind would be better to decipher the data and discover the true cause of the sickness. It could be added that in places that Rabbah (known for his sharpness) and Rav Yosef (known for his broad Torah knowledge) argue, the ruling is like Rabbah in all but three places. We see that in rulings on specific instances, talent outweighs experience, in spite of the fact that the Gemara says that Rav Yosef would be a more fitting Rosh Yeshivah.

Sounds the Same

מֵאֵילַת וּמֵעֶצְיֹן גָּבֶר

From Eilat and from Etzion-gever

(2:8)

 A shul hired a *chazzan* to lead the *davening* for them on Rosh Hashanah and Yom Kippur. A few days before Rosh Hashanah, the *gabbai* spoke with the *chazzan* on the phone to finalize the arrangements. Since the *chazzan* was coming from Teveria, the *gabbai* agreed to rent an apartment for the *chazzan* and his family.

On Erev Rosh Hashanah the *chazzan* set out for Elad, and when he reached the city, he called the *gabbai* to ask for directions. The *gabbai* told him the name of the street and the address, but the *chazzan* could not find his way. He asked people who were in the street, but they could not help him. He had no choice but to call the *gabbai* again.

Frustrated, the *gabbai* asked him which city he was in.

He replied that he was in Elad, of course. The flustered *gabbai* let out a gasp. His congregation was in Eilat!

They both realized that although the *gabbai* had said Eilat, the *chazzan* had heard Elad. Since Eilat is many hours away, and it was Erev Rosh Hashanah, the *chazzan* informed the *gabbai* that he would not be joining them for Yom Tov. The *gabbai* insisted that the *chazzan* must come, for otherwise they will have no *chazzan* or anyone to blow the *shofar*. The *chazzan* claimed that had he known that the job was in Eilat he never would have accepted the job.

Must the *chazzan* go? If not, who must pay for the apartment that was rented for the *chazzan* and his family?

 If the *chazzan's* hearing is normal, and he was misled because the phone line was unclear, he is free from any obligation, as it was not his fault. Even if the *chazzan* is slightly deficient in his hearing, it is still probably not his fault since he never thought that the job was in Eilat.

If it would be possible for the *chazzan* to travel to Eilat, it is certainly a great mitzvah, to enable the congregation to have a *chazzan* and someone to blow the *shofar* for them. Nevertheless, he does not have to exert himself more than other people who ordinarily travel there in order to avail himself to them to allow them to do their mitzvah. This is especially true since traveling to Eilat involves leaving the Biblical boundaries of Eretz Yisrael proper, and the *chazzan* does not have to forgo the benefit of *davening* in Eretz Yisrael on Rosh Hashanah.

פרשת ואתחנן
Parashas Va'eschanan

Wedding Album

כִּי לֹא רְאִיתֶם כָּל תְּמוּנָה
For you did not see any likeness

(4:15)

 Mr. Greenbaum hired a photographer for his daughter's wedding. In the middle of the first round of dancing the photographer fainted and was taken to the emergency room. The wedding continued in the photographer's absence, and all the while many precious moments were not eternalized. May one of the guests use the photographer's equipment to "capture" the wedding on film?

 The Gemara[15] explains that in a case of loss, an employer who has possession of his employee's tools may avoid his loss by using these tools. It is stipulated that this is permissible only if the employee refuses to finish the job without

---

15. *Bava Metzia* 68a.

an acceptable excuse. If the employee became ill, this ruling is not applicable. Therefore it would seem that one may not use the camera without permission from the photographer.

On the other hand, it is likely that the photographer would prefer that his camera should be used to capture the highlights of the evening, since he will be paid to develop the film and print the pictures. In the event that his camera would break, he will be compensated, so he really has nothing to lose. In addition, he certainly would not want to cause pain to the *chassan* and *kallah*, and so one could assume without reservation that the photographer would want them to use his camera. Obviously, if before he was taken to the hospital, the photographer expressed a reluctance to others using his equipment, his wishes must be honored.

A Mitzvah or an Aveirah

וְנִשְׁמַרְתֶּם מְאֹד לְנַפְשֹׁתֵיכֶם

But you shall greatly beware for your souls
(4:15)

 Yitzchak needed to fulfill his obligation to hear the *shofar* on Rosh Hashanah, and he did so in a most distasteful manner. He blew the *shofar* into his friend's ear, causing his friend great discomfort. Did Yitzchak actually fulfill the mitzvah of *shofar* if in effect his action was simultaneously an *aveirah*?

A One who does a mitzvah by means of an *aveirah* has not discharged his obligation.[16] In this case the mitzvah is to hear the *shofar*, and no sin was done in the hearing, rather in the blowing. Perhaps that would be a reason to say that the mitzvah is separate from the *aveirah*.

We could prove this case from a Gemara *in Yerushalmi*.[17] The *Baraisa* states that one who learned of the death of a close relative on Shabbos and immediately tore *kriah*, has discharged his obligation to "tear *kriah*," even though he has desecrated the Shabbos by doing so.

The Gemara questions why this is different from one who ate stolen matzah on Pesach. Why would we not say that he has not fulfilled his mitzvah, since it was accomplished through an *aveirah*? The Gemara resolves this difficulty by explaining that in the case of stolen matzah, the stolen matzah itself is the *aveirah* and one cannot do a mitzvah with an *aveirah*. But when one ripped his garment on Shabbos, although he has certainly done an *aveirah*, the torn garment is not itself an *aveirah*.

The *Ramban* learns from this *Yerushalmi* that if one tears a stolen garment, one would not fulfill this mitzvah of rending his garment upon hearing of the death of a close relative, since then the garment itself would be the object of an *aveirah*.

According to this, since the *shofar* and its sound are not themselves an *aveirah*, even though the person is doing an *aveirah* simultaneously with his mitzvah, it would not prevent him from fulfilling the mitzvah.

The *Sefer Chassidim*[18] writes that one who grabbed a *siddur* from his friend on Rosh Hashanah and used it to pray was chastised by an elderly man for angering Hashem. When he asked the elderly man how to proceed, the man instructed him to ask permission to borrow the siddur and *daven* again, because his first prayer was ineffective!

---

16. *Succah* 30a.
17. *Shabbos* 13:3.
18. 772.

The *Chida* had difficulty with this, as it seems to contradict the ruling concerning one who rent his garment on Shabbos, who has indeed fulfilled the mitzvah. In the case of the *siddur* as well, there was no sin in the prayer, only in taking the *siddur* without permission.

The *Minchas Yitzchak*[19] was questioned regarding a man with a weak heart who was instructed by his doctor not to blow the *shofar* as it could cause his condition to worsen. The man disregarded his doctor's orders and his condition did in fact deteriorate as a result of his blowing. Was this a *"mitzvah haba'ah b'aveirah"*?

The *Minchas Yitzchak* quoted the *Yehudah Ya'aleh*[20] and the *Maharam Schik*[21] who dealt with a similar case. A man was warned by his doctors not to eat matzah and *maror* on Pesach night, lest he put his life in jeopardy. These *gedolim* responded that this would certainly be a case of a *mitzvah haba'ah b'aveirah*. The *Maharam Schik* adds that there is no mitzvah here at all, rather only an *aveirah*. The *Minchas Yitzchak* concludes that certainly in this case, where the man could have heard *shofar* from someone else, to blow for himself would only be an *aveirah,* and not a mitzvah at all.

These cases, however, are not identical to our original question, because in these cases the mitzvah can come only via the *aveirah,* by eating or blowing against medical advice, while in our case the *aveirah* is merely coincidental. Yitzchak has nevertheless fulfilled his obligation of shofar.

———————◆————————

19. Vol. 4, 102.
20. *Orach Chaim* 160.
21. Ibid. 260.

One Reader or Two

אָז יַבְדִּיל מֹשֶׁה

Then Moshe set aside

(4:41)

 There was a *talmid chacham* with a beautiful voice who would read the *Megillah* masterfully every year for his shul. One year he had heart surgery, and he did not have the strength to read the entire *Megillah*. To forfeit his post of reading the *Megillah* would cause him great emotional pain. Should he be allowed to make the *berachos* on the *Megillah,* read one or two chapters, and then step aside and let someone else finish the job, or is it better to find a replacement who could read the *Megillah* in its entirety?

 The *Rema*[22] states that it is fitting that the same person blow all of the *tekiyos* on Rosh Hashanah, as one who starts a mitzvah is instructed to finish it. The *Mishnah Berurah* comments that in shuls where the *minhag* is to divide the *tekiyos* among several people, they may keep their *minhag*, because "the Jews are holy, and have great love for the mitzvos and therefore we will not take away the opportunity from those who wish to take part in the mitzvah." Maybe we could compare *Megillah* to *shofar* and allow the *Megillah* to be read by two people in order not to deprive the *talmid chacham* of his mitzvah.

Nevertheless, perhaps someone else should read the entire *Megillah* from beginning to end, for the *Mishnah Berurah* writes, "If the reader lost his voice in the middle of the *Megillah*, the opinion of the *poskim* is that his replacement need not start the *Megillah*

---

22. *Orach Chaim* 585:4.

from the beginning, as repeating the *Megillah* would be difficult for the congregation."[23]

The *Sha'arei Teshuvah* adds that if the first reader had read only a few *pesukim*, it is not so burdensome to begin again. Also, if the congregation is agreeable to hear the *Megillah* again from its beginning, and Purim is Motza'ei Shabbos, it is better to read it again. If Purim is on a different day of the week, and the congregation is fasting due to Taanis Esther, they may be lenient.

We learn from this that it is desirable that the *Megillah* be read by one person. However, perhaps since we do allow the *Megillah* to be read by more than one person in a case where repeating the *Megillah* would be difficult for the congregation, maybe the pain of a sick *talmid chacham* is also sufficient reason to allow multiple readers. וצ"ע.

It's Not Easy Being Green

וְלֹא תִתְאַוֶּה בֵּית רֵעֶךָ
You shall not desire your fellow's house
(5:18)

 Pinchas has a wonderful study partner in yeshivah and Pinchas would like to learn with him during their intersession as well. For some reason, his partner can learn with him only in his home. The problem is that the home in question is a luxuriously decorated

---

23. See *Sha'arei Teshuvah*.

mansion and every time that Pinchas is there, he is overcome with feelings of jealousy and desire. Does the learning justify putting himself into a situation that severely tests his character?

 Although the final commandment of the *Aseres HaDibros, Lo Sachmod,* is not violated unless one actually attempts to acquire his friend's objects,[24] jealousy and desire are certainly negative attributes. Nevertheless, this is not a valid reason to prevent them from learning together. If one would have to be concerned about such issues, one could not walk to shul lest he see something improper. Alternatively, how could one study with a partner at all, lest their conversation stray to forbidden speech?

The Chofetz Chaim[25] explains a difficult Gemara to shed light on this issue. In *Maseches Chullin*[26] it states: Which profession should one pursue in this world? He should make himself as if he were a mute. The Gemara continues: One might think that one should make himself a mute when it comes to Torah study as well. (The Gemara concludes that, on the contrary, we *are* to speak in Torah.)

How could the Gemara entertain such a possibility? Is the Gemara suggesting that a person should never learn Torah? Rather, explains the Chofetz Chaim, it refers to someone who, by learning with a partner, will have to face the test of speaking forbidden speech. And even so, the Gemara concludes that one should still learn Torah with his partner and the Torah will protect him from sin.

So too, in our case, Pinchas should learn with the *chavrusa.* Beforehand, he should learn *mussar* to remind him of the words of our Sages that teach that running after materialism is the destruction of man, and he should *daven* to Hashem that he be saved from being tested.

---

24. See *Shulchan Aruch, Choshen Mishpat* 359:1.
25. *Shemiras HaLashon, Sha'ar HaTevunah.*
26. 89a.

In a similar vein, the *sefer Lev Chaim*[27] says that even if speaking words of Torah in public may cause the speaker to think highly of himself and become haughty, that should not prevent him from speaking. He should still speak, while trying to control himself to do so for the sake of the Torah and not to glorify himself.

Guard Your Tongue

וְדִבַּרְתָּ בָּם
And you shall speak of them
(6:7)

The Gemara *in Yoma*[28] states in the name of Rava, "One who engages in idle speech is in violation of a positive commandment, as it says, *Vedibarta bam*, 'and you shall speak about them (words of Torah).'" "Them" implies that one may not indulge in idle speech.

The *Sfas Emes* asks: Why did Rava find it necessary to infer the prohibition of idle speech from a *pasuk*? If a person has a constant mitzvah to speak words of Torah, any idle speech is automatically in conflict with the positive mitzvah to study Torah. Even without the inference, from the *pasuk* itself it is implicit that one may not speak idle words, as doing so does not allow him to learn.

Perhaps Rava's inference is relevant in a situation where one may not learn Torah; for example, in an unclean place, if one is in mourning, or one is resting for his

---

27. Vol. III, 102.
28. 19b.

health and needs to take a leave from Torah study. Even though one may not study Torah, one should still not engage in idle speech.

One of the 48 qualities necessary to acquire Torah is minimizing conversation.[29] Some commentaries[30] explain that this actually means to engage (minimally) in conversation in order to rest the brain. Even under such circumstances, one should speak about things that have purpose, and are not idle.[31]

✸rue ✸hinuch

וְשִׁנַּנְתָּם לְבָנֶיךָ
You shall teach them thoroughly to your children
(6:7)

 Shimon sat down in shul to learn with his son on Shabbos afternoon. Someone came into the shul from the adjoining room, where there was a *minyan* for *Minchah*. He told Shimon that they had already taken out the *Sefer Torah*, and that they needed someone to read for them from the Torah. Shimon was unsure if he should oblige. On the one hand, he was already involved in a mitzvah, and was exempt from engaging in another mitzvah. On the other hand, there was a question of embarrassing the Torah, as well as *tircha d'tzibura* (for the *minyan* would have to wait for someone to read for them). Should he

---

29. See *Pirkei Avos* 6:6.

30. See *Orchos Yosher*, Chapter 2, in the name of the Vilna Gaon.

31. Editor's Note: This question is also addressed in *Sefer Chofetz Chaim* (Introduction, *Mitzvos Asei, Be'er Mayim Chaim* 12). He explains that the Gemara seeks to infer that when one speaks idle talk, he not only violates the obligation to study Torah during that time, but is also actively violating a commandment against idle speech.

continue learning, or go read the Torah on behalf of the *minyan*?

 The *Rambam*[32] rules that if one has the opportunity to do a mitzvah that cannot be done by someone else, he should interrupt his learning to go do the mitzvah.

In our case, since reading from the Torah is also *Talmud Torah*, and additionally involves doing kindness for the congregation, it therefore has priority to Shimon's own learning. However, since Shimon is learning with his son, he is also involved in the mitzvah of teaching one's child.[33] In addition, during the time that it takes him to walk to the adjoining room, his son will not be learning at all. Perhaps under such circumstances, Shimon should decline.

The Gemara in *Berachos*[34] tells the story of R' Eliezer who came to shul and found that they were missing one person for the *minyan*. R' Eliezer freed his *eved Cena'ani* to allow him to join the *minyan*. Although normally one is not allowed to free an *eved Cena'ani*, the Gemara explains that for the sake of a mitzvah involving many people it is permitted. In our case as well, Torah reading is a mitzvah involving many people, and perhaps it has priority over Shimon's personal mitzvah.

In truth, there is a difference. Freeing an *eved Cena'ani* is a negation of a positive command.[35] The Gemara permits doing so to allow many people to perform a mitzvah. However, when one is already involved in a mitzvah, and is thereby exempt from other mitzvos, there is no difference whether the second mitzvah is more important or not, since he is exempt anyway.

Although the *Mishnah Berurah*[36] writes that if a *Sefer Torah* is already on the table, and there is no one else who can read for

---

32. *Hilchos Talmud Torah* 3:4.
33. *Kiddushin* 29b.
34. 47b.
35. *Berachos* 47b.
36. 66 § 26.

the congregation, one may even interrupt saying the *Shema,* that rule would not apply here, since we find that one may interrupt the *Shema* for other reasons as well, such as answering *Kaddish* or *Kedushah,* and there is no exemption of being involved in the mitzvah of *Shema.*

Nevertheless, Shimon should interrupt his learning with his son to go read the Torah. The mitzvah of teaching one's son is not only the written word, but to teach proper behavior in Torah and mitzvos. When Shimon is asked to read, he can teach his son the importance of giving honor to the Torah. Although he would love to continue their learning, now he needs to go read for the *minyan,* due to the great importance of the mitzvah. That itself will be a lesson to his son to have the proper appreciation for a mitzvah.

———◆———

Save Some for Me

וְעָשִׂיתָ הַיָּשָׁר וְהַטּוֹב
You shall do what is fair and good
(6:18)

 Naftali and Tzvi lived in Romania. Tzvi asked Naftali to watch a package of diamonds for him. Several days later Tzvi was arrested and forced to admit that he had given the diamonds to his friend. Naftali knew the police would be coming to visit him next and prepared for them to search his house. He knew they would be looking for a package of diamonds and would not leave without it. However, he assumed that the police did not know how many diamonds there were, so he slipped a few out of the package, and hid them where they would not be found. The police came soon after, and, as expected, confiscated the package of diamonds, leaving the remaining diamonds behind.

Now the question is: To whom do the hidden diamonds belong? To Tzvi, because they were his, or to Naftali, since he saved them from confiscation? [Maybe it is comparable to someone who saved his friend's property that has been washed away by the ocean. The property belongs to the one who saved it, and not to the original owner.[37]]

The *Shulchan Aruch* rules:[38] If a fire broke out on Shabbos evening, one may rescue enough food for his three feasts, and he may tell others, "Come save for yourselves food for three feasts." If they wish, they acquire the food from *hefker* since he told them to save it for themselves. The *Mishnah Berurah* comments, had he not told them to take for themselves, the food is not considered ownerless, because he can argue that he could have found Jews who would take it for themselves and return it to him later. The *Beur Halachah* adds that it is not the same as something that has been washed away by the ocean, which is considered ownerless because the owner cannot save it, since here he could have asked a non-Jew, or other Jews, who would have returned it, to save it.

In our case as well, Tzvi will not despair of retrieving his diamonds, because he certainly hopes that Naftali will try to save a few of them. Even if Tzvi never thought of the idea, and it is clear that Tzvi gave up hope of recovering his property, Naftali still needs to return them, because the *Mishnah Berurah* quotes a *Magen Avraham*, that *dina demalchusa* is that *yi'ush* (forfeiture) is not effective. Even though in Romania *dina demalchusa* is that the diamonds belong to the government, that is not binding, since

---

37. See *Bava Metzia* 22b.
38. *Orach Chaim* 334:9.

it constitutes robbery. But the law that *yi'ush* does not apply is a proper custom, as the *Ketzos* explains[39] that one should return property even under such circumstances because it states in the Torah, "And you should do what is proper and good."

It Is Not Yours to Trade

כִּי יִשְׁאָלְךָ בִנְךָ

If your child asks you

(6:20)

An 11-year-old boy, whose parents emigrated from Russia, is learning in a Jewish school and is progressing nicely. He learns *Chumash* and Mishnah, *davens* well, and makes *berachos*. In short, he is advancing in his spiritual growth. One day the boy told his teacher that every Shabbos his father takes him on a trip together with the family, in the family's car.

The boy wants to know what to do. If the teacher will tell the boy to refuse his father's demands, the father may remove his boy from the school and send him to public school instead. Perhaps it would be better to tell the boy not to resist, since he is not the one driving the car, and when he will be older, he will be better able to handle the situation. At this point, however, he might be better off listening to his parents, to ensure that he will have a chance to get a solid Jewish education. What should the teacher advise?

---

39. 259 §3.

A It would appear that the boy should be told the truth, that one is not allowed to travel in a car even if someone else is driving.[40] One may not tell him that it is permissible, even though there is so much at stake. Just as one is not allowed to feed a minor something that is prohibited,[41] one may not instruct him that it is permissible to eat something that is actually prohibited. Even though in our case it is likely that the boy will be taken out of the school, this possibility does not permit violating a prohibition, and we do not have permission to "do business" with the Torah's laws — to violate some, in order to profit elsewhere. The child should be told that it is prohibited to travel in a car on Shabbos, and even if his father thinks that it is permissible, his father is mistaken. If the father forces the boy, the boy should not resist physically because he will not be successful in overcoming his father. Rather, he should react by begging and crying to be allowed to keep the Shabbos.

---

40. See *Chasam Sofer*, Vol. 6, *Likkutim* 97 cited in *Beur Halachah* 404 s.v. *V'ein*.
41. See *Shulchan Aruch, Orach Chaim* 343:1.

פרשת עקב
Parashas Eikev

Maximize Your Potential

אֶת ה' אֱלֹקֶיךָ תִּירָא
Hashem, your G-d, shall you fear
(10:20)

The Mishnah in *Bava Metzia*[42] states that if one has the opportunity to return his father's lost item or his *Rebbi's* lost item, his *Rebbi's* item has precedence. Although his father brought his son into this world, the son's *Rebbi*, who taught him the wisdom of the Torah, is bringing him to the World to Come.[43] Is this Gemara applicable even in a case where the father's lost item is much more expensive than that of his *Rebbi*, or only when both items are of equal value? Similarly, what would the halachah be, if his father was poor, and his *Rebbi* was wealthy? Would the *Rebbi's* item still take precedence

---

42. 33a.
43. If the father pays the boy's tuition, his object takes precedence.

even though it is less significant to him than the father's lost item?

It seems that even under such circumstances, returning his *Rebbi's* lost object takes precedence, even at the expense of returning his father's item. The reason for this is because in addition to the mitzvah of returning a lost item, he is fulfilling another mitzvah as well, the mitzvah to honor one's *Rebbi*. That mitzvah is more important than the mitzvah to honor one's parent, as is explained in the Mishnah. Even though returning his father's item under such circumstances would be a greater mitzvah of *hashavas aveidah*, he will lose out on the mitzvah of giving honor to his *Rebbi*, since there is no mitzvah to honor one's father at the expense of honoring one's *Rebbi*. Although returning his *Rebbi's* item is a lesser mitzvah of *hashavas aveidah,* it is a greater act since it includes the mitzvah of honoring one's *Rebbi*.

————◆◆————

Bar Mitzvah Pose

וּקְשַׁרְתֶּם אֹתָם לְאוֹת
You shall bind them for a sign
(11:18)

Moshe was walking down the avenue one summer evening, when he was approached by the owner of the local photo shop. The photographer, a not-yet-observant Jew, asked Moshe, who was obviously religious, if he would accompany him to the photo store in order to help take a picture. In the rear of the store was a 13-year-old boy on the evening of his Bar Mitzvah. The boy's family was not Torah observant, but his parents, being traditional, wanted him to have a picture of himself wearing *tefillin*. The problem was that neither the parents, nor the photographer, knew how to properly adjust the borrowed pair of *tefillin*. Now they asked Moshe if he could help them. Moshe was not sure what to do. On the one hand, it was already night, and it is forbidden to put on *tefillin* at night.[44] In addition, it seemed disrespectful to use the *tefillin* as a photo prop. On the other hand, a commemoration of his Bar Mitzvah would certainly be special to the boy, and maybe with the passage of time the boy could be brought back to his religion. Should Moshe agree to help the boy put on the *tefillin*?

 Rav Zilberstein decided that it is proper to help the boy don the *tefillin*! The photograph is demonstrative of the love of a mitzvah, and not of disrespect. The parents want to memorialize the occasion of their son wearing *tefillin*. Many *baalei teshuvah* testified that the act of putting on *tefillin* on the day of their Bar Mitzvah made a deep impression on them. A picture of himself wearing *tefillin* will create an emotional connection for the boy to his *Yiddishkeit*.

Putting on *tefillin* at night would be permitted in this situation. The prevailing ruling is that night is considered a viable time for donning *tefillin*, if not for the fact that there is a concern that perhaps one will forget that he is wearing them, and fall asleep while wearing the *tefillin*. Under these circumstances (i.e., it is the night of his Bar Mitzvah, with all of its excitement and fanfare, and he will remove them right after the photo is taken), there may not be a prohibition against wearing *tefillin* at night. The *Shulchan Aruch*[45] has precedented such a possibility, in a case of one who wishes to

---

44. *Shulchan Aruch, Orach Chaim* 30:2.
45. 63:12-13.

travel early in the morning before dawn. He may wear his *tefillin* since there is no concern that he will fall asleep while traveling on the road.

The *sefer Alei Meroros* documents a ruling by Rabbi Yehoshua Aronson, that concentration camp prisoners could don *tefillin* before dawn, when there was no concern that they would fall asleep while wearing them. Those *tefillin* were donned without a *berachah*, and this should be done in our case as well. Unfortunately, this may be this child's only opportunity to wear a pair of *tefillin*.

<hr />

Precious Time

לֹא יִתְיַצֵּב אִישׁ בִּפְנֵיכֶם

No man will stand up against you

(11:25)

 Mrs. Brown was standing on line at the supermarket with a basket full of groceries. A woman approached her and asked if she could go before her, as she had only one item, and will only take a minute. Mrs. Brown had a busy schedule that day, and thought to herself, *What would happen if a few more people would also come with one item, that will really begin to take up my time?* Should Mrs. Brown allow the lady to go ahead of her?

 The *Radvaz*[46] writes, "It makes sense to me that if the case over a penny, that came to *beis din* first, requires great research and takes a lot of time, and the case that

---

46. *Hilchos Sanhedrin* 20:10.

came afterward is very simple, they should adjudicate the second case first in order not to burden the second parties."

Similarly, it would seem that if there is a line of customers with many items each, and one person with just one item, it would be proper to let him go first. However, each case may be different, because sometimes that person may need to pay with a check that needs approval, or to pay with a large bill that requires a lot of change that the cashier will have to collect from several other cashiers, etc. He might wind up taking more time than one of the other customers waiting in line!

פרשת ראה
Parashas Re'ei

Two Mitzvos at Once

לֹא תֹסֵף עָלָיו

You shall not add to it

(13:1)

During Succos a man found a stray cow. He took the cow with him in order to return it to its owner. On the way, the man became hungry and wanted to stop at a nearby *succah* to eat. However, he could not bring the animal into the *succah*. He could not leave the animal outside, since he was responsible to return it. Therefore, since one who is busy with one mitzvah is exempt from performing other mitzvos,[47] he would have to eat outside of the *succah*. Suddenly he had a brainstorm. He would tie a rope from the cow to his own leg, and if the cow would try to escape, or someone would come to take the cow, he would feel the rope tug at him. Is he allowed to use this tactic to perform two mitzvos at once?

---

47. See *Succah* 25a.

As far as the obligation to watch the lost item, as long as the cow is tied well, there is no concern of negligence. However, since he is essentially exempt from the mitzvah of *succah*, maybe he is not allowed to sit in the *succah* because of the prohibition of *Bal Tosif* (adding to a mitzvah)?

*A*The *Avnei Nezer*[48] was asked why one who sits in the *succah* while it is raining is only called a *"hedyot"* (unintelligent) (as doing so is not a valid performance of the mitzvah)[49] and is not in violation of *Bal Tosif*. He answered that *Bal Tosif* applies only when the addition to the mitzvah is in the same vein as the mitzvah itself. For example, the Torah commanded to put four *parshiyos* in one's *tefillin*, and someone wants to put five; the Torah said to keep seven days of Succos, and he wants to keep eight. In contrast, to sit in the *succah* while it is raining is not a quantitative addition to the mitzvos.

Similarly, Rav Elchonon Wasserman in *Kovetz Shiurim*[50] explains that one who is distressed by sitting in the *succah* and is therefore exempt from the mitzvah, and sat there nevertheless, is not in violation of *Bal Tosif*, since the mitzvah is to live in the *succah* like one lives in one's home. One who is distressed is not doing the mitzvah at all, and therefore there can be no addition to a mitzvah that is not being performed at all.

In our case, if he sits in the *succah*, he is doing the actual mitzvah, as it is only the circumstances that cause him not to be obligated. It would seem that there would be a problem of *Bal Tosif*.

Rav Elchonon discusses the nature of the exemption when one who is occupied with a mitzvah is therefore exempt from a different mitzvah; does the exemption just takes away the *obligation*, or does it entirely negate the mitzvah. The difference between the two possibilities would be if one did the second mitzvah

---

48. *Orach Chaim* 467 § 6.
49. See *Rema* 639:7.
50. *Bava Basra* 54.

concurrent with the first mitzvah. If one did so, then according to the first understanding he has done the mitzvah, and therefore it would follow that there is no *Bal Tosif*, since he has done the mitzvah properly. If, however, under such circumstances he has no mitzvah at all, he has not fulfilled the mitzvah of *succah*. After he finishes his first mitzvah (*hashavas aveidah*), he would have to do the mitzvah of *succah* again (for example, on the first night of Succos when one is obligated to eat in the *succah*) and it would seem that he is in violation of *Bal Tosif* as well.

The *Sha'ar HaTziyun*[51] rules that if one who is guarding a lost item, and is therefore exempt from all positive mitzvos, ate matzah on Pesach, he has nevertheless fulfilled his obligation, since he is fit to do the mitzvah, even though he is exempt. As far as making the *berachah* on the matzah there is room for doubt, for how can he say that he is commanded to eat the matzah, when in truth he is really exempt. Therefore, in our case as well, he may eat in the *succah*, although he should not make a *berachah* on the mitzvah of *succah*.

Keeping the Peace

לֹא תִתְגֹּדְדוּ

You shall not cut yourselves

(14:1)

 It was not unusual for a visitor to enter the shul during the week and to request to lead the services. However, the custom of the shul was to *daven* a specific *nusach*.

---

51. 475 § 39.

Even though the visiting *shaliach tzibbur* (literally, messenger of the congregation) was instructed repeatedly not to deviate from the custom of the shul, he insisted on leading the prayers according to his own *nusach*. This incensed one of the shul members, who decided to correct the situation. One bucket of cold water over the prayer leader's head was enough for him to allow someone else to lead the services, as the wet *chazzan* left the shul in shame. Was this justified?

 There are several sources that one may not change from the local custom. The Gemara in *Yevamos*[52] states that there is a Torah prohibition against creating factions within a community. The Gemara in *Pesachim*[53] prohibits veering from the local custom, lest one cause an argument. Certainly a person should not lead the prayers in a manner that is against the will of the congregation.[54]

However, even though the visitor acted incorrectly, this would not permit causing him excessive pain and embarrassment. If they could not persuade him to follow the will of the congregants, they would be allowed to lift him and physically remove him from the shul, as he has no right to be there. Then he would have no claim that he was shamed unfairly, since they were within their rights to do so.

The *Maharsham*[55] leans toward permitting removing one who is *davening Shemoneh Esrei* in the aisle of the shul, when he is obstructing other people. In our case as well, the *shaliach tzibbur* is disturbing the congregation from their *davening* and can certainly be removed before he reaches *Shemoneh Esrei*. However, there would be no permission to shame him in addition to that.

52. 13b.
53. 50b.
54. See *Rema* 53:22.
55. 102 (4).

The *Ateres Moshe*[56] dismisses the claim that the one who poured the water should be excused because he was provoked, as such a claim is acceptable only to excuse a verbal response.[57] He also cites the *Maharshag*[58] that minor changes in the *nusach*, such as whether *Hodu* or *Baruch She'amar* should be recited first, are not a significant breach of custom. He concludes that the one who poured water on the *shaliach tzibbur* is guilty of shaming him, and the entire congregation who were part of such a terrible episode should recite for several days with great intent the prayer of "May it be the will of Hashem that we be saved from brazen people and brazenness."

Questionable Public Relations

עַשֵׂר תְּעַשֵׂר
You shall tithe
(14:22)

An administrator of an organization traveled to America to collect funds. Because his organization was still unknown, he decided to use the following tactic to help promote his cause: He visited a very respected *Rav*, and told him that it was dangerous for a collector to travel with so much cash on hand. He asked if the *Rav* would exchange his personal check for $10,000, in return for cash. The *Rav* agreed.

---

56. Vol. 1, 31.
57. As explained in *Shulchan Aruch, Choshen Mishpat* 420-421.
58. Vol. 2, 67.

When the administrator reached the next community he was given the opportunity to make an appeal in shul. In the middle of his speech praising the work of his organization, he put the *Rav's* check on the table for all to see. Everyone thought the *Rav* had given such a large donation, and decided to follow suit. Now the administrator had second thoughts as to the morality of his actions. Is he required to return the money?

The Gemara[59] entertains the permissibility of someone borrowing an expensive item in order to appear wealthy so people will extend him credit, even if the impression is false. It would seem that such behavior is indeed acceptable.

However, in that case, anyone lending money could consider the possibility that the item was borrowed. Possessing this item does not necessarily reveal the true financial status of its holder. In our story, it is unlikely that people would guess the true motivation behind the *Rav's* check, and therefore the fund-raiser is certainly guilty of misrepresentation.

This question was brought to Rav Elyashiv, who replied: If the donors do not give 10 percent of their earnings to *tzedakah,* the *beis din* could force them to give their share. Therefore, even if the administrator was wrong in what he did, we could consider his actions as coercing someone to give *tzedakah* that they were obligated to give anyway, and the money would not have to be returned.

[Even if the donor had already given his fair share of *tzedakah,* perhaps the money would not have to be returned despite the fact that he was tricked, as the donor does not want to have the money returned to him, once he already designated it for *tzedakah.* צ"ע.]

---

59. *Bava Metzia* 96a.

A Matter of Accounting

עַשֵׂר תְּעַשֵּׂר

You shall tithe

(14:22)

 When someone donates money to a non-profit organization, he is entitled to a tax deduction. For example, if he contributes $1,000 he may save $300 in taxes. How much of his $1,000 can he deduct from *ma'aser kesafim*?

 He may apply $1,000 toward *ma'aser*, since the organization received all of his money. One is allowed to benefit by choosing where to give his *ma'aser*, and one may benefit by receiving a tax deduction as well.[60]

Rav Moshe Feinstein[61] explained that the donor is not getting any new money by giving the *tzedakah*. He is actually keeping his own money as the government agreed not to tax him on the *tzedakah*, because it is deducted from his income. Therefore, he does not have to consider the money he saves as new income. This is in addition to the fact that one is allowed to benefit indirectly, by choosing where to give his money. For example, one may give *tzedakah* to an organization so that the one who runs the organization will feel appreciation toward the donor (as opposed to receiving a gift in return for his donation, which would be considered a direct benefit).

---

60. See *Minchas Yitzchak* Vol. V 34 § 10. He may, however, have to pay *ma'aser* on the amount he benefited.

61. *Igros Moshe, Yoreh De'ah* Vol. I 43.

A Free Mitzvah?

פָּתֹחַ תִּפְתַּח אֶת יָדְךָ

You shall surely open your hand

(15:11)

A. One of the *gedolei hador* issued a check for 1,000 shekels to a *tzedakah* organization to be distributed among the poor for the mitzvah of *Matanos La'evyonim.* A wealthy man bought the check from the organization for 50,000 shekels and framed the check to hang on his wall. Since the check was never cashed, and no money was transferred from the bank account of the *gadol*, has the *gadol* fulfilled the mitzvah of *Matanos La'evyonim*? Since the *gadol's* check generated 50 times its value for *tzedakah*, maybe he has certainly performed the mitzvah.

B. Reuven gave a check to a poor person for *Matanos La'evyonim* and the poor person used the check to buy food. The owner of the grocery store passed on the check to a creditor, and the check was never cashed. Presumably the check was lost. Has Reuven fulfilled his obligation or not, since the money never left his account?

Rav Elyashiv ruled that if someone was obligated to give money to *tzedakah,* he has not fulfilled his obligation if his check was never cashed. In the case of the *gadol hador,* Rav Elyashiv said that the organization should have someone acquire 1,000 shekels from the organization on the *gadol's* behalf, which the *gadol* will return to them to be distributed to the poor. Although the *gadol's* bank account was never diminished, he has fulfilled his obligation with the money gifted to him by the organization.

On the other hand, it is possible that the mitzvah of *Matanos La'evyonim* is different than the general mitzvah of *tzedakah*. The *Ritva* in *Megillah*[62] explains that *Matanos La'evyonim* is not just *tzedakah,* but it is an extension of the *simchah* of Purim. Perhaps the *simchah* has been achieved even if the check was never cashed.

The *Maharil*[63] was asked if one could do the mitzvah of *Matanos La'evyonim* with *ma'aser* money. On the one hand, *ma'aser* money already belongs to the poor and it is therefore not considered as if one had given them anything new. Or, since the essence of the mitzvah of *Matanos La'evyonim* is to make poor people happy, perhaps it does not make a difference to the poor person where the money is from. He is happy that he was chosen to receive the money. The *Maharil* answers that since the *Rabbanim* enacted an obligation of *Matanos La'evyonim*, it is an obligation that cannot be discharged with money that does not belong to the one giving. Therefore *ma'aser* money would not be acceptable currency.

The *K'sav Sofer*[64] argues that the mitzvah of *Matanos La'evyonim* is not a regular obligation that requires one to give of one's own money, since the essence of the mitzvah is to bring joy to the recipient, not necessarily to give of one's money. Evidently the *Maharil* understood that one does have to expend his own money. That is the prevailing opinion of the *poskim*. As long as the check was never cashed, one has not fulfilled the mitzvah.

———◆———

62. 7a.
63. Cited by *Magen Avraham* 694 § 7.
64. *Yoreh De'ah* 112.

My Day Off

וְשָׂמַחְתָּ בְּחַגֶּךָ

You shall rejoice on your festival

(16:14)

 Q A *chazzan* who lived in a different city was hired to come and lead the *davening* in a shul every Shabbos. On Yom Tov he wanted to stay home and spend time with his family and therefore the *chazzan* stipulated that he would come only on Shabbos, and not on Yom Tov. It was not long before Yom Tov and Shabbos coincided, and an argument ensued. The *gabbaim* claimed that since it was Shabbos, the *chazzan* was obligated to come. The *chazzan* claimed that it was Yom Tov, and he was on vacation. Who is right?

 A Since Yom Tov is meant to be a time of *"simchah,"*[65] and the obligation of *simchah* remains even when Yom Tov and Shabbos coincide, it is logical that the *chazzan* should be allowed to stay home. The *chazzan* feels that he cannot rejoice properly with his family when they are away from home, and therefore he is exempt from traveling.

A minor proof that Yom Tov supersedes Shabbos can be brought from the fact that when Shabbos and Yom Tov coincide, the usual Shabbos *davening* is replaced by the Yom Tov text (with additions for Shabbos), and not the other way around.

---

65. See *Shulchan Aruch, Orach Chaim* 529:1.

Dressing Up

וְשָׂמַחְתָּ בְּחַגֶּךָ

You shall rejoice on your festival

(16:14)

 The Cohens are a very special couple, who have been married for many years. One Yom Tov, there was simply not enough money in the house to buy Yom Tov clothing for both Rabbi and Mrs. Cohen. Mrs. Cohen would like her husband to purchase a beautiful frock for himself, so that she can enjoy the Yom Tov with the knowledge that her husband has new clothing. This would also be an honor for the Torah, as her husband is a *talmid chacham*. Rabbi Cohen, however, would like to use the money to buy his wife a dress in honor of Yom Tov. What should they do?

 Rabbeinu Chaim Palagi writes in his *sefer Kaf HaChaim*[66] that regarding quality of food, a husband's needs come before those of his wife. Regarding clothing, the wife's needs take precedence over those of her husband. Therefore, he should buy his wife a dress in fulfillment of the mitzvah of *"Simchas* Yom Tov,"* as it is an obligation for the husband to make his wife happy on Yom Tov.[67] The way a man does so is by buying his wife clothing and jewelry, according to his financial situation.

---

66. 24 b.
67. *Shulchan Aruch, Orach Chaim* 529:2.

פרשת שופטים
Parashas Shoftim

A Profitable Investment

צֶדֶק צֶדֶק תִּרְדֹּף

Righteousness, righteousness shall you pursue

(16:20)

Shimon lent large sums of money to several people and, unfortunately, he was never repaid. His wife is encouraging him to take these people to *beis din* to force them to pay. She insists that it is a mitzvah to adjudicate in *beis din*. However, Shimon knows that the legal process will not be an easy one, and until he sees any money from it, it will cause him a lot of anguish. It may also cause his borrowers to violate mitzvos *bein adam la'chaveiro*. Should he take them to *beis din* so that he will not be considered a fool who throws away that which belongs to him,[68] or should he refrain from legal action, and let Hashem repay him elsewhere?

---

68. See *Chagigah* 4a.

The Gemara in *Bava Basra*[69] tells the story of someone who asked a tenant how he came to live in his present residence.

"I bought it from Levi," he responded.

"Levi is a thief," came the retort.

"But I have witnesses that you approached me one night to acquire land from Levi on your behalf."

"My intention was to acquire the land, to avoid engaging Levi in a legal battle."

Rava concludes that the plaintiff has a legitimate claim since indeed a person is likely to spend money in order to avoid a legal battle.

Rabbeinu Chananel explains that although the land was rightfully his, a person would still spend money to avoid an argument. According to this, it is obvious that forgoing a valid claim is not foolish, for if it were, such a claim would not be accepted.

The son of the Chofetz Chaim writes[70] that his father never brought anyone to *beis din*, even if they caused him significant losses. Whether it was people who bought on credit from his wife's store and never paid, or whether the losses were incurred when he sold his *sefarim* via emissaries, his losses totaled thousands of rubles. Even though his losses upset him, he never argued with anyone. The Chofetz Chaim told his son that he forgives them; since they will not pay in any event, he did not want them to be punished on his account.

The *Rav* from Luna related that he personally witnessed the Chofetz Chaim making an accounting with one of his *sefarim* salesmen. It became apparent that several hundred rubles were missing! The salesman excused himself by saying that his wife was very demanding and that he could not stop her from taking some of the money. Once the salesman had departed, the *Rav* from Luna saw the Chofetz Chaim hurry outside to the salesman's carriage, take a silk scarf from under his coat, and press it into the

---

69. 30b.
70. *Dugma MeiChayei Avi* 65.

salesman's hand! The Chofetz Chaim insisted that he present the scarf to his wife so that his life with her would be easier.

We can deduce from this story that many times it is advantageous for a pious individual to forgo taking people to *beis din*, when doing so may lead to lying, anger, or even *chas v'shalom* cursing the judges!

If, however, being *mevater* will cause someone to become a burden upon the community, i.e., he will have to collect *tzedakah*, he should not be that pious; rather, he should present his case to *beis din* and claim that which is rightfully his, in order not to tax the community.

<hr />

Medical Secrets

לֹא תַסִּיג גְּבוּל רֵעֶךָ
You shall not move a boundary of your fellow
(19:14)

Dr. Kass produces natural remedies that are not available to the public. The formulae for these remedies are all written down in a special notebook. Dr. Levy has an opportunity to access Dr. Kass' notebook. May Dr. Levy read the notebook without the owner's permission in order to study his colleague's wisdom, and enable him to heal others?

The *Halachos Ketanos*[71] was asked by someone whose friend had forbade him to use his book, if merely viewing the book would be considered "use." The *Halachos*

---

71. Vol. 1, 6.

Ketanos responded that although one who merely views, hears, or smells something that has been given to the *Beis HaMikdash* is not guilty of *meilah* (benefiting from something sacred), nonetheless, it is still forbidden to do so. For example, measures were taken so that craftsmen who had to repair the *Kodesh HaKodashim* could not gaze upon their holy surroundings, i.e., they were lowered down in a mostly closed box.

The *Ya'avetz* questions whether the comparison to looking at something that one has been forbidden to enjoy is accurate. In the case of someone who has been denied use of a book, he is not merely looking, because looking is equivalent to using the book!

In Dr. Levy's case, no one actually forbade him from using the book. If he is not planning on taking the knowledge for his own benefit, rather for his patients, perhaps it would be permissible.

The Gemara in *Yoma*[72] tells how R' Yochanan tricked a Roman expert into revealing the cure for a dangerous disease of the gums, and he publicized the information in a *shiur*!

This is all with the understanding that Dr. Levy is only benefitting his patients. If, however, his new knowledge would cause any loss to Dr. Kass, i.e., to take away patients from him, it would be forbidden. Similarly, Dr. Levy may not publicize the information, as doing so would be an infringement on Dr. Kass' business as well (*hasagas gevul*).

The Gemara in *Shabbos*[73] records that Rava did not publicize the cure for cracked skin, in order not to damage the livelihood of Dr. Minumei's sons.

If, however, Dr. Levy wants to learn many secrets from the book so that he can become an expert in the field, it would be similar to doing business with his friend's property, which would also be forbidden. וצ"ע.

---

72. 84a.
73. 133b.

A Help or a Harm I

A. A boy lost the use of both of his kidneys and needed a donor for a transplant. His mother volunteered to give him one of her kidneys. After a series of tests it was found that her right kidney was suitable for the transplant. At great expense, she engaged the services of a top private surgeon. The surgeon erred, and removed her left kidney instead of her right one. After it had been removed, the kidney was checked, and it was found to have a tumor. Had the right kidney been removed, the tumor would have grown, rendering the woman's remaining kidney non-functional. Obviously Hashem had guided the surgeon's hand to save this woman's life. Does the doctor need to pay the woman for damages, for removing the wrong kidney? (Whether the woman needs to pay for this operation, for which she did not hire the surgeon, and which she never intended to have performed, will be the topic of the question in *Parashas Ki Seitzei* [23:4].)

B. Yaakov drove recklessly and collided with Yehoshua's car. Yehoshua was rushed to the emergency room and detained for testing and observation. This caused Yehoshua to miss his airline flight that afternoon. That night Yehoshua found out how lucky he was, as the plane he was scheduled to have taken had malfunctioned and crashed into the ocean, leaving no survivors. Does Yaakov need to pay Yehoshua for damaging his car, or since he saved his life, no payments or apology is required?

C. Rav BenZion Hauseman told an unbelievable story that happened to a member of his family. This man became ill and was hospitalized. There he contracted a fever, and the doctors could not diagnose the illness. When they were taking the patient's temperature with a mercury thermometer, the glass cracked, and the patient swallowed the mercury. They immediately flushed his stomach, at the same time emptying the poison that had been harboring in his body, and bringing the patient immediate recovery. The doctors wrote in the patient's file that it was Hashem's hand that had brought about the patient's recovery.

If someone else had broken the thermometer in the patient's mouth, and that had led to the patient's cure, would the patient be able to claim damages and medical expenses from the one who broke the thermometer, or since it was obvious that Hashem had guided his hand, he would be innocent of all charges?

D. A woman contracted a disease, and lost her power of speech. A few years later, while crossing the street, she was hit by a car, and thrown quite a distance. She suffered multiple injuries, but at the same time something inside her was impacted and slowly she recovered her ability to speak. Does the driver need to pay her for damages, or since he benefited her much more than the damage caused, he does not have to pay?

 The Gemara[74] tells of Rabban Gamliel who accidentally knocked out the eye of his faithful slave, Tevi, an act that should have rendered Tevi a free man.[75] Rabban Gamliel

---

74. *Bava Kamma* 74b.
75. See *Shemos* 21:26.

was very happy about this, as he wanted to set Tevi free and was not allowed to because of the Torah's prohibition against willfully freeing an *eved Cena'ani*.[76] The *Beis Yitzchak*[77] and *Ya'avetz*[78] ask, could Rabban Gamliel be happy when he transgressed the prohibition of hitting one's friend? Even if it was accidental, he still needs an atonement! The *Beis Yitzchak* explains that this supports the opinion of the *Turei Even*, who says that one may allow his friend to hit him, even to the extent that there is no transgression involved. Certainly, Tevi forgave Rabban Gamliel for his actions, since it gained him his freedom. That is why Rabban Gamliel was happy.

According to this, in all of the previous scenarios, it would seem that the victims certainly forgave the actions of the offenders, since in the end, everything worked out for the best.

However, it seems that there is a difference if the action brought about an immediate benefit — even if not immediately apparent — or if the benefit came later as a result of the person's wounds.

Rabban Gamliel's assault on Tevi rendered him a free man immediately, transforming Rabban Gamliel's act into a positive one. If, however, the act had been a negative one, causing pain and damage, and only with the passage of time it resulted in an eventual benefit, the assailant would still be liable for his actions.

The *Mishnah Berurah*[79] explains in a similar context, "We do not have to look toward the future, since the result might not have come." Similarly, this would apply whenever the assailant caused damage, despite the fact that the victim subsequently had a benefit.

Therefore, the surgeon who removed the wrong kidney, which was found to be cancerous, does not need to pay damages since his act is considered a positive one at the same time it was performed.

The reckless driver who caused his victim to miss his flight has to pay, since he certainly damaged him, and only afterward a

76. See *Berachos* 47b.
77. *Yoreh De'ah* Vol. II, 101 § 2.
78. In *Bava Kamma* ad loc.
79. 222:4.

new circumstance arose that retroactively turned his accident into a lifesaver.

In the case of the thermometer, since the entire expense was for flushing the stomach, which was a necessary and positive act at the time, it makes sense that no damage payment would be necessary from the one who broke the thermometer.

In the case of the mute woman, even though the accident restored her power of speech, and therefore it would seem to have been a positive act, in actuality there were two acts at the same time. Her multiple injuries came at the same time that whatever cured her was affected. Each act, causing her injuries and restoring her speech, is judged separately and since one of them was only negative, the driver would be required to pay for the damages despite the simultaneous cure.[80]

(Regarding having to pay for the benefits received, see "A Help or a Harm II," *Parashas Ki Seitzei*, p. 438.)

---

80. See *Chashukei Chemed, Bava Kamma,* page 418, who brings proofs to this point.

פרשת כי תצא
Parashas Ki Seitzei

Finders Are Not Always Keepers

הָשֵׁב תְּשִׁיבֵם לְאָחִיךָ

You shall surely return them to your brother

(22:1)

 Akiva found a lost object, and now had the opportunity to fulfill the mitzvah of *hashavas aveidah*. Afterward he regretted having found it, as he was very busy, and could not take time from his work to do the mitzvah. Akiva met his friend Effy and asked him if he would like to do the mitzvah instead of him. Effy was elated at the opportunity, and went directly to call the owner to arrange the return of the lost item. The owner told Effy that he no longer needed it, and he wanted Effy to keep it. Does Effy get to keep it, or maybe the owner wanted the finder to keep it, in which case it belongs to Akiva?

The *Shulchan Aruch* rules:[81] If one sent a messenger to buy something with a set price, and the seller gave the messenger extra merchandise, the messenger and the one who sent him split the additional merchandise. If the price is not fixed, everything belongs to the one who sent him. Had Akiva sent Effy to buy something on his behalf that would have been the halachah.

However, in our case, Effy was not a messenger, at least not for Akiva. Effy was acting on behalf of the owner of the lost property. When Akiva relieved himself of his obligation, he also forfeited any rights he had to the mitzvah. Therefore Effy deserves to keep the item.

In addition, the mindset of the owner is certainly to gift the one who actually intended to return the item, not the one who decided that he did not have the time.

Where Is Your Gratitude?

וַהֲשֵׁבֹתוֹ לוֹ

And you return it to him

(22:2)

A man of highly questionable character was walking down the street when he noticed a very expensive automobile parked at the curb. He could not resist the temptation, and within seconds he had broken the lock

---

81. *Choshen Mishpat* 183:6.

and started the car with the skill of a professional thief. As he drove away, he noticed something moving in the back seat. He quickly turned around and saw a semiconscious child who was blue in the face and having difficulty breathing. The man immediately turned the car around to drive to the nearest hospital.

At the hospital, he related the following story. He had been walking down the street and had noticed a child in the back of the car, who looked like he was in distress. At that point, he broke into the car, and drove straight to the hospital.

The doctors, with the help of Hashem, were able to save the child, and the hospital staff was able to locate the parents. The parents came and thanked the man profusely for saving their child. As the father escorted the "hero" from the hospital, he noticed that the lock on the car door was completely broken. The father turned to the man and said, "You know, a lock on an expensive car like this costs a few thousand dollars! Please pay me for the damage you did!" The rescuer/thief answered, "What? I just saved your child's life! What do you want from me?"

What is the halachah in such a case? Does the rescue absolve the rescuer/thief of the obligation to pay for the damage done to the car during the attempted theft, or not?

 It must be ascertained if the determining factor of a man's deed is his actions or his intent. The Gemara in *Menachos*[82] relates an argument concerning a man who threw a net into the ocean on Shabbos to catch some fish, and his net indeed caught several fish, as well as a child who was in danger of drowning. Rabbah said the man is innocent, while Rava said that he is not. Rabbah's reasoning is that we look at the man's

82. 64a.

action, while Rava's reasoning is that we look at his intent. The halachah is like Rabbah, as is written by the *Rambam*.[83] According to this, the man who rescued the child should not have to pay for the damage to the car, as all rescuers are exempt from damages that occurred during their rescue.[84]

As Long as It Stands

כִּי תִבְנֶה בַּיִת חָדָשׁ

If you build a new house

(22:8)

Chanina and his younger brother Yosef were heirs to their father's estate. The father left a large piece of land with one large house and one small house. Yosef offered Chanina that he could take the larger house on the condition that if the house would need to be rebuilt, they would build two houses of the same size, and each of them would receive one. Chanina lived in the larger house for years. As the house aged, its walls began to crack. Chanina wants to pour concrete support beams to keep the house intact, but Yosef claims that doing so is like rebuilding the house. Who is right?

Rav Elyashiv answered that Chanina may not build new supports for the house. The Rav's source is in *Shulchan Aruch*.[85] Just as a widow is supported from the estate of

83. *Hilchos Shegagos* 2:15.
84. *Sanhedrin* 74a.
85. *Even HaEzer* 94:1,2.

her late husband, she is also given living quarters, or alternatively she may live in the house where she had lived with her husband. If her quarters collapse, the heirs are not required to rebuild them. Without permission from the heirs she may not even rebuild them herself, nor may she repair the cracks or add to the structure. She has to live there as is, or leave.

This is because her rights to the house exist only for as long as it stands, and she may not enhance the capability of the house to stand. In our case as well, Chanina may not build supports for the house.

The *Netziv* in *Meishiv Davar*[86] ruled in a similar case, based on *Tosafos* in *Bava Metzia*[87] which states that any addition to the house is considered a new building, even if one uses the same stones as before.

<hr />

A Help or a Harm II

לֹא יָבֹא עַמּוֹנִי וּמוֹאָבִי

An Ammonite or Moabite shall not enter
(23:4)

 In the case where the surgeon removed the wrong kidney that was found to be cancerous,[88] does the woman need to pay for the operation that saved her life, or since the doctor had no intent to give her this benefit, she does not need to pay for his carelessness?

In the cases of the thermometer, as well as the case of the mute woman, since they would be willing to pay

86. 3:69
87. 79a.
88. See "A Help or a Harm I," *Parashas Shoftim*, (p. 430).

for the benefits, perhaps they should pay for the "service" that was provided?

 The Gemara in *Sanhedrin*[89] tells the story of Geviha ben Pesisa who argued with an apostate. Geviha had a hunched back, and the man threatened to give Geviha such a hard kick that it would straighten out his back. Geviha replied, "If you would do that, you would be a great doctor who could demand a great fee!"

The *Chida* comments on this Gemara, that even though the *Rema* rules[90] that one who does a favor for his friend may indeed ask to be paid, that is only if he had intention to benefit the recipient. If, however, the act was done with the intent to do damage, and inadvertently caused a benefit, no payment is due, since we know his true intent. Geviha did not really mean that the person would deserve payment, but that he would gladly pay him, even though he had intended to hurt and not to heal.

The *Dubno Maggid* expresses the same idea. There is a mitzvah not to let the nations of Ammon and Moav marry into the congregation of Israel. The Torah explains that the reason for this is because these nations did not greet the Jews with bread and water after the Exodus from Egypt, and because they hired Bilaam to curse the Jews. The Torah adds that Hashem did not want to hear Bilaam's curse and changed the curse into a blessing. The *Maggid* asked, Why was this last detail necessary to relate here? He answered with a parable.

There was once a merchant who traveled with a loaded wagon through the forest, and was accosted by a robber. The robber left the merchant in the forest, and rode off with the wagon. At the edge of the forest, the robber was caught and brought for trial. The robber insisted to be paid for his services, because the forest was a dangerous place, filled with robbers and wild animals, and it was

---

89. 91a.
90. *Choshen Mishpat* 264:4.

his expertise that resulted in the wagon traveling safely though the forest. The judge laughed. "You took the wagon through the forest in order to take it for yourself. If it were left to you, the merchant would have nothing. Certainly he does not owe a thing."

Moav might have thought that it was unfair that the Torah should push them away. After all, because of them, the Jews were blessed three times by a prophet. The Torah refutes this claim. The Jews owe Moav nothing. They wanted the Jews to be cursed, and it was only Hashem Who prevented this. The only gratitude due is to Hashem, not to Moav, who had absolutely no intention to benefit the Jews.

According to this, in cases B, C, and D (see "A Help or a Harm I," *Parashas Shoftim,* p. 430), where the person did an act of damage, no payment is due. Additionally, in the first case, the surgeon intended to do good, and despite the fact that he made a mistake, no damage was done. Rav Elyashiv ruled that since the woman benefited from the operation, she needs to pay. However, she is not required to pay for an operation in which the kidney is intended for transplant, which requires a special surgeon. Rather, she should pay the price one would pay to a regular surgeon to take out a cancerous kidney. If the woman will claim that for such an operation she would not have taken a private surgeon, rather one from the medical group to which she belongs, we would have to decide if she is telling the truth, since we see that at times she does choose to engage the services of a private surgeon.

Structural Defect

כִּי יִקַּח אִישׁ אִשָּׁה חֲדָשָׁה

When a man marries a new wife

(24:5)

 Zevi rented an apartment for himself and his new wife. They quickly discovered that in addition to themselves, there was a mouse occupying their living quarters. His wife is terrified and refuses to live there. Can Zevi claim that renting the apartment was a *mekach ta'us* (a transaction made under a misconception) and renege on his contract?

 Even though in Talmudic times it seems that it was common to have mice in the house,[91] today the standards have changed. Many women are terrified of mice, and it is certainly a defect in the apartment for which one could nullify the contract. However, if one could rid the apartment of mice by hiring an exterminator, the mice would not be considered a defect. If the mice were present before they signed the contract, it would be the owner's responsibility to pay for the exterminator, since this is a skilled labor. (In *Bava Metzia*[92] we learn that the owner is responsible for the lock on the door as well as anything that requires a craftsman to fix.) If extermination is not effective, it would seem the renter could nullify his lease.

————◆-◆-◆————

91. See *Pesachim* 8b.
92. 101b.

Cardboard by the Pound?

אֶבֶן שְׁלֵמָה וָצֶדֶק יִהְיֶה לָךְ

A perfect and honest weight shall you have

(25:15)

A certain bakery was known for its exquisitely beautiful, as well as sumptuously delectable, tortes, which were sold for a not-insignificant amount of money. The owner of the bakery would carefully place the cake in a box and weigh the torte in the box. The cardboard box is much less expensive than the fancy cake, yet the bakery charges the same price per pound for both. Is that dishonest?

To one who has learned the Gemara in Shabbos,[93] it would seem that there is no problem with the bakery's practice. Rabbi Yishmael taught that one may mix in a measure of preservative into the grain without concern. Even though he sells the grain by weight, and the preservative is cheaper than the grain, since the preservative is necessary to keep the grain from spoiling, one may consider it as part of the grain.

Along these lines one could say that since the box is necessary to keep the cake intact, it may be sold as part of the cake.

However, there is a difference. The preservative is mixed with the grain well before the grain is measured. At the bakery the cake is put into the box right before it is weighed. There is no reason to protect the cake before weighing it, as opposed to afterward. Therefore to weigh the cake with the box is problematic.

---

93. 31a.

If the bakery insists on protecting the cake before placing it on the scale, they should deduct the weight of the box and charge a fair price for the box, separately. A less desirable method would be to print a sign saying that their practice is to charge for the box according to the price per pound of the cake.

However, if this is common practice in all bakeries, and everyone knows that this is how cakes are weighed, there is no problem of dishonesty.

פרשת כי תבוא
Parashas Ki Savo

An Incomplete Present

וְשָׂמַחְתָּ בְכָל הַטּוֹב

You shall rejoice with all the goodness

(26:11)

Menachem purchased travel insurance in preparation for a trip abroad. The terms of the insurance were
such that in the event that medical treatment would be
required, Menachem must pay the expenses, and he
would be compensated based on the receipts he provided to the company. Each receipt required a $50 co-
payment from Menachem.

Toward the end of Menachem's trip, he became
ill and consulted a doctor. The doctor never charged
less than $200, but because he was so impressed
with Menachem's personality, and he realized that
Menachem was a tourist, he gave Menachem a discount,
and charged him only $100. However, the receipt that
the doctor provided stated the usual fee of $200.

When Menachem returned home he was unsure of

how to collect from the insurance company. He could be reimbursed only if he would submit the bill, but upon receipt of the bill for $200, they would pay him $150 — $200 minus the $50 co-payment — when in reality, he had only paid $100. Can he take the extra $50 and consider it a gift from the doctor, since the doctor knew that Menachem had insurance? Perhaps he is only entitled to $100 since that is the amount he paid? Alternatively, maybe he is only entitled to $50, since he must meet his co-payment of $50?

 It seems that Menachem is not entitled to collect an extra $50 that he never paid to the doctor. The basis for this is the ruling of the *Rema*[94] that states: If someone gave 50 gold coins to an agent to settle with his creditors, and the agent was able to settle for 25 gold coins, the excess coins belong to the original owner. Since the coins were always his, they do not become the property of the agent. Certainly in our case, Menachem, who never even saw the extra $50, cannot acquire it! The fact that he was given a receipt for $200 does not entitle him to additional money. In the *Rema's* case there may have also been outstanding bonds for 50 gold coins, and the agent was able to buy them for 25 gold coins. Even so, he is not allowed to keep the additional money.

One may argue that Menachem is not an agent representing the insurance company, but had a separate dealing with the doctor, and a business deal with the insurance company. The fact that the doctor gave him a discount is unrelated to his agreement with the insurance company, which agreed to pay him for the receipts he provides.

However, the *Shach*[95] does not concur with this argument. The *Shach* quotes the *Divrei Rivos,* who ruled in the following case:

---

94. *Choshen Mishpat* 183:9.
95. Ad loc. § 17.

Reuven sent Shimon as his agent to borrow money from a gentile. Shimon informed Reuven that the gentile is charging 10 percent interest for the loan, and Reuven agreed to the terms. Reuven subsequently discovered that the gentile is charging only 5 percent interest, and Shimon decided to keep the other 5 percent for himself. Shimon claims that he borrowed the money from the gentile for himself, and he is lending the money to Reuven at 10 percent interest. The *Divrei Rivos* ruled that since Reuven never intended to pay interest to Shimon, Shimon cannot take money that was never intended to be given to him. In our case as well, the insurance company only intended to pay for Menachem's out-of-pocket expenses, not for his business deals. Therefore, Menachem is not entitled to take money that he never spent, since the insurance company never agreed to sponsor such a transaction.

Nevertheless, Menachem may indeed be entitled to collect the $100 that he spent, despite the fact that he is obligated to cover $50 of the cost himself. The rationale is that the doctor intended to give a gift to Menachem, and not to the insurance company! The reason the insurance company required co-payment is to ensure that their client will not go to the doctor unnecessarily. In this case, Menachem really did need the doctor's services. In addition, the insurance company benefited from the discount that Menachem received. Menachem could have refused the discount and the company would have had to pay $150. The company would be willing to pay Menachem $100 so that they should not have to pay $150, had he declined the discount.

In practice though, it seems that the insurance company would not agree to such an arrangement, in order to prevent other people from fraud. Therefore Menachem would have to pay the $50 he originally agreed to pay.

However, since the doctor wanted to give Menachem a present, and not to benefit the insurance company, perhaps Menachem should request $150 from the insurance company, and send the doctor the additional $100. On the other hand, although the doctor's intent was to benefit his patient, even if Menachem did not have any benefit from the doctor's generosity, and only the insurance company benefited, maybe that is the true will of Hashem, that the company should profit. וצ"ע.

Honoring One's Parent: At What Price?

אָרוּר מַקְלֶה אָבִיו וְאִמּוֹ

Accursed is one who degrades his father or mother

(27:16)

Q **An insurance agent** informs his clients that he is selling a savings plan to provide money for the weddings of their children. In truth, the policy is actually life insurance. As the policy is paid yearly, it accumulates value, and can be cashed in for more than the value paid as premiums. The insurance company pays interest for being able to use the money collected in premiums, in return for not having to pay the death benefit. If his clients would know the truth, they would not be interested in such a policy, as many people do not want to consider their mortality and do not wish to carry life insurance. Is it permissible for the agent's son to expose his father's dishonesty, since it is *lashon hara l'to'eles,*[96] or, since he is speaking ill about his parent, it would be

96. Speaking negatively about someone else for a constructive purpose; see *Chofetz Chaim, Klal* 10.

considered a violation of honoring one's parents, and is forbidden even for a positive reason?

 This question is deliberated by the author of *Shalmei Nissan*[97] who quotes one of the *poskim* who forbids speaking ill of one's parents even for a constructive purpose. Although one who defames others for a constructive purpose is not a gossiper, one who defames a parent is in violation of *kibbud av va'eim* as well as including himself in the curse of one who embarrasses a parent.[98] These transgressions are not permitted, even if they are being violated for a constructive purpose.

It would seem that this opinion is in contradiction to the Gemara in *Megillah*,[99] which relates how Rachel Imeinu told Yaakov Avinu that her father was a conniver and he would not consent to them getting married. It is an apparent difficulty that Rachel spoke *lashon hara* about her father if one may not do so even for constructive purposes.

There seem to be four reasons to permit doing so in Rachel's case.

1) This incident took place before *Matan Torah*. She was therefore not obligated by the Torah's law to honor her parent. Even though children are obligated morally to do so out of appreciation,[100] and such is their custom, however in a case where there is a constructive purpose, it would be permissible for Rachel to warn Yaakov about her father, as she did.

2) The propriety of honoring her father is outweighed by her preventing her father from stealing from Yaakov, since she is saving her father from a true sin.

3) Rachel was not required to forgo marrying Yaakov for the sake of honoring her father. The obligation of honoring one's parents does not include forfeiting one's spouse.[101]

---

97. *Koveitz Kol Torah*, Nissan 5761.
98. *Devarim* 27:16.
99. 13b.
100. See *Igros Moshe, Yoreh De'ah* 2:130.
101. See *Yoreh De'ah* 240:25.

4) The *Rema*[102] rules that one is not required to honor a wicked father. Although one may not cause pain to a wicked father, nevertheless to degrade one's father behind his back would not cause any pain and is certainly just an issue of honor.

Nevertheless, it would seem that one may even speak *lashon hara l'to'eles* about one's parents, and the son could indeed warn his father's clients. This may be inferred from the *Sefer Chassidim*,[103] who writes that if a child sees someone entrusting an item for safekeeping with the child's parent, and the child knows that his parent is not to be trusted, then if the owner of the item is honest and intelligent, the child should tell him not to leave the item in the parent's care, and tell him the truth. If the owner of the item is not honest and intelligent, the child may just say not to leave the item there, without revealing negative information about his parent.

It would seem the reason to permit this is in order to save the parent from a transgression. If a father was sick, and the only way to heal him was to undress him and cause him embarrassment, it is obvious that the son could do so to save his father's life. Similarly, one could speak ill about his parents in order to save them from suffering eternally, due to their sins.

---

102. *Yoreh De'ah* 240:15.
103. Chapter 1087.

Just Desserts

בָּרוּךְ פְּרִי בִטְנְךָ

Blessed shall be the fruit of your womb

(28:4)

A woman arrived in the delivery room, without her husband, in an advanced stage of labor. After the birth, the doctor happily told the woman, "*Mazel Tov!* You have given birth to a healthy baby girl!" The woman burst out crying. When the doctor asked her why she was so upset, she responded that she already had six daughters at home, and she had received strict instructions from her husband to go to the hospital by herself, and if the baby would be a girl, she should not inform him nor should she bring the baby home!

The doctor calmed the woman and assured her that with Hashem's help, everything would work out for the best. The doctor left the room to call the husband and wished him a hearty *Mazel Tov* on the birth of a baby boy! The doctor's tone turned serious when he quickly added that the husband should come to the hospital without delay and proceed immediately to the doctor's office, even before visiting his wife. The husband did as he was instructed, and was soon facing the doctor across his desk. The doctor offered the father a glass of water, and instructed him to remain calm.

The doctor explained that the child was born with several birth defects. The doctor began to list a litany of problems, starting with one leg being longer than the other, and continuing with more serious problems. Finally he concluded that the baby had a serious problem in the brain, but that the most worrisome was the serious defect in the baby's heart, for which the baby was to be operated on in the coming hour.

This was too much for the man to bear. He buried his face in his hands and cried bitterly. He confessed that it was all his fault for causing his wife so much pain, and not having the proper gratitude to Hashem for his six wonderful daughters. Instead of thanking Hashem, he had only been interested in having a son. What would have been so terrible, asked the father, if he would have had a healthy baby girl, like his six daughters at home?

"It is true," said the doctor. "You need to repent for not thanking Hashem for His blessings that He showered upon you. However, for now, you have not been punished. *Mazel Tov, Mazel Tov!* You have had a healthy baby girl!"

After the stunned father recovered from this second shock, he thanked the doctor for helping him to appreciate Hashem's kindness, and he thanked Hashem for all the kindness that He bestowed upon him.

Did the doctor have the right to cause the father such pain in order to open his eyes?

The Gemara in *Bava Basra*[104] says that Penina's intentions were for the sake of Heaven. She would taunt Chana, who had not been blessed with children, in order to spur Chana to pray for a child. Even so, Penina was punished, and every time Chana bore a child, Penina buried two of her own children.

Rav Chaim Shmulevitz explained that although Penina had a compelling motive for what she did, nevertheless, she caused Chana terrible anguish. Causing someone pain is like sticking one's hand in a fire. Regardless of one's intention of doing so, he will surely

---

104. 16a.

get burned. Where does that leave the well-meaning physician?

 The doctor did a tremendous mitzvah. The father was not acting properly, and it is permissible to cause him pain. The Gemara in *Bava Metzia*[105] explains that there is a prohibition against verbally abusing one's friend. For example, if one's friend is beset with tragedies, they should not tell him, as Iyov's friends told him, that he deserves it.

The *S'ma*[106] explains that Iyov's friends did tell him so, because Iyov had complaints to Hashem for His behavior. In our case as well, the father is ungrateful for Hashem's kindness, and may be pained to set him straight.

In contrast, Chana was innocent of any wrongdoing and did not deserve to be pained by Penina.

An additional proof can be brought from the Gemara in *Shabbos*.[107] Rav had traveled by boat on a river whose waters were contaminated. Shmuel was an expert doctor and realized that Rav had drunk from the water and been infected. Shmuel decided to cure Rav surreptitiously. He invited Rav to his house and served him foods that would have a laxative effect on Rav, yet he did not tell Rav where he could go to relieve himself, so that it would take Rav time. Shmuel's purpose was for everything in Rav's system to be thoroughly expelled. This caused Rav great discomfort, although it ultimately cured him. We learn from Shmuel that one may cause his friend pain when his intent is to benefit him.[108]

---

105. 58b.
106. 228 § 6.
107. 108a.
108. Although Rav was angered by Shmuel's behavior, this is because he did not realize Shmuel's intent (*Ben Yehoyada*).

פרשת נצבים
Parashas Nitzavim

Good Things
Come Anyway

אַתֶּם נִצָּבִים הַיּוֹם כֻּלְּכֶם
You are standing today, all of you
(29:9)

A. **Mrs. Fine dreaded shopping** before Yom Tov because she knew what the check-out lines were like. Her daughter offered to take the shopping cart with just a few items and stand in line, while her mother continued shopping. That way they could make the most of their time. Is that the proper way to act?

B. Saadia was waiting on line at the pharmacy when his neighbor Tzadok walked in and dejectedly surveyed the long line. He asked Saadia if he was last, and when he replied in the affirmative, Tzadok announced that he was after Saadia, and would return in time for his turn. Twenty minutes later, Saadia was next in line, and

Tzadok returned. At least half a dozen people had arrived in the interim, and were perturbed when Tzadok insisted that he was after Saadia. Is he allowed to keep his place, even if he did not wait there?

 The *Meiri* in *Sanhedrin*[109] implies that there is no firm source for the concept of waiting in line as the determining factor in the right to be first. Such things are not under the purview of law; they are, rather, commonly accepted practices considered to be proper behavior. Therefore, such a practice as waiting in line is not always binding, and sometimes there is reason to deviate from the order of the line, e.g., to let a sick person go before one who is healthy, or to allow an orphan or widow or a *talmid chacham*, to precede all others. According to this guideline, the proper behavior and accepted custom will have to be determined for each individual circumstance, in order to decide if the "place-saving" in question is acceptable.

Since the normal way to shop is to fill one's shopping cart before standing in line, and if everyone would save a place in line while they shopped, it would create havoc, it makes sense that to do so is improper. Therefore, one should complete his shopping first, and only then stand in line.

In the case of the pharmacy, where everyone is standing and waiting for their turn to get their prescriptions filled, it does not make a difference to anyone if someone uses his time productively instead of standing idle. If people are upset, it is only because they are jealous. However, he should ask the person before him in line to notify those who come afterward that someone else is before them, so they will not mistakenly think that the line is shorter than it really is, and be disappointed when the person returns.

———◆———

109. 32b.

In the Footsteps of Our Sages

וְהַנִּגְלֹת לָנוּ וּלְבָנֵינוּ

But the revealed [sins] are for us and our children
(29:28)

Harav Shlomo Goldstein is an erudite *talmid chacham* and is held in great esteem by the members of his community. The *Rav* accepted an invitation to officiate as the *Mesader Kiddushin* for the Greens' son. After the *chupah*, Mr. Green requested that the *Rav* should kindly stay on, and grace the wedding meal with the honor of his presence. The *Rav* had a very busy schedule, but agreed to stay a little longer in order to give pleasure to his hosts.

As the *Rav* was preparing to leave, one of the wedding guests whispered to the *Rav* that this wedding was supposed to be mixed seating (men and women) and the fact that the men and women were separated by a *mechitzah* was only due to the *Rav's* presence. As soon as the *Rav* leaves, the *mechitzah* will be removed.

The *Rav* is unsure if he should leave the wedding as he planned, in order to deliver his regularly scheduled class at shul, or perhaps he should stay at the wedding in order to prevent the wedding guests from a serious breach of modesty and other transgressions. What should he do?

It would seem that the *Rav* should cancel his *shiur*, and preserve the proper conduct at the wedding. The Gemara in *Chullin*[110] relates that Abaye, who was

---

110. 133a.

a Kohen, was so busy teaching his students that he never had a chance to attend *Bircas Kohanim* in shul. Yet the Gemara in *Succah*[111] tells the story of a man who proposed to a woman that they should travel together before the morning's light. Abaye, who overheard this conversation, volunteered to follow them in order to prevent them from any wrongdoing on the way. Abaye followed them for three *parsaos* (9 miles), until eventually the man and woman parted ways.

Even though Abaye was so occupied with his students that he could not even attend *Bircas Kohanim*, he still found the time to prevent a man and woman from possible misdeed. It takes approximately three-and-a-half hours to walk three *parsaos*, and Abaye had to undertake the return trip as well. If so, Abaye probably missed delivering his morning *shiur*, which was set for the time that the rest of the congregation *davens Shacharis*. It seems clear from this that the *Rav* should skip delivering his *shiur* in order to maintain proper conduct at the wedding.

One could argue that Abaye had an obligation to rebuke the man for his plan, and therefore he had a responsibility to prevent them from sin, but in our case it is possible that the *Rav* has no such obligation. The *Beur Halachah*[112] writes, "It is logical that the ruling of the *Rema,* that one must object to someone who wishes to transgress a prohibition that is explicit in the Torah, applies only if the transgression is an occasional one. If, however, the people involved have thrown off the yoke of Heaven completely, like those who publicly violate the Shabbos or those who eat *tereifeh* wantonly, they have lost their status of Jews as far as the obligation to rebuke them."

Nevertheless, it is still worthwhile to cancel the *shiur* for the sake of the wedding guests, as they have not thrown off the yoke of Heaven completely. The Gemara in *Eruvin*[113] relates the story of

---

111. 52a.
112. 608 s.v. *Aval.*
113. 69b.

someone who walked in public on Shabbos while holding a per-fumed sachet, in a place that had no *eiruv*, which is a transgression of carrying on Shabbos. When this man saw R' Yehudah HaNasi in the street, he covered the sachet out of embarrassment in front of the esteemed *Rav*. R' Yehudah declared that such a person is considered to be a *mechallel Shabbos b'tzin'ah* (one who violates the Shabbos in private, but is not willing to do so publicly). In our case as well, the people are embarrassed to act this way in the *Rav's* presence. If the *Rav* will stay and draw the wedding guests closer to *Yiddishkeit*, he will receive the blessings of Abaye, as he is following Abaye's example of taking time from learning to prevent others from sinning.

Practice Makes Perfect

וְשַׁבְתָּ עַד ה' אֱלֹקֶיךָ

And you will return unto Hashem, your G-d

(30:2)

Congregation Eitz Chaim hired Chaim Goldberg, a 14-year-old boy, to read the Torah for them on Shabbos, as their regular reader would be away. After the reading, Chaim realized he had made an error, such that the congregation had not fulfilled their obligation. Everyone had already gone home, and it was too late to call them back. Does Chaim have to refuse his payment from the shul?

If the congregation is meticulous in their Torah read-ing, Chaim cannot take the money, since he did not do the job for which he was hired. However, since almost the entire reading was correct, and they only need to reread three *pesukim* (as one may not read less than three *pesukim*, even though they only need to fix one word[114]), he may be paid for the whole reading, minus three *pesukim*.

Rav Chaim Kanievsky said that he should be paid for the length of time he read, and deduct the time needed to read three *pesukim*.

If, however, the congregation is not that stringent about their Torah reading, and they only want that the Torah should be read, whether they fulfill their obligation or not, Chaim could keep the entire payment, since his reading satisfied his employers. (This is true especially if there is talking during the reading.)[115]

More than the question of money, Chaim needs to ask himself, how can he do *teshuvah* for causing the congregation not to fulfill their obligation? If he did not prepare properly, he is responsible for the loss of the mitzvah of the entire congregation!

— ◆ —

---

114. See *Shulchan Aruch, Orach Chaim* 282:7.
115. What if the Rabbi and some others are careful but others are not? Rav Zilberstein answered that the Rabbi usually does not pay, but if he does, or others do, then the money should be deducted.

Mitzvos Take Time and Money

כִּי הַמִּצְוָה הַזֹּאת

For this commandment

(30:11)

 What do catering halls do with the leftover food after a *simchah*?

There are some halls that dispose of all of the food if the *baalei simchah* do not want it. The rationale of the caterer is that he needs to prepare fresh food for the next wedding. Nobody wants last night's leftovers. To package the food in order to send it to needy people would mean hiring extra workers, an expense that exceeds the value of the food. Does this justify wasting edible food?

 The Responsa *Hisorerus Teshuvah*[116] writes, "If preserving something that has use requires expending time and effort, there is no prohibition of *Bal Tashchis* (wasting resources). One may even chop down a tree if he needs to use its place.[117]

"There is actually a difference between these cases, however.

"When one needs the location of a tree, or if the wood of the tree is worth more than its fruits, chopping down the tree is not a destructive act, and therefore there is no prohibition. When one needs to spend time or money in order to preserve the food, he is not wasting time or money. He is using his time or money to do a

---

116. Vol. IV, *Choshen Mishpat* 35.
117. One should consult a *Rav* for exact parameters.

mitzvah. There is no precedent that 'wasting' one's time has priority over wasting one's property."

It can be inferred from the words of the *Hisorerus Teshuvah* that there would be no license for a caterer to throw away good food for the sake of saving money.

Rav Elyashiv suggested a possible defense for the caterer's practice, based on the *Chayei Adam*[118] in the laws of *tzitzis*. If one is changing his *tzitzis* strings to more beautiful ones, he may untie the old ones and dispose of them (in a respectful manner). The *Chayei Adam* suggests that if it is difficult to untie the strings, he may instead cut them off. It is not considered *Bal Tashchis* since he has no intention to be destructive. He supports his view with the Gemara in *Bava Basra*,[119] where Bava ben Buta instructed King Hordos to renovate the *Beis HaMikdash*. According to the Gemara's second answer, the *Beis HaMikdash* was in good condition, and to break even one stone of the *Beis HaMikdash* is a Torah prohibition.[120] Yet since Hordos' intention was to rebuild, it was not considered a destructive act. The *Sefer Chassidim*[121] writes along these lines as well, concerning replacing a page of a *Sefer Torah*.

Rav Zilberstein pointed out to Rav Elyashiv that there seems to be a difference between the cases. In the case of the *tzitzis* strings the intent is to replace them with strings that are more beautiful. Hordos' motivation was to beautify the *Beis HaMikdash*. In the case of the *Sefer Chassidim* as well, the intention is to replace the page of the *Sefer Torah* with one that is more beautiful. In contrast, the caterer is throwing out good food, an act which is purely destructive.

Rav Elyashiv responded that the proof of the *Chayei Adam* is difficult to understand. It is impossible to renovate any building without demolishing the previous structure. In the case of the *tzitzis*, one always has the option of untying the strings. If so, how

---

118. 11:32.
119. 3b.
120. See *Devarim* 12:4.
121. 879.

could the *Chayei Adam* compare the two cases? It must be that it was obvious to the *Chayei Adam* that one does not have to expend time in order to avoid ripping the old strings. The point of the proof was that it is not considered disrespectful to the mitzvah, just as in the case of the *Beis HaMikdash* it is not considered destructive to demolish its stones, when the intent is to rebuild it more beautifully.

According to this, if saving the food involves expenditures, discarding it might be justified.

פרשת וילך
Parashas Vayeilech

Maximizing Your Potential

וְעַתָּה כִּתְבוּ לָכֶם

So now, write for yourselves

(31:19)

It has been less than a year since Meir's father's *petirah*, and Meir would like to do something to increase his father's merits in heaven. He has a limited budget for this project, and he has two possible options. Meir's father had recorded many pages of ideas that he thought of in the course of his learning, and with the talents of a good editor, the thoughts could be arranged into a *sefer*. However, such a work would not attract the attention of the public, and only Torah scholars from the extended family would really gain from, and appreciate it. Alternatively, Meir could invest in classic *sefarim*, i.e., Gemaras and *Shulchan Aruchs*, which are greatly needed by the local *batei midrash*. Meir wants to know which option would bring his father greater pleasure: to have his *chiddushim* (original Torah thoughts) published, even though their audience will be a limited one, or to donate *sefarim* that will be used on a constant basis.

The Gemara in *Yevamos*[122] explains the *pasuk*,[123] *I will dwell in Your tents in [two] worlds,* by asking: Is it possible for a person to live (simultaneously) in two worlds? Rather, Dovid HaMelech said to Hashem, "Master of the World, may it be Your Will that people should quote me in their learning," as R' Yochanan said in the name of R' Shimon bar Yochai, "Any scholar who is quoted in this world, his lips speak in his grave."

The *Chasam Sofer* had no desire to have his *sefarim* published, as he held that there was no obligation to do so.

In contrast, *Sefer Chassidim*[124] writes that if Hashem revealed a novel Torah thought to someone, and he did not write it down to share it with others, he has stolen from He Who revealed it to him. The *Reishis Bikkurim* said that publishing one's works is included in the obligation of teaching Torah. Similarly, Rav Moshe Feinstein wrote that if one is capable of publishing his work to benefit others, he must do so in order to teach Torah to others.

However, this is only applicable to a *sefer* that will provide a widespread benefit. A *sefer* that will not help the masses is probably not included in the mitzvah, and it would be more advantageous to spend the money for more useful *sefarim*.

If instead of asking what would be better for his father, Meir would ask what **he** should do, it would be obvious that he should print his father's work. By doing so he will fulfill the mitzvah of *kibbud av* (honoring his father) [125] as is apparent from the Gemara in *Yevamos*, and the *Sefer Chassidim*.

---

122. 96b.
123. *Tehillim* 61:5.
124. 530.
125. See *Shu"t Teshuvah Me'Ahavah* Vol III, 19.

Another advantage in printing his father's *sefer* is that doing so may hasten the final Redemption. Rabbi Shlomo Kluger (introduction to *Tuv Ta'am VaDa'as*) writes that every new *sefer* brings the *"geulah"* closer. This is alluded to by Shlomo HaMelech in *Koheles.*[126]

———◆◆◆———

A Sure Sign

וְעָנְתָה הַשִּׁירָה הַזֹּאת לְפָנָיו לְעֵד

Then this song shall speak up before it as a witness

(31:21)

Binyamin Silver was a very wealthy and successful businessman who had laboriously worked his way up the corporate ladder. His son was born later in his career with a silver spoon in his mouth, and did not share his father's hard-work ethic. Unfortunately, his son's lack of enthusiasm expressed itself in his religious commitment as well.

His son, now a teenager, walked into his father's office and asked his father to fund a vacation through several European countries. Binyamin told his son that he would happily fund the trip if his son promised to put on *tefillin* every day. The son promised and extended his hand. Binyamin, a shrewd businessman, countered that he would give his son an advance to pay for part of the trip, and if he received confirmation that his son indeed donned his *tefillin* every day, he would transfer

126. 12:12.

the balance of the money to cover his son's expenses for the remainder of the trip.

"How will you transfer the money?" his son asked.

"I will find a way," his father assured him.

The son took the money and set off to pack his bags for his trip.

A few days later the son phoned Binyamin in his office and asked him to transfer the funds.

"Are you wearing your *tefillin* every day?" asked the father.

"Dad! I promised you I would, didn't I?" came the reply.

"Then don't worry, the money will come," promised Binyamin.

A few days later the scenario repeated itself: a desperate phone call with a request for the promised money, Binyamin's questioning his son about his *tefillin*, and the son's assurance that he was keeping his part of the deal.

"Okay," said Binyamin, "the money will come."

The money never came. The son was disgruntled with his father's insensitivity, leaving him stranded in Europe without any money, and he had no choice but to use his return ticket and come home.

Binyamin's son entered the house, and began shouting at his father.

"How could you have abandoned me in a foreign country without a penny! You promised you would send me money. How could you lie to me like that?"

Binyamin ignored his son's hysterics. "Did you put on *tefillin* every day?"

"I told you a hundred times, I put on *tefillin*. What do you want from me?"

"Please bring me the *tefillin*," said Binyamin.

The son unpacked his *tefillin* bag.

"You see, I had them the whole time!"

The father picked up the *tefillin* bag and slowly unzipped it. Binyamin withdrew a large wad of bills from the side of the *tefillin* bag, and his son shriveled in shame. He realized that he had dug his own hole, and promised his father, sincerely this time, that from now on, he would wear his *tefillin* every day.

The Gemara in *Sanhedrin*[127] states that a scarf that has been designated to hold *tefillin*, and has been used to hold them, may not be used to hold money. Was Binyamin allowed to insert the money into the *tefillin* bag to verify his son's commitment to the mitzvah? Perhaps doing so is for the mitzvah's sake and should therefore be permitted?

 R' Shlomo Zalman Auerbach ruled[128] that one may leave a mirror in one's *tefillin* bag if it serves the purpose of aiding in the placement of one's *tefillin*, as it is considered a mitzvah accessory. The bag was designated to hold the mitzvah object and all of its necessary components.

Perhaps Binyamin's money was also considered an accessory to the mitzvah, although in truth there is a clear difference. The mirror is an aid to the actual performance of the mitzvah. The money, in contrast, is to fund the son's adventures and has only a secondary function, to insure the son's fulfillment of the mitzvah.

However, there are several other reasons to allow the placement of the money in the *tefillin* bag.

1) If the *tefillin* bag already contained a mirror, or a bottle of *tefillin* paint, it is as if it was never designated specifically for *tefillin*. The *Beur Halachah*[129] states that one who keeps his *tallis* in the

127. 48a.
128. *Halichos Shlomo*, Chap. 4, § 34.
129. 42:3.

same bag as his *tefillin* may even put in non-mitzvah items as well.

2) Nowadays, when our *tefillin* have covers, the *Mishnah Berurah*[130] rules that there is no problem of placing other things in the *tefillin* bag. (The *Minchas Elazar*[131] and *Divrei Yatziv*[132] differ, since the knots on the straps remain uncovered, and have the same halachic status as the *tefillin*.)

Under Surveillance

לָקֹחַ אֵת סֵפֶר הַתּוֹרָה

Take this Book of the Torah

(31:26)

 A shul owned a very expensive *Megillas Esther*, and several times burglars had attempted to steal it. Someone suggested that a small hole be drilled in the *aron hakodesh* where the *Megillah* was kept, and a small security camera be installed in order to photograph the burglars. Would such a measure be permissible, or is it a lack of respect to the *aron hakodesh*?

 Rav Elyashiv responded that any action taken to safeguard *tefillin* or *Sifrei Torah*, even if it involves disrespect, is permitted. The Gemara in *Berachos* states[133] that one may bring *tefillin* into the lavatory in order to protect them. *Rashi* explains that the safety of the *tefillin* is more important than their

---

130. 34, 4: *Beur Halachah "Shtei."*
131. Vol. I, 27.
132. Vol. I, 48.
133. 23a.

honor. Since one is obligated to protect his *tefillin* from mice or thieves, that takes precedence over treating them with respect. This means that it is not considered disrespectful, since his intention is to protect them.

Similarly, the *Shulchan Aruch* writes[134] that one must treat a *Sefer Torah* with respect. If, however, one is afraid of thieves, one may even place the *Sefer Torah* on a donkey's back and ride on top of it. According to this, one may drill a hole in the *aron hakodesh* for security purposes.

However, this comparison is not exact. We only find that one may take *tefillin* into a lavatory to safeguard that particular pair of *tefillin*, or to sit on a *Sefer Torah* to protect the *Sefer Torah* itself. In our case, we want to allow drilling a hole in the *aron hakodesh* which is essentially meant to serve the *Sifrei Torah*, to protect something else, i.e., the *Megillah*. Would that be permissible?

Rav Elyashiv maintains that the possibility exists that if the thieves will be successful in stealing the precious *Megillah*, they will attempt to steal *Sifrei Torah* as well. It should not make a difference if one is trying to protect that particular *Sefer Torah* or a different one.

In addition, one way to honor the Torah is to ensure that its mitzvos are observed. Therefore, preventing the thieves from stealing the *Sifrei Torah* cannot be regarded as a lack of respect to the Torah.

---

134. 282:1,3.

פרשת האזינו
Parashas Ha'azinu

A Captive Audience

הַאֲזִינוּ הַשָּׁמַיִם וַאֲדַבֵּרָה
Give ear, O heavens, and I will speak
(32:1)

There are *talmidei chachamim* who share their wisdom with others by delivering a *shiur* to their fellow passengers on an intercity bus ride. The participants enjoy the learning, and their otherwise boring trip is transformed into a spiritually uplifting experience. Occasionally there are a few passengers who protest that they would rather sleep or learn something else, and the *shiur* disturbs them. Does the *"maggid shiur"* have to consider their feelings and refrain from saying the *shiur*?

The Gemara in *Bava Basra*[135] relates the edict of Yehoshua ben Gamla, that *chadarim* be opened to teach children in every state and every city. Based on this, the Gemara says that neighbors who share a courtyard may not object

---

135. 21a.

to the opening of a *cheder* in one of the houses on the basis of the noise that will result. The *Shulchan Aruch* rules[136] that neighbors cannot prevent one another from making their house into a *cheder* or from doing any other mitzvah. According to this, a mitzvah as great as communal learning on a bus, which is a merit for all involved, as it is a public demonstration of honoring Hashem as well as safeguarding people from wasting their time or engaging in forbidden speech, cannot be restricted.

However, the *Pischei Teshuvah*[137] qualifies that although one may open a *cheder* on his own property, opening a *cheder* on a shared property is prohibited, since most people would not be willing to become a partner in a house in which many outside children come and go. If so, perhaps a bus is considered shared property, and one may not make it into a classroom.

Upon closer examination, a crucial difference will be realized. To share one's room with a *cheder* on a constant basis is something that most people cannot tolerate. However, a *shiur* on a one-hour bus ride is something that most people could tolerate, and many people would enjoy. Therefore we return to the original ruling that one may not object to the *shiur*. In the case of the *cheder*, if the *cheder* does not open on the shared property, they will find another place for the *cheder*, but the bus is an irreplaceable opportunity, to make the most of what would otherwise be wasted time by many people.

There was once a young man in a yeshivah who learned out loud. The neighbors complained that he should lower his voice. The Chazon Ish ruled that the neighbors cannot complain, because Torah study may not be hindered because of a concern for depriving others from sleep. Certainly, during travel — which is a time of danger[138] — the collective merit of all those learning in the *shiur* has priority over people's sleep.

---

136. *Choshen Mishpat* 156:3.
137. Ad loc. § 2.
138. See *Rashi* to *Bereishis* 42:4.

Do I Have To?

עִם חֵלֶב כִּלְיוֹת

As fat as kidneys

(32:14)

 A dialysis patient deteriorated until the point of kidney failure and the doctors say that he will not live more than a week unless he undergoes a kidney transplant. There is a healthy candidate who is a potential donor for this patient. Is there an obligation for someone to donate his kidney in order to save his friend's life?

 The *Recanti*[139] writes that if a governor threatened a Jew that unless the Jew allows him to sever one of the Jew's limbs, which presents no danger to one's life, he will kill another Jew, some say that the Jew must allow his limb to be amputated. A proof of this can be brought from the Gemara in *Avodah Zarah*[140] that permits medical treatment for the eyes on Shabbos since an eye disease could be life threatening. One may infer that a non-life-threatening limb could not be treated on Shabbos (in a way that constitutes a desecration of Shabbos), even if that would mean losing the limb. According to this, if Shabbos may not be desecrated in order to save a limb in a case where this poses no threat to life, yet one may desecrate Shabbos in order to save the life of his friend, logic dictates that certainly one would have to forfeit a limb in order to save his friend's life!

---

139. 470.
140. 28b.

The *Radvaz*[141] maintains that doing so is a magnanimous act, but would not be mandatory. He elaborates as to why the logic of the *Recanti* is not conclusive, and maintains that the ways of the Torah are pleasant. It is unthinkable that a person would have to allow himself to be maimed so that someone else should not kill his friend. Therefore it is strictly an act of piety, and fortunate is the one who is capable of performing this *chesed*. However, if there is any danger to the donor, it would be an act of foolishness![142]

Perhaps the discussion above is relevant to a limb that, if missing, would affect his daily life. A missing kidney, however, does not limit its donor in any way unless something happens to the remaining one *chas v'shalom*. He may live till 120, *b'ezras Hashem*, with his remaining kidney without complications.

Maybe in such a case, even the *Radvaz* would concede that one must donate his kidney.

However, it would seem that there is no such obligation, as the operation itself has an element of risk, and one does not have an obligation to risk his life in order to save his friend, although doing so is certainly a great mitzvah.[143]

---

141. Vol. III, 627.

142. See *Pischei Teshuvah, Yoreh De'ah* 157 § 15; *Chasan Sofer, Kesubos* 61b.

143. See *Mishnah Berurah* 329 § 19.

פרשת וזאת הברכה
Parashas V'zos HaBerachah

Mass Labor

וְזֹאת הַבְּרָכָה
And this is the blessing
(33:1)

 The administrator of the shul was very pleased that the shul was bustling with activity. People came throughout Succos to *daven* and to learn. But the piles and piles of *sefarim* that needed to be returned to the shelves were overwhelming. When one person came forward and agreed to tidy the shul for $100, the administrator jumped at the opportunity.

Immediately following *Maariv* after *Simchas Torah* the volunteer gave a bang on the *bimah* and talked about how one needs to treat *sefarim* with the proper respect, and how praiseworthy is one who does kindness and returns *sefarim* to their proper places. He asked everyone to take just five minutes to clean up the many *sefarim* scattered around the shul. The administrator was stunned. He had never intended to pay to have the shul members return the *sefarim*! Does the volunteer deserve to be paid?

 The *Yerushalmi*[144] tells the story of 300 *Nezirim* who were obligated to bring three offerings each but could not afford to pay for them. Shimon ben Shetach was able to exempt 150 from their obligation by nullifying their original vows. He was not successful in finding a way to absolve the vows of the other 150. He sent a message to the king, "There are 300 *Nezirim* who need a total of 900 animals for offerings. If you will give half, I will give the other half." The king sent his donation of 450 animals. Subsequently, someone spoke *lashon hara* to the king, claiming that Shimon ben Shetach had not given anything! The king was furious, and Shimon ben Shetach had to flee. When Shimon ben Shetach eventually returned, the king asked him, "Why did you trick me?" Shimon ben Shetach replied, "I did not trick you. You gave from your money, and I gave from my wisdom!"

According to this, the volunteer may deserve payment for his instrumental role in cleaning up the shul. However, even if he deserves his payment, he is still guilty of tricking the congregation by asking them to do kindness with the shul, and show respect for the *sefarim*, when in reality, they were doing his job for him! If they would know that he was being paid for their work, they would not have been willing to participate.

When Rav Nissim Karelitz heard this ruling, he added that since he fooled the congregation, he does not deserve to be paid, because he was never hired to mislead anyone.

---

144. *Berachos* 7:2.

Giving Tzedakah at the Proper Time

תּוֹרָה צִוָּה לָנוּ

The Torah that was commanded to us

(33:4)

 A poor man entered the *Kissover Kollel* and asked one of its members, who was sitting by the door, if he would mind collecting money for the poor man's family. The poor man explained that since he knew several of the *Kollel's* members, he would be embarrassed to collect personally. Should the *Kollel* member take half an hour from his learning to collect *tzedakah* for the poor man?

 It would seem that even the poor man himself should not collect *tzedakah* while the *Kollel* is in session, as doing so will disturb their Torah learning. The *Kollel* was established to promote Torah learning, not to facilitate the collection of *tzedakah*.

Rav Wosner writes[145] that although mitzvos take precedence over learning when the mitzvos cannot be done by others, in this case the *Kollel* members would be happy to give *tzedakah* after they finish learning. It is just for the convenience of the collectors that they want to disturb the *Kollel's* learning. Under such circumstances there is no requirement for the *Kollel* to interrupt their learning to give *tzedakah*. This is not considered a mitzvah that one has the opportunity to do only during their learning time.

---

145. *Shevet HaLevi,* Vol. X, 157.

In addition, taking time from his learning may border on stealing, as the sponsors of the *Kollel* want its members to learn. If the member agrees to collect, he must deduct this time from his attendance, and his pay must be docked accordingly, but he certainly has no obligation to do this for the poor man's sake.

Another reason why the *Kollel* member should not collect *tzedakah* during his learning time is because he obligated himself to support his wife when they married each other, and the only reason she agrees that he may learn Torah instead of taking a job with a greater income is because she appreciates the value of his learning, and that is her sacrifice for the learning of Torah.[146] Therefore he has no right to collect *tzedakah* during the time that he is scheduled to learn for the benefit of their family.

The Most for Your Money

לְעֵינֵי כָּל יִשְׂרָאֵל

Before the eyes of all Israel

(34:12)

 Simchah Cohen bought the honor of *Acharon Chazak* for $300. There were other Kohanim in shul, and the plan was to call a different Kohen first for the first *aliyah*, and Simchah would be called for *Chazak*. However, by the time they opened the Torah to start the reading, all the other Kohanim had left the shul, and the *gabbai* had

---

146. See *Berachos* 17a.

no choice but to call Simchah for the first *aliyah*, and to give *Chazak* to someone else. Under the circumstances, Simchah refused to pay the $300. Is he justified?

 It would seem that *Chazak* belonged to Simchah, and the mitzvah remained his. Although someone else was given the *aliyah*, the mitzvah, as well as its rewards, remain Simchah's. As the *Chasam Sofer*[147] writes about *Kaddish*: "If someone said someone else's *Kaddish*, the *Kaddish* still benefits the soul for whom it was supposed to be said!" Therefore it would seem that Simchah should pay his pledge even though someone else was called for the *aliyah*.

When the question was posed to Rav Elyashiv, he maintained that when one pledges to give money for an *aliyah*, his intent is only if he is actually called for the *aliyah*.

On the other hand, the *Magen Avraham*[148] writes that the *minhag* in Österreich was to pay any pledge, even if the person was outbid and his friend captured the mitzvah. Even though this is not our *minhag*, it still lends support to the reasoning of the *Chasam Sofer*.

Rav Elyashiv also added another reason for Simchah to pay: The first *aliyah* of Kohen is more of an honor than *Chazak*, since through it one does the mitzvah of giving honor to the Kohen by calling him first. It would therefore be proper to pay, since he received an *aliyah* that has greater value than *Chazak*.[149]

Despite this, people presume that *Chazak* is the more significant *aliyah*. Therefore we can only say that it would be befitting for Simchah to pay his pledge even if he is not actually obligated.

---

147. *Yoreh De'ah* 345.
148. 306 § 15.
149. The reason why Rav Elyashiv felt that Simcha should pay, as opposed to the case of "Hashem Knows" (*Parashas Bamidbar*, p. 324) where a child usurped the man's right to open the *aron hakodesh*, is due to the fact that Simchah received the *aliyah* of Kohen, which is of greater value. In the other case, the man received nothing in return.

Glossary

Acharon Chazak – the person called to the Torah at the completion of one of the five Books of the Torah

Arba'ah Minim – the Four Species

Aron Hakodesh – Holy Ark

Arvus – responsibility that all Jews have for each other's observance of the mitzvos

Aufruf – a pre–wedding event in which the groom is called to the Torah the Shabbos before the wedding

Aveirah – sin

Baal(as) Teshuvah – returnee to his/her heritage, i.e., religious observance

Bal Tashchis – the prohibition against wasting something of value

Bal Tosif – the prohibition against adding on to the requirement of a mitzvah

Batel – nullified

B'dinei Shamayim – an obligation between the person and Hashem

Bedi'avad – once the deed was done

Beheimah – animal

Bein adam la'Makom – between man and Hashem

Bein adam la'chaveiro – between man and his fellow man

Bein hazemanim – intersession

Beis din – Rabbinical Court

Beis HaMikdash – Holy Temple

Berachah (pl. *Berachos*) – blessing

Bircas Kohanim – the Kohen's blessing to the congregation

which is part of the repetition of Shemoneh Esrei

Bitul mekach – nullification of a sale

Bitul Torah – negation of Torah learning; wasting time that should be used to learn Torah

Bris – circumcision

B'val Yomar – restricted from being said

B'yedei Shamayim – a punishment meted out by Heaven

Chachamim – wise people, sages

Chag – holiday

Chalitzah – a ceremony to sever the marriage requirement between a man and his late brother's wife, when the brother died without leaving any children.

Chassid – very pious individual

Chassan – groom

Chatzitzah – interposition

Chazzan – cantor

Cheder (pl. *Chadarim*) – *Torah institution for children*

Cherem – ban

Chesed – kindness

Chiddushim – original Torah thoughts

Chillul Hashem – desecration of Hashem's Name

Chiyuv – lit., obligation. Also used to refer to a mourner for a parent, who has precedence to be the chazzan.

Chupah – wedding canopy

Davening – praying

Din Torah – Jewish court

Dina demalchusa – government law

Eliyahu HaNavi – Elijah the Prophet

Erev Shabbos – Friday afternoon

Eved Cena'ani – a non-Jewish slave who is bought from gentiles

Gabbai (pl. *Gabbaim*) – aide to a Rebbe; man in charge of running a shul

Garmi – a more directly caused damage; see *gerama*

Gazlan – thief

Gedolei Hador – leaders of the generation

Gemach – *an* organization founded to provide community service; free loan society

Geneivas da'as – deceit

Genizah – a respectful form of disposal of holy items

Gerama – an indirectly-caused damage for which Beis Din will not obligate one to pay, although he is still liable according to the Heavenly Beis Din

Get (pl. *Gittin*) – Jewish divorce contract

Goy – gentile

Hashavas Aveidah – returning a lost object to its owner.

Hefker – ownerless property

Hezek re'iyah – damage caused by one neighbor looking into his friend's property, thereby preventing his friend from using his property for anything that requires privacy

Hezek shemiah – damage through listening

Hiddur mitzvah – glorification of a mitzvah

Kabbalas P'nei HaShechinah – greeting the presence of Hashem

Kabed es Hashem Mehon'cha – Honor Hashem with your wealth

Kaddish – memorial prayer for the deceased

Kallah – bride

Kapparah (pl. *Kapparos*) – atonement

Kesubah – marriage contract

Kezayis – olive-sized piece

Kibbud Av VaEim – honoring one's parents

Kiddush Hashem – sanctification of Hashem's Name

Kiddush Levanah – blessing the new moon

Kinyan – literally, an acquisition; usually a transfer of an object or a contract to make a verbal agreement a physical reality

Kodesh HaKodashim – The Holy of Holies

Kohen – Jewish priest

Korech – sandwich of matzah and *maror* eaten at the seder

Kvatter – the one who brings the baby into the room where the circumsion is taking place

Lashon Hara – evil gossip

Lashon Hara L'to'eles – speaking negatively for a positive purpose

Lechatchilah – to perform a mitzvah in the most preferable way

Lechem hapanim – showbread used in the service of the Beis HaMikdash

Lehavdil – differentiating between the holy and mundane

Levayah – funeral

Lifnei iver – placing a stumbling block in front of one who is blind; used in conjunction with enabling someone to sin

Ma'aser Kesafim – the practice to give 10 percent of one's earnings to tzedakah

Mafkir – to relinquish ownership

Maftir – the final aliyah

Maggid Shiur – one who delivers a Torah lecture

Mahn – manna

Malkos – flogging

Maror – bitter herbs

Mashlim – the final Torah-reading

Matan Torah – the giving of the Torah at Sinai

Matir neder – to annul a vow

Mechallel Shabbos b'tzin'ah – one who violates Shabbos in private, but not in public

Mechilah – forgiveness; giving permission for someone to do something harmful to you

Mehudar – beautiful

Meis mitzvah – Jewish corpse that has no one responsible for its burial

Mekach ta'us – a sale conducted under false pretenses or in error

Melachah – a Biblical desecration of Shabbos

Mevater – to forgo that which belongs to you

Middas Sodom – wickedness

Mi'd'Oraisa – of Biblical origin

Mi'd'Rabbanan – according to the Rabbinic enactment

Min – apostate

Minhag – common practice

Mishlei – King Solomon's Book of Proverbs

Mispallelim – congregants

Mitzta'er – literally, "in pain"; an exemption from sitting in the succah

Mitzvah – Torah commandment

Mitzvah haba'ah b'aveirah – a commandment fulfilled via a transgression

Mizbe'ach – Altar

Mochel – forgive; to forgo one's right; to grant permission to expose his shortcomings

Nashim – women

Nasi – the leader of the Jewish people

Navi – prophet

Nazirim – a nazirite, one who has vowed to abstain from grape products, haircutting and defilement by a corpse.

Neder – vow

Neshamah – soul

Oneis gamur – totally not at fault

Parah Adumah – red heifer, used in certain ritual purification processes

Paroches – the curtain in front of the Aron Hakodesh

Pasuk (pl. *Pesukim*) – Scriptural verse

Pasul — invalid

Parshiyos – paragraphs; weekly Torah readings

Pe'ah – the corner of the field that is not harvested so that it can be picked by poor people

Petirah – demise

Pidyon Haben – redeeming a firstborn son

Pikuach Nefesh – a case of life and death

Plishtim – Philistines

Poskim – halachic authorities

Rabbanan – our Rabbis

Rachmana litzlan – Heaven save us

Rachtzah – ritual washing of the hands at the Pesach Seder

Rebbi – teacher

Rechilus – talebearing

Rishonim – earlier halachic authorities

Ruach HaKodesh – Divine Inspiration

Sandek – the one who holds the baby during the bris

Sefer (pl. *Sefarim*)– holy book

Seudah – feast

Seudas Shabbos – a Shabbos meal

Shadchan – matchmaker

Shalom Bayis – domestic tranquility

Shas – Talmud

Shechinah – Presence of Hashem

Shidduch – marriage proposal

Shinui – changing the form

Shiur – Torah lecture

Shlishi – third; the third aliyah of the Torah reading

Shochet – ritual slaughterer

Shomer Shabbos – Sabbath observer

Siddurim – prayer books

Siman – identifiable marking, that can be used to claim a lost object

Simchah – rejoicing; festive event

Sinas Chinam – baseless hatred

Sonei Matanos Yichyeh – One who despises gifts will live

Talmid Chacham (pl. *Talmidei Chachamim*) – Torah Scholar

Tanna – a scholar of the Mishnah

Tefachim – handbreadths

Terumah – portions assigned for the Kohen

Teshuvah – repentance

Tircha D'tzibura – causing the congregation extra bother

Tochachah – reproving his friend

To'eles – constructive purpose

Torah Shebe'al Peh – The Oral Law

Torah Shebichsav – The Written Law

Tereifah – unkosher due to bodily defects which will cause the animal to die within 12 months

Tza'ar baalei chaim – the prohibition against causing pain to animals

Tzedakah – charity

V'ahavta l'rei'acha kamocha – Love your neighbor as yourself

Yaakov Avinu – the patriarch Jacob

Yahrtzeit – anniversary of one's death

Yamim Nora'im – High Holy Days

Yerushalayim – Jerusalem

Yetzias Mitzrayim – the Exodus from Egypt

Yid – Jew

Yiddishkeit – Judaism

Yi'ush – Giving up hope on retaining ownership, Usually applies to a lost object.

Zeh neheneh v'zeh lo chaser – when one benefits from another, and his friend does not lose out.

Zerizus – expedience; alacrity

Sources

The discussions in this work are based on selections from
Rabbi Yitzchok Zilberstein's multi-volume *Chashukei Chemed*.
The listing below directs the reader to the volume and page number
where the discussion appears in the original.

Sefer Bereishis

Parashas Bereishis
Pure Profit   Megillah 364 (See also Sanhedrin 215)
Family Loyalty   Megillah 222
Manufacturer's Instructions   Succah 295
Professionalism and Emotion   Kesubos 639

Parashas Noach
Vegetables a la Mode   Shabbos 707
Granting Permission Against One's Will   Kesubos 46
Natural Resources   Shabbos 315

Parashas Lech Lecha
Irreplaceable Tefillin   Succah 352
Social Security   Bava Basra 66
But You Promised!   Gittin 208
Applying the Lessons We Learn   Pesachim 639

Parashas Vayeira
Speed Versus Beauty   Yoma 66
Overbooking   Gittin 469
Medical Ethics   Megillah 365

INDEX / 483

Personal Responsibility . . . . Succah 370
Parental Rights . . . . Yoma 457
Chanukah Gelt! . . . . Megillah 136

Parashas Chayei Sarah

Everyone Has One . . . . Bava Basra 234
A Doctor With No Compunctions . . . . Kesubos 613
Be Careful Whom You Ask . . . . Kesubos 372
A Match Made in Heaven . . . . Bava Basra 522

Parashas Toldos

No Place Like Home . . . . Bava Basra 127
The Money-Making Umbrella . . . . Bava Metzia 106
Sign on the Microdotted line . . . . Gittin 47
Car Switch . . . . Bava Kamma 535
Overlooked, but Not Forgiven . . . . Bava Kamma 232
Eisav's Kibbud Av . . . . Yoma 261
Easy as Pi . . . . Bava Metzia 304

Parashas Vayeitzei

My House for a Slice of Bread . . . . Kesubos 589
Who Owes Whom . . . . Gittin 205
Would You Mind Moving, Please . . . . Bava Kamma 193
Fair Exchange Is No Robbery – Or Is It? . . . . Berachos 44
Does Family Always Come First? . . . . Bava Metzia 220
The Walls Have Ears . . . . Bava Basra 45
True Honor . . . . Kesubos 611

Parashas Vayishlach

Doing Kindness at the Expense of Others . . . . Kesubos 546
Are There Free Rides? . . . . Bava Kamma 588
An Underhanded Acquisition . . . . Bava Metzia 324

Parashas Vayeishev

May We All Hear Good News . . . . Megillah 190
Are All Men Created Equal? . . . . Shabbos 84
Misdirected Renovation . . . . Bava Kamma 612
Stop – Thief! . . . . Berachos 268
You or Me? What's the Difference? . . . . Kesubos 560
The Right Place at the Right Time   Bava Metzia 50 (also Bava Basra 612)
Advertising . . . . Bava Metzia 550

Parashas Mikeitz

Picture Perfect I . . . . Gittin 457

Health Insurance — Bava Metzia 452
Picture Perfect II — Gittin 457
Birds of a Feather — Sanhedrin 568
Finders Keepers — Pesachim 39

Parashas Vayigash
Buy in Bulk — Bava Kamma 92
Best Buy — Kesubos 641
Practice Makes Perfect — Succah 97

Parashas Vayechi
Quiet Contribution — Shabbos 654
Right Address, Wrong House — Megillah 147
Eviction Without Notice — Bava Basra 215
Hashem Runs the World — Sanhedrin 495

Sefer Shemos

Parashas Shemos
Free Babysitting — Yoma 590
Misplaced Gratitude — Shabbos 83
100 Percent Leather — Pesachim 439
It's the Ambiance — Gittin 329
A Matter of Faith — Bava Basra 77

Parashas Va'eira
The Right Match — Gittin 316
Measure for Measure I — Kesubos 145
The Oldest Trick in the Book — Sanhedrin 514
Conditional Air — Sanhedrin 428

Parashas Bo
The Absolute Truth — Yoma 429
True Service — Yoma 483
Subtle Lighting — Bava Kamma 144
Into the Fire — Pesachim 370
Whose Matzah Is It? — Pesachim 276
How Much Would You Give to Do a Mitzvah? — Pesachim 607
Leil Shimurim — Bava Metzia 397
There Is No Place Like Home — Pesachim 643

Parashas Beshalach

Buckle Your Seatbelt! — Bava Kamma 54
Determining Your Budget — Succah 84
Mitzvah Accessories — Succah 389
In Honor of Shabbos — Bava Basra 75

Parashas Yisro

High-Volume Service — Succah 424
A Difficult Mitzvah — Bava Metzia 308
True Honor — Yoma 227
The Best Seder — Pesachim 637

Parashas Mishpatim

The Best Things in Life Are Free — Kesubos 370
The Man Who Cried, "Ambulance!" — Megillah 187
Medical Expenses I — Gittin 311
Medical Expenses II — Gittin 312
Dangerous Shame — Shabbos 542
False Security — Bava Metzia 239
In Absence of X-Ray Vision — Pesachim 145
Check Changing — Kesubos 548
Being Holy at Someone Else's Expense — Megillah 157
Majority Rules — Sanhedrin 34
Israeli Healthcare — Yoma 160
The Whole Truth — Bava Metzia 237

Parashas Terumah

A Modern-day Holdup — Bava Basra 218
Unnecessary Money — Kesubos 609
Undue Dues — Pesachim 511
The Dye Is Cast — Shabbos 360
Priorities — Gittin 250

Parashas Tetzaveh

Defective Merchandise I — Bava Metzia 341
Defective Merchandise II — Bava Metzia 342
Peace Plan — Megillah 238

Parashas Ki Sisa

Rare Photos — Shabbos 722
Minimizing the Damage — Pesachim 188
It's for the Kids — Kesubos 48
Phone Home — Bava Metzia 40

It's a Living   Bava Kamma 168

Parashas Vayakheil
A Diagnosis in Honor of Shabbos   Bava Metzia 328
Fare is Fair   Kesubos 616
A Living Torah   Shabbos 561

Parashas Pekudei
It Pays to Be Nice   Bava Kamma 605
Whose Mitzvah Is It?   Gittin 252
An Expensive House Call   Sanhedrin 191
Going the Extra Mile   Bava Basra 384
Shul Business   Yoma 283

Sefer Vayikra

Parashas Vayikra
A Father's Blessing   Yoma 48
The Privilege of Ownership   Yoma 220
The First or the Most   Yoma 135

Parashas Tzav
One Dizzy Chicken   Yoma 414
No Time to Eat   Pesachim 148
Can You Take It With You?   Pesachim 277

Parashas Shemini
You Have the Right to Remain Silent   Berachos 391
Please Pass the Ketchup   Kesubos 58
To Eat or Not to Eat   Yoma 530
Mandatory Attendance? I   Pesachim 348
Bac-Os   Pesachim 304

Parashas Tazria
The Preferred Sandek   Yoma 96
Family First   Gittin 250
Care for Tefillin   Sanhedrin 562

Parashas Metzora
Classified Information   Sanhedrin 175
Service Call   Kesubos 66
Trojan Couch   Bava Kamma 309

Color Coordination — Bava Kamma 342
Wet Paint — Bava Basra 59

Parashas Acharei Mos
It's Only Water — Yoma 234
Special Delivery — Sanhedrin 295
The Yolk Is on Whom? — Bava Metzia 205
To Call or Not to Call I — Yoma 555
To Call or Not to Call II — Yoma 556

Parashas Kedoshim
A Business Expense — Bava Metzia 43
Driver's Test — Shabbos 660
A Choice of Mitzvos — Megillah 51
Mandatory Attendance? II — Shabbos 203
Keeping Your Co-workers — Yoma 53
Uh! Uh! Nu! — Pesachim 614

Parashas Emor
Kiddush Hashem — Yoma 274
Priorities — Yoma 526
Which Mitzvah to Choose — Succah 356
The Chofetz Chaim's Preference — Yoma 305
Cramped Quarters — Succah 41
The Best Way to Live — Succah 43
Oops! Sorry — Bava Kamma 165

Parashas Be'har
Conflicting Interests — Bava Basra 52
Too Cheap to be True — Megillah 152
A Misinformed Seller — Yoma 230
Seller Beware — Kesubos 592
Your Life Has Priority — Succah 350

Parashas Bechukosai
The Right to Remain Silent — Bava Basra 128
Measure for Measure II — Kesubos 586
Absolute Value — Megillah 362

Sefer Bamidbar

Parashas Bamidbar

Going Down? — Bava Metzia 347

Hashem Knows — Yoma 199

Parashas Nasso

An Outstanding Loan Payment — Bava Kamma 248

Would You Care For Another Cheese Blintz? — Gittin 156

Shalom Bayis — At What Cost — Bava Kamma 223

Parashas Beha'aloscha

Age Before Beauty — Gittin 230

Steak Out — Sanhedrin 143

Sensitivity — Sanhedrin 78

Parashas Shelach

The Situation Is Not So Grave — Bava Metzia 144

Too Easy — Bava Kamma 235

To Give Him Another Chance — Bava Kamma 509

Parashas Korach

Know Your Place — Bava Basra 437

We Want to Pay! — Gittin 305

A Picture Is Worth … — Kesubos 524

Taking a Risk to Do Mitzvos — Succah 360

Parashas Chukas

Seize the Moment — Yoma 41

In the Absence of a G.P.S. — Pesachim 164

"Has Anyone Seen My Contacts?" — Bava Basra 388

You Get What You Pay For — Bava Kamma 140

Caution in Repaying a Loan — Kesubos 568

Theft Deterrent — Bava Kamma 558

Accidental Insurance — Bava Metzia 81

Parashas Balak

Be Kind to Animals — Bava Kamma 178

Using the Law for Your Own Purposes — Bava Basra 34

Parashas Pinchas

Shul Policy — Megillah 311

Jackpot! — Megillah 83

Priority to Be Chazzan   Succah 474

Parashas Mattos
False Alarm?   Pesachim 336
Expensive Garbage   Kesubos 246
And You Shall Be Clean   Megillah 212

Parashas Mas'ei
Metered Parking I   Megillah 142
Metered Parking II   Megillah 143
Defensive Driving   Bava Kamma 627
With a Broken Heart   Kesubos 303

Sefer Devarim

Parashas Devarim
Picking Your Mitzvos   Sanhedrin 56
One in the Hand …   Sanhedrin 58
First Come …   Sanhedrin 62
Preferential Treatment   Sanhedrin 184
Talent Versus Experience   Berachos 396
Sounds the Same   Gittin 337

Parashas Va'eschanan
Wedding Album   Bava Metzia 333
A Mitzvah or an Aveirah   Bava Kamma 234
One Reader or Two   Megillah 46
It's Not Easy Being Green   Bava Metzia 42
Guard Your Tongue   Yoma 163
True Chinuch   Gittin 377
Save Some for Me   Shabbos 596
It Is Not Yours to Trade   Kesubos 56

Parashas Eikev
Maximize Your Potential   Sanhedrin 57
Bar Mitzvah Pose   Bava Kamma 75
Precious Time   Sanhedrin 69

Parashas Re'ei
Two Mitzvos at Once   Succah 148
Keeping the Peace   Berachos 107
Questionable Public Relations   Bava Metzia 406

A Matter of Accounting	Bava Basra 76
A Free Mitzvah?	Megillah 138
My Day Off	Gittin 372
Dressing Up	Pesachim 413

Parashas Shoftim
A Profitable Investment	Sanhedrin 36
Medical Secrets	Sanhedrin 311, Pesachim 208
A Help or a Harm I	Bava Kamma 415

Parashas Ki Seitzei
Finders Are Not Always Keepers	Bava Basra 449
Where Is Your Gratitude?	Pesachim 383
As Long as It Stands	Shabbos 573
A Help or a Harm II	Bava Kamma 418
Structural Defect	Shabbos 624
Cardboard by the Pound?	Bava Kamma 635

Parashas Ki Savo
An Incomplete Present	Sanhedrin 499
Honoring One's Parent: At What Price?	Megillah 161
Just Desserts	Sanhedrin 522

Parashas Nitzavim
Good Things Come Anyway	Sanhedrin 60
In the Footsteps of Our Sages	Sanhedrin 545
Practice Makes Perfect	Yoma 86
Mitzvos Take Time and Money	Sanhedrin 520

Parashas Vayeilech
Maximizing Your Potential	Sanhedrin 131
A Sure Sign	Sanhedrin 275
Under Surveillance	Megillah 329

Parashas Ha'azinu
A Captive Audience	Bava Basra 129
Do I Have To?	Sanhedrin 241

Parashas V'zos HaBerachah
Mass Labor	Bava Kamma 146
Giving Tzedakah at the Proper Time	Sanhedrin 239
The Most for Your Money	Succah 358

This volume is part of
THE ARTSCROLL SERIES®
an ongoing project of
translations, commentaries and expositions on
Scripture, Mishnah, Talmud, Midrash, Halachah,
liturgy, history, the classic Rabbinic writings,
biographies and thought.

For a brochure of current publications
visit your local Hebrew bookseller
or contact the publisher:

Mesorah Publications, ltd

4401 Second Avenue
Brooklyn, New York 11232
(718) 921-9000
www.artscroll.com